THE NEWS
SHAPERS

THE NEWS SHAPERS

The Sources Who Explain the News

LAWRENCE C. SOLEY

PRAEGER

New York
Westport, Connecticut
London

Library of Congress Cataloging-in-Publication Data

Soley, Lawrence C.
   The news shapers : the sources who explain the news / Lawrence C.
Soley.
    p.   cm.
   Includes bibliographical references and index.
   ISBN 0-275-94033-0 (alk. paper)
   1. Reporters and reporting—United States. 2. Attribution of
news—United States—History. 3. Journalism—United States—
Objectivity. 4. Television broadcasting of news—United States—
Objectivity.   I. Title.
PN4781.S65   1992
070.4 '3 '0973—dc20   91-33606

British Library Cataloguing in Publication Data is available.

Library of Congress Catalog Card Number: 91-33606
ISBN: 0-275-94033-0

First published in 1992

Praeger Publishers, One Madison Avenue, New York, NY 10010
An imprint of Greenwood Publishing Group, Inc.

Printed in the United States of America

The paper used in this book complies with the
Permanent Paper Standard issued by the National
Information Standards Organization (Z39.48–1984).

10 9 8 7 6 5 4 3 2 1

CONTENTS

TABLES

PREFACE

Academic books that are written to be accessible to the general reader are often criticized by reviewers for the popular press for being too dry and stodgy or by academic reviewers for containing more entertainment than information. Although I was aware of and tried hard to avoid the pitfalls that await writers who try to hike the middle ground between scholarship and readability, I am not sure that I succeeded. If I failed, as so many others have, I assume all responsibility. If the book is both readable and informative, the credit belongs to the many individuals who provided substantive and editorial assistance on this project.

Foremost among these individuals is my longtime friend and collaborator, Marc Cooper. Without Marc's advice and assistance, this book would never have been written. He and I worked together on "All the Right Sources" for *Mother Jones* magazine, which eventually received the Sigma Delta Chi award for research about journalism. That article led Marc and me to discuss a book-length study of news shapers. The discussions led to this book. As fate would have it, Marc got assigned to other stories before the book was ever started. He was therefore unable to commit to a long-term book project. Although unable to find time to help write the book, Marc nevertheless provided me with information and insights about new shapers during the period when he was gainfully employed on other projects. For this I am indebted.

I am also indebted to Anne Jett, who consistently provided me with good advice and comments. Many of her thoughts and recommendations have been incorporated into the book. Another University of Minnesota colleague to whom

I owe a word of thanks is Don Gillmor, who patiently read and edited the first academic version of *The News Shapers*. He did this shortly after arriving at the Gannett Center for Media Studies at Columbia University, where he was a visiting fellow from 1989 to 1990. I am especially thankful for his feedback, given the other responsibilities he had at the Gannett Center and the alternatives that New York City offers to reading an academic treatise.

Finally, I am grateful to the editors at *City Pages, Dissent*, and several other journals, who provided me with editorial advice on articles that have found their way, in part, into this book. At *City Pages*, I would like to thank Steve Perry and Monika Bauerlein, who edited "Leaders of the Pack" (October 24, 1990), "The Spin Doctors of War" (January 30, 1991), and several other articles that focused on news shapers. At *Dissent*, I wish to thank Irving Howe and Maxine Phillips, who critiqued and edited "Thinking Right," which appeared in the Summer 1991 issue of their journal. A final word of thanks goes to Doug Foster, Rich Reynolds, and others at *Mother Jones*, Craig LaMay at the *Gannett Center Journal*, and Robin PanLener at the *Journal of Public Communication*, whose publications carried articles on the news shapers.

THE NEWS
SHAPERS

1

SHAPING THE NEWS

During the predawn hours of December 20, 1989, U.S. troops launched a surprise invasion of Panama in an effort to depose Gen. Manuel Noriega. The troops neutralized Noriega's army, but the general escaped. After eluding capture for five days, Noriega surfaced at the Vatican Embassy in Panama City, where he had taken refuge.

As the invasion story unfolded, ''CBS Evening News'' turned to ''consultant'' Fred Woerner for analysis. Woerner explained to CBS news viewers on December 21 that Noriega planned to take U.S. citizens as hostages for use as bargaining chips. The consultant appeared again on December 22, stating that the United States needed to remain in Panama even after ousting Noriega, despite pressure to withdraw by members of the Organization of American States. On December 27, Woerner warned CBS viewers that Noriega remained a threat, even though he was unarmed and in the Vatican Embassy.

Viewers were also informed that Noriega's residence contained 20 kilos of cocaine and pictures of Adolf Hitler, which turned out to be false. However, they were not told that retired Gen. Fred Woerner was the former commander of the 193d Infantry Brigade in Panama which led the invasion, or that he was an architect of the December 20 military action. Woerner retired on July 20, 1989, six months after he criticized the Bush administration for not having a clear policy regarding Noriega (*New York Times*, February 24, 1989, A3, and July 21, 1989, A4). Dan Rather instead described Woerner as a ''former chief of the U.S. Southern Command in Panama'' (CBS-December 22, 1989), and this was done on only one occasion.

Fred Woerner is one of the "new shapers" that the media go to for inside information, background, or predictions concerning the outcome of still-unfolding stories. News shapers differ from news makers, who are part of a bona fide news event. News makers include criminals and victims, government officials, candidates for office, military leaders, terrorists and their hostages, foreign dignitaries, and leaders of advocacy organizations. These individuals are clearly identified as representing specific sides within situations of controversy or conflict. In effect, news stories are reports about what these individuals have said or done.

News shapers, on the other hand, are presented as detached analysts. Woerner was described as a "CBS consultant." The networks also describe their news shapers as political scientists, experts, or scholars. They are presented as nonpartisan, even if they have long histories of partisanship. Some news shapers are former government officials; some are former politicians. Despite this, they are frequently described with impartial titles such as a specialist, journalist, or economist. What distinguishes news shapers from other individuals who appear on newscasts or are quoted in newspaper stories is that they are not part of the event. Their sole function is to provide commentary or analysis, although their statements are never described as such.

When the Iran-Contra affair was in the news, the networks turned to David Gergen for expert commentary. Like General Woerner, Gergen popped up on a newscast for a few seconds to give it some shape, disappeared, and then reappeared on another night. He appeared five times on ABC, four times on CBS, and six times on the NBC evening news during 1987. Gergen was usually described as editor of the *U.S. News and World Report*. He is the quintessential news shaper, appearing frequently on network evening newscasts and almost every other national news program. Gergen is a permanent fixture on the "MacNeil/Lehrer NewsHour" and a frequent guest on Sunday morning news programs like "This Week with David Brinkley."

Gergen's appearances as a network news shaper began on June 21, 1980, when NBC asked him to comment on presidential candidate Ronald Reagan's tax cut proposal and President Jimmy Carter's options in responding to it. Gergen commented that Carter's credibility would be hurt if he, too, advocated a tax cut. Carter's attempt to balance the "budget has now become a mirage; it's moved further into the future. How is he going to come forward with a tax cut without having first balanced the budget? That's the box he's in now," Gergen declared.

During his debut, NBC described David Gergen as the editor of *Public Opinion* magazine. *Public Opinion* was never identified as the publication of the American Enterprise Institute (AEI), a conservative public policy organization where Gergen was a "resident fellow." Nor was it mentioned that Gergen worked as a primary campaign adviser to Reagan's eventual running mate, George Bush. To the viewer, it appeared that David Gergen was simply a journalist.

David Gergen is the quintessential news shaper, because he attended and taught at a private, Ivy League university, was associated with a former Republican administration, worked at a conservative Washington, D.C., "think tank," and carries the mantle of journalist. He is currently an editor of the *U.S. News and World Report* magazine, which is how he is described during most of his news appearances. On the few newscasts where he is accurately described as an "ex–White House communications director" or "former White House aide," the fact that he worked for Republican administrations is never stated.

Not only did Gergen work under Presidents Nixon and Ford, but he was also one of the powerhouses of the Reagan administration. He worked as President Reagan's White House staff director from January to June 1981 and then worked as a communications director for the president until 1983. Following this tour of duty, Gergen went to the John F. Kennedy School of Government at Harvard University as a resident fellow and from there to the *U.S. News and World Report*.

As a result of these assignments, Gergen can be called a think tank fellow, an academic, a former government official, a journalist, or simply an "analyst," who objectively comments on news events. During 1987 and 1988, the networks used Gergen two dozen times to shape their news. Never once was he identified as a Republican partisan or Reagan booster, which he clearly was. Gergen's worship of President Reagan was not difficult to ascertain. In the *New Republic*, Gergen wrote:

Reagan has a chance of becoming even more of a national father figure than he already is. Of course, he cannot abandon his roots either as a conservative or a Republican. But the man who Sidney Blumenthal has aptly called the Chairman Mao of the Republican Party could make himself the force that binds the country together and points it towards larger purposes. (1984, 18)

All of the frequently appearing news shapers have backgrounds that are similar to Gergen's. They have ties to a handful of right-wing Washington think tanks such as the Heritage Foundation, AEI, and Center for Strategic and International Studies (SIS) and elite publications such as the *Washington Post, New York Times*, or *Times* magazine and graduated or taught at private, eastern universities. Individuals associated with public universities or left-of-center think tanks such as the Institute for Policy Studies are rarely used as news shapers. News shapers comprise a separate, elite class of individuals who provide the analysis for much of the national and international news that we view and read.

Typical of this group is William Schneider, who appeared 72 times on all three major networks' evening news programs between 1987 and 1989. Schneider also served as a regular political analyst for National Public Radio's (NPR's) "Morning Edition" during the same period. He shaped the news on a dizzying array of topics for the networks: the Strategic Defense Initiative (CBS–February 7, 1987), Gary Hart's presidential bid (ABC–May 7, 1987), Supreme Court nominations (CBS–September 5, 1987), Mexico's president (CBS–July 5, 1988), tax policy (NBC–November 12, 1988), Jim Wright's ethics (CBS–April 13, 1989), ambassadorial appointments (CBS–July 29, 1989), the Housing and Urban Development (HUD) scandals (CBS–August 13, 1989), the war on drugs (ABC–August 15, 1989), and abortion rights (NBC–October 14, 1989), to name but a few subjects. Schneider commented on at least as wide an array of topics for NPR's "Morning Edition."

Schneider was also continually present in the print media. Between 1987 and 1989, he wrote 58 opinion articles for the *Los Angeles Times*, which were syndicated to numerous other daily newspapers. He also wrote a weekly column for the *National Journal*. However, Schneider's real influence comes from shaping, rather than writing about, the news. Print journalists go to him as often as broadcast journalists to get analysis. He was also quoted by the Associated Press in 77 wire stories between 1987 and 1989. The *Boston Globe* (December 1, 1987, 29) reported that "so far this year, Schneider has been quoted more than 300 times in publications tracked by a computer system—including the *New York Times, Washington Post,* the *Christian Science Monitor* and the major news magazines." *Newsweek* (May 27, 1987, 5) reported that "Schneider showed up 10 times . . . on national television and in national print media" during the week that Gary Hart withdrew from the presidential race.

When the news media revealed that Sen. Joseph Biden was reciting a speech of Neil Kinnock as though it were his own, Schneider became one of the most frequently cited and caustic critics of Biden. On the ABC news (September 16, 1987), Schneider said: "His character has been his strongest suit. It's what the man sells. Now, we have a chance to see his real character." The *New York Times* interviewed and quoted "campaign expert" Schneider the next day. Three days later Schneider's thoughts about Biden popped up in the *Boston Globe* and four days later in *USA Today*. Although the media described Schneider as a detached "political analyst" and "political scholar," he was actually a player in the game: Schneider gave Biden the tape of Kinnock's speech that was later plagiarized (*Columbia Journalism Review*, November/December 1987, 29). No news report carried this fact.

The media go to Schneider for quotes because he is part of the close-knit Washington network that includes the Capitol reporters who seek him out. Other than that, his academic credentials are similar to those of hundreds, perhaps thousands, of current and former professors. Schneider received graduate degrees from Harvard University, where he taught until 1979. While a professor, Schneider published a few articles in journals such as the *American Behavioral Scientist* and *Foreign Affairs*.

Schneider went from Harvard to the Hoover Institution, one of several right-wing think tanks on the west coast. While there, he wrote several articles for the Institute for Contemporary Studies, a rightist think tank founded by Caspar Weinberger and Edwin Meese to promote Ronald Reagan's presidential bid. Schneider also found a home for his writings in Norman Podhoretz's magazine of rightist thought, *Commentary*, and the AEI's organ, *Public Opinion*, founded by David Gergen. These publications, not journals like the *American Journal of Political Science* or *American Political Science Review*, provide Schneider with credentials that impressed the media.

From Hoover, Schneider went to the AEI as a "resident scholar." It was at the AEI that Schneider's prominence grew, largely as a result of AEI propaganda. Between 1980 and 1985, Schneider wrote ten articles for *Public Opinion* magazine. During those years, AEI literature touted Schneider as the author of three books: *The Radical Center, From Discrimination to Affirmative Action*, and *The Confidence Gap* (see *Public Opinion*, April/May 1980, p. 1, and August/September 1985, 1). Only *The Confidence Gap* was actually published. He was the secondary author of this book.

Despite having a fairly ordinary résumé, Schneider, along with other media-recognized experts, has ridiculed the credentials of others—even those with credentials similar to their own. When asked by reporter Richard Berke about another conservative policy organization, the Heritage Foundation, Schneider responded, "I am not impressed by their scholarly credentials, but I am impressed by their political savvy. They know how to advance their cause" (*New York Times*, November 21, 1988, B10). When finally asked by TV critic James Warren to respond to reports that his own scholarly credentials were a bit exaggerated, Schneider refused to comment (*Chicago Tribune*, February 25, 1990, V2).

What Schneider lacks in academic accomplishments he makes up for in other ways. He's white, associated with a conservative think tank, and has degrees from a private, eastern university. As a columnist for the *Los Angeles Times*, Schneider can also be described as an elite journalist. These are the essential ingredients of the often-quoted new shapers. Had Schneider been an appointee in a previous presidential administration, he might have been quoted even more by the media. Most important he is always willing to criticize the Democratic party, liberals, and minorities.

William Schneider made his news shaper debut on CBS on February 14, 1984, where he discussed the unpopularity of organized labor and how labor union support would hurt Mondale's presidential bid. Schneider's comments were so liked by the network news team that they invited him back on March 28 to comment about the negative advertising being used in the Democratic primary race. During the Democratic convention, he appeared on ABC and CBS. In both appearances, Schneider spoke about the gay caucus within the Democratic party and how gay support would hurt Mondale's campaign.

William Schneider made seven network appearances in 1984. That number climbed to 23 in 1987 and to 35 in 1988. The networks described him as a political scientist, political analyst, expert, and AEI spokesman. In no appearance was the AEI correctly described as a conservative organization.

Schneider's analyses are typified by the following quotes. On the ABC evening news (July 30, 1987), Schneider claimed that "most Democrats agree that it would be suicidal to put Jesse Jackson on the ticket." Eight months later on ABC's "This Week with David Brinkley" (April 3, 1988), Schneider claimed that Jesse Jackson would be "poison to the Democratic ticket." On Pat Schroeder's bid for the presidency, Schneider commented, "I think it's risky to nominate a woman for the top of the ticket and the Democrats know it." Schneider denigrated Gary

Hart's character, saying, "Americans have learned over the years that character, judgment, integrity are as important as issue positions. As we've seen with many presidents, issue positions can change but character is much harder to change" (ABC–September 16, 1987).

In effect, Schneider attacked almost every Democratic presidential candidate. He even attacked the Democratic party as an organization, saying, "Reagan has created a new coalition in American politics and it is holding together for George Bush, because the coalition sees one simple threat: liberals. The higher the political office, the more ideology matters. And the more ideology matters, the worse Democrats do" (CBS–November 7, 1988).

The elite group of news shapers to which Schneider belongs is not only homogeneous in terms of education, associations, ethnicity, and gender, but it is also very small. Approximately 90 individuals dominate political discourse about national and international events. The analyses of these 90 individuals constantly appear on the network evening newscasts, the "MacNeil/Lehrer Newshour," NPR's "Morning Edition," and Sunday morning news programs and in metropolitan daily newspapers. It is impossible to avoid hearing or reading their comments that shape the news.

2

BIASED REPORTING OR
BIASED SOURCES?

The media have always been criticized for being politically biased, but criticism intensified after Vice Pres. Spiro Agnew claimed that the news media were "giving the American people a highly selected and often biased presentation of the news" (Kenworthy 1969, 1, 24). According to the vice president, network news reports were slanted against the Nixon administration, but were uncritical of Nixon's opponents: "[The media] can make or break by their coverage a moratorium on the war. They can elevate to national prominence within a week. They can reward some politicians with national exposure and ignore others." Agnew suggested that the networks were elevating extremists like Stokely Carmichael to prominence while ceaselessly attacking the president:

How many marches and demonstrations would we have if marchers did not know that the ever-faithful TV cameras would be there to record their antics for the next news show? . . . In this search for excitement and controversy, has not more time gone to the minority of Americans who specialize in attacking the United States—its institutions and its citizens?

Agnew added that he was not advocating censorship, only exposing the biases of the media.

Following the vice president's attack on the media, several books appeared that claimed to document the anti-Nixon bias of the network news programs. The Arlington Press, a conservative publishing company, issued *The Left Leaning*

Antenna (1971) by Joseph Kelley and *The Gods of Antenna* (1976) by Bruce Herschensohn, a former Nixon administration official. Both claimed that the media provided false reports about President Nixon and other conservatives while failing to report the misdeeds and conspiracies of the political left.

Joseph Kelley, for example, claimed that the shootings of students at Kent State University by National Guardsmen in 1970 were the outgrowth of a leftist plot to sabotage an important military research project, not panic on the part of Guardsmen:

One of the buildings that the radicals wanted to destroy housed a research project of special interest from a military standpoint. This was the Liquid Crystal Institute, one of two such projects in the United States, and one in which the Soviet Union had evinced considerable interest. (1971, 104)

According to Kelley, "the world-be Lenins and Che Guevaras" in Students for a Democratic Society (SDS), a radical student group, organized the demonstrations as part of a conspiracy to destroy the militarily important research facility at Kent State University. The media never reported the SDS plot when reporting on the Kent State shootings, because the media "felt the same way as the New Left about President Nixon, Vice President Spiro Agnew and other members of the administration" (105).

TV Guide reporter Edith Efron published *The News Twisters* (1971), an allegedly objective study of network news coverage of the 1968 presidential campaign. Efron concluded that the networks were "massively slanted against Richard Nixon," airing seven times as many anti-Nixon as pro-Nixon stories. Her conclusions were arrived at by reading transcripts of network news broadcasts and coding them as to whether they exhibited anti-Nixon, pro-Humphrey, pro-black militant, or other biases.

CBS responded to *The News Twisters* with a study of its own. The CBS study examined Efron's research method and concluded that it was "seriously flawed. And it draws erroneous prejudiced and unsupportable conclusions" (Columbia Broadcasting System, 1971, 137). The rebuttal claimed that Efron intentionally distorted her own data to reach conclusions that were consistent with Agnew's criticism. For example, Efron claimed that "network reporters in alliance with Democratic-liberal politicians portrayed Hubert Humphrey as a talkative saint studded over with every virtue known to man," while Richard Nixon was "not portrayed as a human being at all but is transmogrified into a demon out of the liberal id" (1971, 55). Despite her claim that the media treated the Democratic candidate favorably, her data indicated that CBS broadcast 2,388 words in favor of and 2,083 words against Hubert Humphrey. NBC, according to Efron's own analysis, broadcast only 1,852 words in favor of Humphrey, but 2,655 words against him.

Reviews of *The News Twisters* that appeared in academic research journals voiced the same criticisms of the book as CBS. A review in *Journalism Quarterly*, a publication devoted to research in mass communications, concluded:

There are at least two problems with her "original" method of analyzing news stories for "bias." The first is that any clue[s] to her criteria of what was pro or con on the issues which she selected to study . . . are extremely subjective. . . .

The other problem was the visual interpretation by the viewer. She worked only with words and disregarded the visualization entirely. Yet she introduced a concept of "forcefulness" which turns out to be so much bunkum. (Kuczin 1972, 192)

The year following publication of *The News Twisters*, the American Institute for Political Communication (AIPC, 1972) conducted a study that examined biases in network news coverage of the 1972 presidential primary campaign. The newscasts were coded by whether they exhibited pro-Humphrey or pro-McGovern biases using a technique similar to that employed by Efron (1971). The board of directors of the AIPC consisted primarily of Humphrey supporters—individuals like AFL-CIO leader Lane Kirkland. The study predictably found that the network news reports were pro-McGovern and anti-Humphrey.

Robert Stevenson, Richard Eisenger, Barry Feinberg, and Alan Kotok (1973) tried to replicate Efron's study, but instead found that her conclusions were more biased than the network reporting that she allegedly exposed. For example, Efron concluded that an October 17 report on CBS was anti-Nixon. She summarized the report as "reporter says Nixon, if elected, would be an obstacle to peace" (1971, 283). The summary was based on the following report by Marvin Kalb:

KALB: The strong possibility of a bombing halt does not appear to be a political stunt, designed to win votes for Hubert Humphrey. It is the result, first, of an obvious softening in Hanoi's policy, and second, in the President's willingness to see it and act upon it. . . . High officials who have been wrapped up in the Vietnam agony for years are hopeful that Hanoi will accept, because they believe the North Vietnamese would prefer to deal with a lame duck Lyndon Johnson than with the current frontrunner, Richard Nixon.

Stevenson et al. (1973) reviewed the CBS transcripts that Efron used in her study, but were unable to reproduce her findings. On the contrary, these researchers concluded that CBS's reporting was evenhanded during the 1968 presidential campaign. Stevenson and his colleagues also suggested that the techniques used by Efron for assessing bias were largely subjective, producing biased rather than objective results.

Even though Stevenson and his colleagues demonstrated that the methods employed by Efron and the AIPC are unreliable, politically conservative researchers continue to use the same methods. Several studies published by the AEI, a conservative policy organization, employed Efron's method. Michael Robinson, Maura Clancey, and Lisa Grand (1983) examined "policy news" that appeared "in the 'soft news' portions of the national press" during the first two months of 1983. Their study was published in *Public Opinion*, the AEI's journal. According to these researchers, only two network news stories during this period were favorable to President Reagan, while 27 were "directly negative." Robinson, Clancey, and Grand also counted the number of words that were pro-

and anti-Reagan, just as Efron did with news reports concerning Richard Nixon. Not surprisingly, the researchers found that press reports were 20 times more negative toward the president than positive.

Maura Clancey and Michael Robinson coded the ''spin'' or ''tone'' of comments made by network journalists during 200 broadcasts about the 1984 presidential campaign. This study, like the previous one, appear in *Public Opinion* magazine. The researchers alleged that ''Ronald Reagan's bad press total was ten times greater than his good press total,'' while the Mondale-Ferraro ticket received more good than bad press (1985, 50). These were almost the same ratios reported by Efron (1971, 32–33) for the 1968 election. She claimed that the networks spoke 10.5 anti-Nixon words for every pro-Nixon word, but more good than bad words about Hubert Humphrey.

The Video Campaign, a book published by the AEI and coauthored by AEI ''adjunct scholar'' S. Robert Lichter, along with Daniel Amundson and Richard Noyes, claimed that the networks were not totally objective during the 1988 presidential campaign, either. In *The Video Campaign*, Lichter, Amundson, and Noyes coded presidential election stories that were aired by the networks between February 8, 1987, and June 7, 1988. They found that Democrats received slightly more positive assessments than Republicans (i.e., 56 percent to 54 percent), but many more positive assessments when only the statements by reporters were coded (i.e., 64 percent to 54 percent). The researchers also claimed that ''the most liberal of the major candidates in each party received better coverage than any of the competitors'' (1988, 99).

S. Robert Lichter was also coauthor, with Stanley Rothman and Linda Lichter, of an earlier book, *The Media Elite*, which also asserted that the mass media are liberally biased. This book attempted to document the liberal political views of journalists and then demonstrate that these liberal views are present in news stories. Predictably, the book found that most news stories about politically controversial issues favor liberal positions. Of stories about school busing to achieve integration, over 55 percent were found to be probusing, whereas less than 45 percent were found to be antibusing. Concerning nuclear safety, about ''60 percent of all judgments coded were negative, and 40 percent positive'' (1986, 205), affirming the authors' beliefs that the media more frequently express liberal than conservative viewpoints.

Lichter also heads the Center for Media and Public Affairs, a Washington-based organization that publishes *Media Monitor*, one of several publications that allegedly exposes liberal media bias. The best known of the other publications is *AIM Report*, which is issued twice monthly by Reed Irvine's Accuracy In Media (AIM). Founded in 1969 to document Vice President Agnew's allegations, AIM has evolved into an activist organization, raising money for Oliver North and Richard Secord's libel suit against author Leslie Cockburn and making recommendations to readers about how to best complain to advertisers and publishers about ''liberal media bias.'' AIM also produced a documentary about press coverage of the Vietnam War that aired on Ted Turner's WTBS superstation and some public broadcasting stations.

Another rightist publication is *MediaWatch*, the most conservative, rabid, and rhetorical of the right-wing media-bashing reports. *MediaWatch* was created in 1987 by L. Brent Bozell III, a nephew of William F. Buckley, Jr., and former leader of the National Conservative Foundation. *MediaWatch* is published by the Media Research Center, which Bozell heads. *Between the Lines*, which bills itself as "The Conservative Watchdog of the Establishment Media," appeared in 1988, a year after Bozell's group went into business. It also claims to document liberal media bias. Finally, the Media Institute, another rightist outfit, sporadically publishes pamphlets that allegedly document the media's antibusiness bias.

In 1987, in response to the ever-growing number of organizations dedicated to "exposing" liberal bias, Fairness and Accuracy In Reporting (FAIR) was founded. This left-wing version of AIM publishes *Extra!*, which exposes the conservative biases of the mass media. In 1990, a second left-wing publication concerned with media bias appeared. The publication, *Lies of Our Times*, is almost exclusively devoted to exposing inaccuracies in the *New York Times*.

Because of the subjectivity inherent in the methods employed by Efron (1971), Robinson, Clancey, and Grand (1983), Clancey and Robinson (1985), Lichter, Amundson, and Noyes (1988), and others intent on exposing "media distortions," another method was developed by scholarly researchers for assessing bias—coding the sources, not the messages, that appear in news segments. This approach, unlike the others, removes subjectivity from the coding process by analyzing the individuals interviewed by the media, rather than interpreting what these individuals said. This content analytic approach consists of coding news sources by their gender, political party affiliation, place of residence, race, or profession.

Leon Sigal (1973) was one of the first researchers to study the sources used by reporters. His study examined the sources in stories published in the *New York Times* and *Washington Post*. Among sources appearing in these newspapers, U.S. government officials were the most frequently cited. U.S. officials, who were defined as members of the three branches of the federal government, constituted nearly one-half of the sources in 2,850 news stories. Among U.S. officials, members of the executive branch were the most frequently used. Only 2 percent of all sources were from the federal judiciary, and 6 percent were from Congress. The next largest category was foreign officials, who comprised 27.5 percent of the sources, followed by nongovernmental Americans, who comprised 14.4 percent of the sources. The remaining sources were state and local government officials (4.1 percent), journalists (3.2 percent), nongovernmental foreigners (2.1 percent), and sources whose affiliations could not be ascertained (2.4 percent).

As part of a larger study of press coverage of the Kennedy administration, Montague Kern, Patricia Levering and Ralph Levering (1983) examined the sources in front- and inside-page foreign policy crisis stories in five newspapers: the *New York Times, Washington Post, Chicago Tribune, St. Louis Post-Dispatch*, and *San Francisco Examiner*. In the sample, 50.1 percent of the 11,246 sources were foreign officials. The largest group of domestic sources was Kennedy administration officials, who constituted 30.1 percent of the sample. The next largest group was other domestic political leaders, who comprised 12.8 percent of the sample, and "interest group" spokespersons, who comprised 3.3 percent of the sample. Interest groups were defined as business, labor, religious, peace, and "patriotic" organizations.

Joseph Dominick (1977) coded a sample of network news programs telecast between 1973 and 1975 according to their geographic source. He found that two-thirds of the total national news reports came from three places: California, New York, and Washington, D.C. About half of all national news minutes focused on Washington. The Midwest, Southwest, and Southeast were undercovered compared to their percentages of the U.S. population, and two states—Pennsylvania and Ohio—were "grossly" undercovered. Dominick concluded that there were biases in the selection and origination of news stories, but did not claim that they were intentional. Instead, he suggested that the biases were most likely the result of where the networks base their news teams. The networks have crews in cities like New York, Washington, and Los Angeles, which explains why so much news originates from these locations.

The study by Dominick was replicated and extended by D. Charles Whitney, Marilyn Fritzler, Steven Jones, Sharon Mazzarella, and Lana Rakow (1989), who coded the sources and types of news in a sample of network newscasts that aired between 1982 and 1984. Like Dominick, Whitney et al. found regional biases in network news reports: the Northeast and Pacific were overrepresented, while the Midwest, Southwest, and Southeast were underrepresented. The researchers also found that women were underrepresented as news sources, accounting for just 13.6 percent of the appearance by identifiable sources.

Whitney et al. found that government officials were the most frequently cited of any source, accounting for 28.2 percent of all appearances. Spokesmen for businesses also appeared frequently. They accounted "for one of eleven of the sources used and just under a third of all institutional sources" (1989, 170). Like businessmen, "other professionals" appeared often, accounting for 19.3 percent of all network news sources. The "other professional" category included attorneys, medical doctors, university professors, and sports figures. The high representation of this category is not surprising, because the researchers coded all news segments, including reports on sports, entertainment, medicine, and religion.

These researchers found that representatives of political, women's rights, civil rights, human rights, and labor groups rarely appeared as sources on the network news. Spokespersons for all these groups combined accounted for only a twentieth of all sources.

Jane Brown, Carl Bybee, Stanley Weardon, and Dulcie Straughton (1987) examined the diversity and types of sources cited by the *New York Times,* the *Washington Post,* and four North Carolina newspapers during "two randomly constructed six-day weeks" of 1979 and 1980. Brown et al. found that women were rarely used as sources. U.S. government officials, on the other hand, constituted 31 percent of the sources used. U.S., foreign, state, and local officials together constituted 55.4 percent of all sources cited. "Affiliated" U.S. citizens constituted 24.4 percent of the sources. An affiliated citizen was defined as an individual associated with a labor union, public interest group, university, political party, or medical, religious, or business institution.

Tony Atwater and Norma Green (1988) examined the sources used in network television coverage of the TWA hijacking of June 1985. They coded every type of source who appeared, including government officials, former government officials, hostages, hostages' families, journalists, "average citizens," and experts. They found that hostages and their relatives comprised 53 percent of the sources, while U.S. government officials comprised only 15.7 percent of sources. Surprisingly, the networks relied more on non-news maker sources—former officials, journalists, experts, and other citizens—than on government sources. The non-news makers comprised 15.8 percent of the networks' sources.

Another study that examined news sources was conducted by William Hoynes and David Croteau (1989) for FAIR, the liberal media watchdog group. Hoynes and Croteau examined and coded categories of individuals who appeared on ABC's "Nightline" between January 1, 1985, and April 30, 1988. The study found that women and blacks rarely appeared. Blacks accounted for 6.2 percent and women accounted for 10.3 percent of "Nightline" guests. Hoynes and Croteau also found that three-fourths of the appearances were by "elites," a very broad category that included former and current government officials and "professionals."

Hoynes and Croteau concluded that "Nightline" systematically excluded citizens who opposed U.S. foreign policy, leaders of public interest organizations such as Ralph Nader, and spokespersons of the political left. To these charges, "Nightline" executive producer Richard Kaplan replied that the events of the day, not he or Ted Koppel, determined the show's guests. Kaplan insisted that "news makers" were invited on, not individuals that he preferred (Gerard 1989, 18).

An analysis of defense and terrorism experts on the "MacNeil/Lehrer NewsHour" was conducted by Edward Herman and Noam Chomsky (1988). This study employed more narrowly defined source categories than used by Hoynes and Croteau (1989) or Whitney et al. (1989), but included news makers as well as other sources. Herman and Chomsky distinguished current from former U.S. government officials and distinguished among types of professionals. Academics, journalists, consultants, representatives of "conservative think tanks," and "other" professionals were separately coded, demonstrating that news shapers are identifiable as a distinct group.

Herman and Chomsky found that former and current government officials appeared with equal frequency on the "MacNeil/Lehrer NewsHour." Current officials accounted for 20 percent of the appearances, as did former officials. Journalists accounted for 25.8 percent of the appearances. The next most frequently appearing sources were academics (i.e., professors) and representatives of "conservative think tanks" like the CSIS.

FAIR, the politically liberal media watchdog group, examined the discussants who appeared on the "MacNeil/Lehrer NewsHour" during a six-month period between February 5, 1989, and August 4, 1989. They found that nineteen individuals appeared as guests more than twice. Of these, five were journalists, two were associated with think tanks, two were university professors, and eight were U.S. congressmen or senators. Secretary of defense Dick Cheney and Common Cause president Fred Wertheimer also appeared more than twice. Of the senators and congressmen, three were Democrats and five were Republicans. Only two of the nineteen were women. Overall, 94 percent of the guests were white and 94 percent were male.

FAIR also found that the "MacNeil/Lehrer NewsHour" relied heavily on representatives of two conservative Washington think tanks, the AEI and CSIS: "AEI fellows appeared six times and CSIS fellows appeared eight times," according to FAIR.

"NewsHour" executive producer Lester Crystal claimed that there was "flaw after flaw" in the FAIR analysis, but never detailed the flaws except to note that FAIR "didn't credit the lengthy tape reports we have." AIM director Reed Irvine, the best known conservative critic of the media, also defended the "MacNeil/Lehrer NewsHour," stating that "MacNeil/Lehrer" got "the best people available instead of using some affirmative-action criterion" (*Los Angeles Times*, May 21, 1990, F8). What Irvine didn't mention was that the people who were available usually came from his hometown of Washington, D.C., or the surrounding area.

One problem with the Hoynes and Croteau (1989) and FAIR (1990) studies is that they did not distinguish news makers from news shapers, as "Nightline" producer Richard Kaplan accurately pointed out. News makers, such as government officials, are individuals who are the legitimate focus of the news. They are distinguishable from news shapers, who provide background or analyses for viewers but are not the focus of the news.

This study examines the political affiliations, institutional associations, and "expertise" of the individuals whom the networks and other news media have chosen to shape their news. It differs from previous studies that have analyzed news sources primarily by distinguishing news makers from news shapers and by identifying and profiling the individuals who shape the news.

The importance of identifying news shapers is underscored by research evidence that suggests that network television news shapers significantly affect public opinion. Benjamin Page, Robert Shapiro, and Glenn Dempsey (1987) examined the responses to public policy questions that were obtained from surveys administered about three months apart. They then coded the sources and statements made during network news broadcasts within three-month intervals. The sources that they analyzed included news announcers, presidents, interest group spokespersons, and "experts." Experts were defined by Page, Shapiro, and Dempsey as former government officials, think tank spokespersons, and academics, who appeared to have no financial or political stakes in the issue on which they were commenting. Analysis of changes in public opinion showed that "expert" commentary was a significant determinant of the public opinion shifts.

3

OBJECTIVITY AND THE SELECTION OF NEWS SOURCES

During the nineteenth century, journalism and political advocacy were intertwined. Journalists opposed or supported slavery, labor unions, women's suffrage, and wars and annexations in the pages of their newspapers. Many of the most famous nineteenth-century journalists, such as William Lloyd Garrison, Frederick Douglass, Horace Greeley, and Edwin Godkin, were more advocate than journalist. Garrison and Douglass were abolitionists and Greeley was a political radical, while Godkin was an advocate of laissez-faire economics but activist government social policy. Godkin, who was editor of the *New York Evening Post*, founded the *Nation* to promote "whatever in legislation or in manners seems likely to promote a more equal distribution of the fruits of progress and civilization" (Ogden 1907, p. 237).

Even Joseph Pulitzer and Edward W. Scripps were advocates. The first issue of Pulitzer's *New York World* contained a statement of purpose and a ten-point platform. The statement of purpose declared that the newspaper would "always fight for progress and reform, never tolerate injustice or corruption, always fight demagogues of all parties, never belong to any party, always oppose privileged classes and public plunderers . . . [and] never be satisfied with merely printing the news" (Tebbel 1974, 286-287). The platform proposed taxes on luxuries, inheritances, large incomes, and monopolies. It supported punishing corrupt officials and employers who coerced employees into voting for political candidates. Scripps was a self-proclaimed "people's champion," who spoke out for the rights of the working class (Emery and Emery 1988).

At the turn of century, advocacy moved from news stories to editorial pages, where it has since stayed. News reporters of the twentieth-century claim to be politically detached and "objective," unlike journalists of the previous era (Schudson 1978). To modern journalists, objective means "an allegiance to the nonpartisan pursuit of factual accuracy" (Roshco 1975, 44).

The degree to which journalists claim to be objective appears to be a function of their power and status within the profession. Reporters are less likely to express beliefs in objectivity than editors or publishers. During the 1960s and 1970s, the differences in outlook between reporters and editors were particularly extreme. *New York Post* reporter Bryna Taubman openly declared that "she cannot be objective today," and Raleigh *News and Observer* reporter Kerry Gruson insisted that "objectivity is a myth." At the same time, Kerry's father, Sydney Gruson, who was assistant to the publisher at the *New York Times*, asserted that "pure objectivity might not exist, but you have to strive for it anyway." Abraham M. Rosenthal, the *New York Times'* managing editor, informed his staff that "the duty of every reporter and editor is to strive for as much objectivity as possible." *Wall Street Journal* publisher William Kerby advised his employees that they should not do "anything which might in the public eye cast the slightest doubt on the impartiality of news coverage" (Sesser 1969). Not surprisingly, an empirical study of journalists' attitudes found a negative correlation between responsibility in news organizations and attitudes toward advocacy journalism (Johnstone, Slawski, and Bowman 1972).

Some journalists, like former NBC News president Reuven Frank, go even further, claiming that the news media actually "mirror" occurrences in society. According to this view, the news media so closely reflect events that it is difficult for citizens to distinguish between actual events and news reports about them. When citizens become outraged about events, they direct their outrage at the media, which brought them the news, rather than at the actual source of their anger. Frank (1969) refers to this as "transference." If society is threatened by crime, economic upheaval, or social disorder, individuals feel that it is the media that threaten them.

Another part of this theory suggests that partisan viewers find the news media's objectivity frightening. Partisan viewers believe that the media must also be partisan. This suggests that critics who shout about "media bias" are themselves biased, opposing objectivity. Frank used the logic of this theory to defend NBC's coverage of the 1968 Democratic party convention in Chicago. According to him, critics of the coverage were opposed to the protesters and NBC's objective reporting:

If such young protesters are as unpopular as I think in the United States today, it seems to me worth suggesting that by showing their confrontation with police without at the same time denouncing them we may have appeared, to those that loathed them, as supporting them. This was made worse by showing them being beaten. The normal reaction of most Americans is sympathy with victims, any victims in any situation. . . . People who hated the victims were revolted by their own sympathetic reactions. This revulsion was transferred to the medium, television. (1969, 91)

It is the news media's detachment and objectivity, rather than biases, that upsets partisans, according to this view.

In the "mirror theory" of news reporting, sources are individuals who either make news or function as "surrogate observers" for journalists. Surrogate observers are needed because there are more things that occur than any journalist can observe (Roshco 1975, 84). Because sources function merely as conduits of information to the objective journalist, there can be no claim that the media use biased sources.

For the news media, the claim of objectivity is primarily a shield against criticism (Tuchman 1972). As Reuven Frank (1969) demonstrated, the objectivity defense can also be turned into an effective offensive weapon. All criticism can be dismissed as simple political partisanship.

Despite claims to objectivity, research does show that there are systematic biases in the selection of sources by journalists. Whitney et al. (1989) and Brown et al. (1987) found that government officials are used more frequently than any other type of source in print and broadcast news reports. Whitney et al. and Hoynes and Croteau (1989) discovered that women rarely appear as sources in network television news stories. They also found that representatives of civil rights, human rights and labor groups are underrepresented as sources. White males associated with elite institutions were found to be the most frequently used sources in studies conducted by FAIR (1990), Herman and Chomsky (1988), and Hoynes and Croteau (1989). These studies demonstrate that news reports do not simply mirror society. Women comprise over half of the U.S. population, blacks comprise over 12 percent, while labor unions represent about 20 percent of the work force, yet members of these groups are rarely among the sources chosen by journalists. If the media simply mirror societal events, representatives of these groups would appear more frequently in the news than they currently do.

From the standpoint of objective journalism, these research results do not diminish the argument that the news media merely reflect occurrences. Journalists contend that white males associated with elite organizations are the most frequently cited sources because they are the most newsworthy. As Bernard Roshco argued:

Big "names" make news not only because they tend to know more than lesser names but also because they usually do what concerns more people. Sources thus become newsworthy as they wield more power, thereby functioning as increasingly important "causes of social arrangements." In this sense, the biggest "name" of all for the American press and its mass audience is the president of the United States. (1975, 75)

"Nightline" producer Richard Kaplan dismissed the Hoynes and Croteau (1989) study of sources using this argument (Gerard, 1989, 18).

Even when this explanation for the documented biases in the composition of news makers is accepted, it does not apply to news shapers, who are not part of a news event and are not direct "causes of social arrangements." While journalists might argue that the news shapers whom they select are more knowledgeable than alternative sources, this argument is not one of objectivity, but rather one of credentials. The burden of proof is therefore placed on journalists to prove that their news shapers are knowledgeable. In the case of news makers, this proof is usually self-evident. The chairman of the Joint Chiefs of Staff is unquestionably better informed about U.S. military tactics than any outsider, the secretary of state is better informed about U.S. foreign policy strategy than almost anyone else, and the Senate majority leader is no doubt better informed about legislative affairs than any alternative source. In the case of news makers, it is also clear that they have partisan associations. The chairman of the Joint Chiefs speaks for the U.S. armed forces, not pacifist groups, the secretary of state is part of the elected administration, and the Senate majority leader represents either Democrats or Republicans, but not both.

The expertise of news shapers is not necessarily self-evident, nor is the direction of their partisanship. Despite the news media's anointing individuals with the title of "expert" or "analyst," there are reasons to doubt many news shapers' expertise. For example, "CBS Evening News" (February 4, 1988) described former Fleet Street writer Ronald Payne as a "terrorism expert," even though Payne has described himself as "a well-experienced hack [who] will go anywhere and can avoid cliches" (*Contemporary Authors*, vol. 97-100, p. 427). Payne coauthored a number of paperbacks about terrorism, including *Terror: The Western Response* (1980), *Terror! The West Fights Back* (1982), and *Counterattack! The West's Battle Against Terrorists* (1982), which apparently caused CBS to confer the title of "terrorism expert" upon him. However, none of his books contain footnotes, documentation, or other proof that they are anything other than pulp fiction. (Payne's books, in addition to having similar titles, repeat the same message: the U.S.S.R. is the principal sponsor of international terrorism.)

In some cases, the mass media have been known to provide news shapers with expert-sounding credentials when the individuals' accomplishments are much more modest. For example, the *New York Times* described AEI spokesman Norman Ornstein as the "author and editor of dozens of books and monographs" (July 15, 1985, 12), while the *U.S. News and World Report* described him as the "author of seven books on government" (January 28, 1985, p. 53). Ornstein, in fact, never authored one book by himself; he coauthored one book titled *Interest Groups, Lobbying and Policymaking* in 1978 (Cooper and Soley 1990). Three years after being crowned as a "leading political authority" by the *U.S. News and World Report*, Ornstein also coauthored a summary of a nationwide Gallup poll titled "The People, Press and Politics."

Ornstein's rise as a leading news shaper was chronicled by the *Washington Monthly*, which dubbed him "The King of Quotes." According to this magazine, Ornstein was quoted by the media a few times in the late 1970s, slightly more often during 1980 and 1981, but increasingly during the middle 1980s, so that by 1986 he was "quoted more than 300 times by major print organizations and at least as often by smaller newspapers," and "appeared about ten times on 'Nightline' and 30 times on 'The MacNeil/Lehrer NewsHour' in addition to frequent appearances on the CBS 'Morning News,' National Public Radio, and NBC's 'Today Show' '' (Waldam 1986, 34). During his 'Nightline' appearances, Ornstein was described as a "congressional scholar," "tax policy expert," and "political scientist," while the *New York Times* described him as an "economist," "political analyst," and expert on "congressional–White House relations." He commented on regulation of the National Football League for *Sport* magazine, labor policy for *Fleet Owner*, and abortion for *Ladies Home Journal*.

On the NBC news (March 22, 1989), Ornstein explained how he rose to prominence as a news shaper: "One of the things I've found is that the more of this I end up doing, the more I end up doing." What Ornstein described is what political scientists, communication researchers, and sociologists describe as the "status conferral function" of the mass media. This theory was introduced by Paul Lazarsfeld and Robert Merton, who observed that

the mass media confer status on public issues, persons, organizations and social movements. . . . Recognition by the press or radio or magazines or newsreels testifies that one has arrived, that one is important enough to have been singled out from the large anonymous masses, that one's behavior and opinions are significant enough to require public notice. (1948, 101)

As media attention increases, so does status, and as status increases, individuals attract more media attention.

If viewers are mesmerized into believing that news events and televised reports are synonymous, reporters become convinced of the expertise of news shapers merely because other journalists have quoted them. The reason why reporters constantly interview Norman Ornstein is not his credentials—Ornstein admits that "there are lots of other political scientists out there who have a staggering understanding of Congress, and there are plenty who are brighter than I am"—it's because other journalists have used him. One Washington reporter who never used Ornstein as a source claimed that she "felt like an idiot for not having known to call him. . . . I just hadn't realized he was a big cheese" (Waldman 1986, 36, 39). That's what is meant by status conferral . . . and "pack journalism."

Status is conferred by the media, not news shapers' insights or accuracy. In fact, news shapers can be wrong, but their status increases anyway. In 1980, Ornstein predicted that the Democrats would lose only four or five Senate seats. They lost twelve and control of the Senate. He also predicted that major tax legislation would never pass. It did. And a few months prior to the presidential campaign that made Willie Horton a household name, Ornstein said, "Maybe I'm stretching this a bit too far, but the point is that the broader public has begun to get a different image of black Americans" as a result of Jesse Jackson's presidential campaign (Minneapolis *Star Tribune*, April 28, 1988,1A).

Even when news shapers clearly have some knowledge about a topic, there is no reason to believe that they are detached and objective, despite being presented as such. Norman Ornstein is associated with the conservative AEI and admits to being a "political moderate" (*New York Times*, July 15, 1985, 12). There is no evidence that he is neutral toward liberal or radical policy proposals. Stephen Hess, a senior fellow at the Brookings Institution who reports that he was used as a news shaper 301 times by television reporters and 789 times by print journalists in 1988 (Hess 1989), has a long history of Republican activism. He worked as a staff assistant to President Eisenhower, an assistant to the Senate Republican whip, a deputy assistant on urban affairs to President Nixon, editor of the 1976 Republican National Platform, and a member of several Republican party committees. Hess's Republican credentials are never disclosed by reporters who interview him. He is always described as a Brookings Institution "scholar" or "political analyst." And David Gergen, who was simply described as editor of *Public Opinion* magazine by NBC, was actually a campaign strategist for George Bush immediately before an appearance as a network news shaper (NBC—July 21, 1980) and a Reagan adviser immediately afterward. Following Reagan's election victory, Gergen joined the president's White House staff. That's hardly what most people think of when they hear the words "detached" and "objective."

EXPLAINING SOURCE SELECTION

In *The Boys on the Bus*, Timothy Crouse described the activities of journalists during the 1972 presidential campaign. He concluded that "campaign journalism is, by definition, pack journalism" (1972, 15). Reporters follow candidates around in groups, are fed the same lines, hear the same rumors, and write the same stories. Many times reporters "arrive at their answers just as independently as a class of honest seventh graders using the same geometry text" (44). If a reporter comes up with a different story than everyone else, editors are immediately suspicious of it. For these reasons, most news reports sound the same.

At other times, the direction of the pack is determined in a hierarchical fashion, with *New York Times* reporters on top and reporters from small newspapers on the bottom. According to Crouse, the "experienced national political reporters, wire men, and big-paper reporters, who were at the top of the pecking order, often did not know the names of men from smaller papers, who were at the bottom" (7). Because small-paper reporters want to move up to the big time, they follow the lead of journalism's heavyweights. During the 1968 election, this hierarchical structure doomed George Romney's presidential bid. The *New York Times* reported that Romney confessed to being "brainwashed" about Vietnam on a Detroit television talk show, and "the networks, always guided by the *Times*, picked it up. The papers in Romney's home state of Michigan, chagrined at having missed such a big local story, compensated by turning it into a monumental issue" (Crouse 1972, 184).

The careers of national news shapers are created in the same way that Romney's elective political career was destroyed. Norman Ornstein started his career as a political pundit by writing a book review for the *Washington Post*, then a few more reviews, and then op-ed pieces. Once legitimized by the prestige press, he graduated to appearances on public broadcasting, and finally to the networks. The rise of William Schneider was similar. He worked as a polling consultant with the *Los Angeles Times*, wrote op-ed pieces based on the polls, and then graduated to writing his own column. After being ordained by the *Los Angeles Times*, Schneider was ready for the networks.

Although pack journalism explains why Stephen Hess, William Schneider, and Norman Ornstein are interviewed over and over again by reporters, it does not explain why news sources are almost always white, male, and from elite institutions. The simplest explanation for the homogeneity among news sources was offered by sociologist Herbert Gans (1979), who observed that journalists "find it easiest to make contact with sources similar to them in class position, as well as race, age, and other characteristics" (125).

Several studies have shown that journalists of the 1970s and 1980s differ greatly from those pictured in Ben Hecht's *The Front Page* (1928) or described by Leo Rosten (1937) in *Journalism Quarterly*. Rosten surveyed 127 Washington reporters and found that 60 finished college, 36 had some college training, 8 never finished high school, and 2 never went to high school. These journalists had stereotyped worldviews, lacked analytic skills, and were blue-collar rather than academic in outlook.

A 1978 survey of journalists conducted by Hess (1981) found that Washington journalists were white, male, well educated, and disproportionately from the Northeast region of the United States. Males not only outnumbered females by a four-to-one ratio, but were much more likely to work for the pack-leading, high-prestige news organizations. Even when women worked for prestige media, they often got the low-prestige assignments, such as regulatory and domestic agencies. Ninety-three percent of the reporters surveyed were college graduates, 33 percent had graduate degrees, and over 6 percent held law or doctorate degrees. Washington reporters were very likely to have attended "selective" universities such as Columbia and Northwestern, and this likelihood increased with the prestige of the medium for which they worked. Finally and not surprisingly, the overwhelming majority of Washington reporters were white. Fewer than 5 percent were black.

During 1979 and 1980, Lichter, Rothman, and Lichter (1986) conducted interviews with 238 reporters, columnists, bureau chiefs, and editors from three weekly news magazines, television networks, the *New York Times*, the *Wall Street Journal*, and *Washington Post*. The characteristics of this sample were almost identical to those reported by Hess: 95 percent were white, 79 percent were male, and 93 percent were college graduates. Moreover, 55 percent had postgraduate education, 78 percent had an individual income exceeding $30,000, and 40 percent had fathers who were in professional occupations.

The findings of Hess and Lichter, Rothman, and Lichter differed mainly in their descriptions of journalists' political views. Hess found that 42 percent of Washington journalists described themselves as liberals, 39 percent said that they were middle-of-the-road, and 19 percent identified themselves as conservatives.

Interestingly, 46 percent claimed that they were more conservative than the rest of the press corps, suggesting that reporters accept the stereotypical view that reporters are liberal, even though more than half claim that they are not (1981, 87).

By contrast, Lichter, Rothman, and Lichter report that 54 percent of their sample were politically liberal. The method that these researchers used to classify the respondents has been criticized for drawing inferences about "journalists which do not accurately reflect the answers they gave to the survey questions" (Gans 1985, 31) and for violating "basic survey methodology by first inferring people's opinions from answers to single questions, and then treating their answers as strongly felt opinions" (Whitney 1987, 871). Lichter, Rothman, and Lichter tried to classify their respondents politically based on several questions and subjective tests, rather than allow the journalists to classify themselves. It is this method of classification that aroused the criticism fron Gans and Whitney.

Notwithstanding the debate concerning the political viewpoints of reporters, these surveys reveal an upscale, highly educated, and well-paid newsroom. According to former *New York Times* correspondent John Herbers, salaries continued to escalate during the late 1970s and early 1980s, so that by the mid-1980s Washington journalists had become a "moneyed elite" (Doyle 1990). They not only get hefty salaries, but are increasingly in demand as speakers for corporations, industry groups, lobbyists and other organizations. Well-known journalists get anywhere from $4,000 to $20,000 for their speeches. Commentator George Will reportedly receives between $12,000 and $15,000 for each of the 40 or so speeches that he gives each year, boosting his annual income to over $1 million (Willrich 1990).

Given the demographic characteristics of elite reporters, it is not surprising that they use white, male elite members as their primary sources. Reporters, editors, and bureau chiefs of prestige media have much more in common with businessmen, government leaders, and sociologists from Harvard University than with African-American social workers. It should not be surprising that journalists are more likely to go to businessmen, government leaders, or Ivy League academics for comments about crime than to African-American social workers or probation officers.

It is the degree to which sources mirror the characteristics of reporters that is surprising. Dominick (1977) and Whitney et al. (1989) found that a disproportionately large percentage of stories originate in the Northeast, where the largest percentage of reporters were born and raised. Hoynes and Croteau (1989) found that blacks accounted for only 6.2 percent of "Nightline" guests. This is almost the same percentage of prestige journalists who are black. Lichter, Rothman, and Lichter (1986) found 21 percent of their sample of journalists to be female, and 13.6 percent of the sources in Whitney et al.'s (1989) sample of network television sources were female. If "mirror theory" exists at all, it needs to be reformulated, stating that news events and sources most closely reflect the demographic characteristics of reporters, not society. Based on this theory, news shapers should be upper-income, white males from the Northeast with Ivy League educations.

ALTERNATIVE EXPLANATIONS

Washington journalists might be demographically and psychographically similar to Hollywood screenwriters, but this doesn't mean that news stories, like television sitcoms, are fiction. News stories reflect a reality, but one that is socially constructed. As Gaye Tuchman observed, reporting "is the act of constructing reality itself rather than a picture of reality" (1978, 12). This reality is increasingly constructed by well-paid elite members who work for corporations dedicated to producing profits, not informed readers, and many reporters are aware of this. When ABC correspondent Sam Donaldson refused to divulge his income to another reporter, saying it "would hurt his credibility as 'the guy in the trenchcoat' " (Willrich 1990), he highlighted this problem. The massive salaries of Dan Rather ($2.3 million), Tom Brokaw ($1.7 million), and Peter Jennings ($1.8 million) suggest that they have little in common with the average American. Their reality is that of the rich and famous.

Long before Washington journalists became a moneyed elite, social scientists observed that "objective reporting" served to legitimize the status quo (Tuchman 1978). "Objective reporting" perpetuates the status quo because it does not criticize the existing social order and because it relies heavily upon sources from legitimated institutions, such as businesses, government, trade groups, and professional associations. Spokespersons from these legitimated institutions are referred to as "conventional sources" by journalists (Strentz 1989). These spokespersons are routinely contacted by journalists, which is why they are called "conventional sources."

Members of anti–status quo groups are viewed as unconventional sources. They are rarely used as news sources because legitimated institutions generate far more stories and "information than the news media can accommodate" (Strentz 1989, 124). Reporters never admit that they avoid using unconventional sources because of the sources' anti–status quo viewpoints. Instead, reporters argue that legitimated institutions do more that is newsworthy and therefore deserve more media attention. Spokesmen from legitimated institutions are therefore used as sources more often than those from nonlegitimated institutions.

Not only are reporters taught that using conventional sources is the standard practice of journalism; they also know that editors serve as enforcers of this practice. Reporters who wish to get their stories published must use these sources. Stories that do not are usually killed (Tuchman 1972).

This helps to explain why Whitney et. al. (1989) found that spokesmen for businesses appear frequently on network news programs, but consumer activists do not. It also explains why professionals who are affiliated with universities, law firms, hospitals, or other legitimated institutions appear with regularity, but spokespersons from women's and civil rights groups rarely appear. When advertising regulation is discussed, spokesmen from the government, American Association of Advertising Agencies, American Advertising Federation, and Association of National Advertisers will be used as sources, but members of Action for Children's Television (ACT) and similar groups will not be used.

Because the day-to-day activities of unconventional groups are not considered newsworthy by the press, unconventional groups find it necessary to stage ''newsworthy events'' in order to publicize their cause. This explains why anti-status quo groups are always staging demonstrations or sit-ins, or getting arrested. While these events are newsworthy and temporarily focus media attention on the group and its cause, the actions only reinforce journalists' perceptions that these groups are not legitimated, making it more difficult for them to become conventional sources, which is what they actually seek.

This explanation for source selection suggests that news shapers will also be drawn from legitimated institutions. Former government officials, university professors, and representatives of public policy think tanks will be called specialists or experts on the environment, but spokespersons for Greenpeace, Clean Water Action (CWA), and Citizens for a Better Environment (CBE) will not. Greenpeace, CWA, and CBE spokespersons are called environmental activists, regardless of their credentials. In this world, a scientist with a doctorate in marine biology is described as an activist if affiliated with Greenpeace, but a think tank spokesman with a masters degree in chemistry or economics is called an expert.

This theory of legitimated institutions also suggests that the more closely associated an organization is with other legitimated institutions, the more frequently its spokespersons will be used as news shapers. Thus representatives of AEI, which receives its financial support from corporations and corporate foundations, will produce more news shapers than the Economic Policy Institute, a think tank that receives much of its financial support from labor unions. Likewise, elite, private universities will supply many more news shapers than public institutions like the University of California at Berkeley, which has an academic reputation equal to or better than that of most private east coast colleges. This is because former officials like David Gergen, Henry Kissinger, and Zbigniew Brzezinski frequently teach at private eastern universities after leaving government. Their presence at Harvard, Georgetown, or Columbia further legitimates these universities.

While these explanations of news shaper selection are consistent with the practice of ''objective journalism,'' Hess (1989, 1990) has offered a different explanation for news shaper selection—journalists, particularly, broadcast journalists, are dishonest. Rather than testing a hypothesis to find out whether it's true or false, journalists simply ''marshal facts or quotes'' that are consistent with their presumptions. Information that is inconsistent with the slant of their stories is discarded. According to Hess (1989, 1990), who is frequently used as a news shaper, producers call ''to check me out, asking enough questions to know whether I am likely to say what they are after. If I don't respond appropriately, they say they'll get back to me. Which normally means they won't'' (1990, 22). The producers continue to call around until they find someone who will say ''the magic words that they are looking for.''

Some journalists have virtually confessed to Hess's charges. Jack Nelson, head of the *Los Angeles Times*' Washington bureau, said, ''When you are going to make an opinionated kind of statement, particularly in the news columns, editors insist you attribute it to someone other than yourself—so you go shopping.'' When asked by *New York Times* reporter Barbara Gamarekian (1989, 10) whether reporters shop for someone ''who reflects [their] point of view,'' Nelson responded, ''It happens.''

Hess's (1989, 1990) charges of dishonesty are not new, but he does have a unique explanation for why broadcast journalists have become the most dishonest of all journalists: The spate of takeovers has put many broadcasting operations under financial pressure. The financial pressure has meant reduced staffs and fewer stories, so that fewer interviews are conducted. When reporters do conduct an interview on tape, they want it to be usable. Because each story that is broadcast can use only one or two interviews, producers find themselves shopping for statements that are consistent rather than contradictory. This pressure has produced a new attitude or ethic among broadcast journalists—locate the statement that you need and then go out and tape it. Hess claims that this ''shopping'' is less likely to occur in print journalism, where information collection is less costly and there are fewer time constraints.

While print journalists might not shop around to find the ''right'' quote, they have become so reliant on certain sources that they simply don't contact others. This has caused reporters to miss major stories like the savings and loan bankruptcies, according to Ellen Hume (1990). *Los Angeles Times* reporters became so reliant on Norman Ornstein's opinions and quoted him so often that the paper placed a moratorium on using him. *Times* reporter Robert Shogun typified this reliance on Ornstein. He told *Washington Monthly* editor Steven Waldman, ''I just trust his judgement. If I were going to buy a used car I'd call him'' (Waldman 1986, 37). Because of this dependence, Shogun and other members of the pack failed to uncover the Iran-Contra Affair, the savings and loan bankruptcies, the HUD scandals, and other major stories.

Washington-based reporters do not seem to realize the problem that their reliance on a small number of Washington-based news shapers has produced. Reporters have used the same, familiar news shapers to comment on the Iran-Contra deal, HUD scandals, ethics violations, and savings and loan failures, even though these news shapers had no knowledge about these problems until others revealed them. The irony is that the news shapers learned about these events by reading about them in the reporters' newspapers.

NEWS SHAPERS: REIFYING THE WORLD

Tuchman (1978) concluded that journalists' methods of identifying and interacting with sources objectify and reify social events. Objectification and reification refer to the presentation of social occurrences such as civil disorders, environmental disasters, and economic activities as events that are outside of human control. These events are presented as naturally occurring processes.

Reification is the extreme case of objectification, where "the objectified world loses its comprehensibility as a human enterprise and becomes fixated as a non-human, non-humanizable inert facticity" (Berger and Luckmann 1967, 89). Reification presents socially produced events as processes that are "akin to fluctuations in weather" (Tuchman 1978, 214). Within this process of reification, news shapers are an essential, and perhaps the most important, component. "Experts" are used by reporters to explain social and economic events to news consumers, just as meteorologists explain the weather. Sociologists, economists, and environmental "experts" serve the same function for social processes that meteorologists serve for weather: they provide expertise about complex phenomena that news consumers would presumably not understand if it weren't for these individuals' analyses. When consumers understand the phenomenon, the need for news shapers presumably disappears.

The primary function of news shapers, according to journalists who use them, is to provide analysis that is comprehensible to readers and viewers. News shapers, according to this view, provide background and commentary about phenomena that are otherwise difficult to understand. If news shapers are used to provide analyses about everyday political events, it suggests that reporters view political events as unfathomable to the average citizen. The more frequently the news media use news shapers, the more they imply that events are explainable only by experts—individuals who "have done it or studied it or clearly have been academic observers of it for years," as Sam Donaldson (1990, 24) put it. "You just don't go ask the man on the street" to explain these events.

The use of "experts" rather than the "man on the street" creates an objectified image of politics: It is understandable to experts, who succinctly explain the process and problems to news consumers. The by-product of this is depoliticization and dysfunction. Depoliticization occurs because the political process is reified and nonparticipatory. According to the picture painted by the media, politics consists of events such as stump speeches, debates, and commercials that are part of a complex strategy. The strategies are too complex for the average citizen to understand, which is why experts are called upon to explain them. Citizens learn who won a debate from experts or from polls that analysts describe. "Political scientists" explain why a candidate emphasizes one issue over another and why a commercial will be effective. The passive reception of predigested media messages becomes a substitute for political involvement, while simultaneously creating a world in which politics is an arena reserved exclusively for experts. In this arena, there are no grassroots activists or citizen-campaigners. If this theory of news shapers and depoliticization is correct, the increased use of news shapers should be related to decreased political participation.

Moreover, this theory suggests that news shapers have a vested interest in reifying the political process and diluting grassroots politics. If grassroots politics indeed existed, the grassroots activists, not news shapers, would become the center of the media's attention. The interest that news shapers have in being in the media spotlight is not just psychological; it's also economic. News shapers, like Washington journalists, are frequently paid to make speeches before groups. Although they get only a fraction of what big-name journalists are paid, news shapers can still get several thousand dollars per speech. Without the media spotlight, this source of easy income would evaporate.

Dysfunction occurs because citizens, who have limited contact with the U.S. political process to begin with, receive almost all of their political information from the media. This information is shaped by "experts," who reduce the news consumers' need to independently assess occurrences. This explains why news shapers have a significant effect on public opinion (Page, Shapiro, and Dempsey 1987): They shape the news that is delivered to a politically immobilized public. Experts provide citizens with a superficial knowledge about events, and this knowledge becomes a substitute for political involvement. As Lazarsfeld and Merton (1948) described it, citizens substitute knowing about a problem for doing something about it. The news shapers encourage citizens to understand the complicated world of politics but do not encourage citizens to get involved. News shapers produce an elitist picture of politics that serves to reinforce their own status as "experts." It assures that news shapers, not the "man in the street," will provide political analysis.

The dysfunctional and depoliticizing aspects of news shapers are clearly discernible from their comments. Long before any presidential primary or caucus was held, William Schneider (ABC–July 30, 1987) declared, "Most Democrats agree that it would be suicidal to put Jesse Jackson on the ticket . . . a minority candidate or someone who's controversial could endanger their prospects and they're just not in the mood to do that." In essence, Schneider recommended that Jackson supporters sit out the 1988 election. Moreover, Schneider painted an elitist, reified picture of politics, where political events are as predetermined as an eruption from Yellowstone's Old Faithful geyser.

Tuchman also suggests that "news presentations soothe the news consumer even as they reify social forces" (1978, 214). This is particularly true of news shapers, who are presented as "experts" with a commanding knowledge about social problems and processes. To citizens, it is soothing to know that there are experts out there who understand and are able to solve problems. Because the experts can solve the problems, it decreases the need for citizen participation in problem solving, further eroding participatory democracy.

4

THE NETWORK
TELEVISION NEWS
SHAPERS: A COMPARISON
OF 1979–1980 WITH
1987–1988

Except for Atwater and Green's (1988) study of sources used during news coverage of the June 1985 TWA hijacking, no study has examined the extent to which news shapers are used in network television reports. Atwater and Green found that 10 percent of the networks' sources were former U.S. officials, experts, or journalists.

To determine how frequently network reporters use news shapers in other stories, a study of two samples of network news programs was conducted. One sample consisted of six weeks of programming that was randomly selected from that airing between January 1, 1987, and December 30, 1988; the other was selected from newscasts airing on the same dates between January 1, 1979, and December 30, 1980.[1] The purpose of the samples was to determine the frequency with which news shapers appeared and whether their use has increased or decreased during the last decade. Within these two sample periods, a record was kept of the name and title of every news shaper who appeared. News shapers were defined as follows:

Former Politicians and U.S. Government Officials: people who are no longer in government, including the advisers, aides, speech writers, and press secretaries of former politicians and officials

Economists: individuals described as "economists" and "economic analysts" or "industry analysts" by the networks

Think tank spokespersons: individuals who are associates of foundations, centers, or institutes that conduct research and publish policy papers

Experts, Analysts, and Consultants: individuals who were described by the networks as
such in newscasts, except when described as economic or industry analysts

Journalists: editors, reporters, columnists, and broadcast news reporters who work for
U.S. media but do not work for the networks

Academics: individuals described as professors, political scientists, historians, or sociologists
or whose title is not given but who are described as spokespersons or representatives of universities

Other: including lobbyists, pollsters, psychiatrists, and teachers who provide background
information but are not involved in the news event.

Between 1979-1980 and 1987-1988, which comprised the periods from which
the two samples were drawn, major changes occurred in news-gathering
technology, the political environment, and network ownership and structure. The
technological changes in news gathering that took place between 1979 and 1987
have been many. The automated library was introduced, allowing reporters to
identify people to interview, get angles and ideas, and conduct quick background
research before starting a story (Hansen, Ward, and McLeod 1987). Remote video
and satellite news-gathering technology has allowed reporters to travel greater
distances to obtain stories and interviews, while home satellite, video cassette
players, cable, and low-power television have provided increased competition
for broadcast news. In the political environment, there was a change from a
Democratic to a Republican administration. The latter change is important con-
sidering Sam Donaldson's claim that the reason news shapers' opinions range
from "middle-of-the-road to slightly to the right . . . is a reflection of the prevailing Washington power structure, and the political winds" (1990, 45). If Donaldson
is correct, more left-of-center news shapers should have been used during
1979-1980, when a Democratic administration was in power. Finally, between
1979 and 1987, network ownership changed hands. Capitol Cities, Inc., purchased
ABC in 1985, NBC was purchased by General Electric in 1986, and CBS fell
into the hands of financier Laurence Tisch after fighting a takeover battle with
Cable News Network (CNN) owner Ted Turner in 1986. These ownership changes
are important, according to Hess (1990), because the takeovers placed financial
constraints on news gathering that had not previously existed.

In addition to these changes, there has been a substantial change in the frequency with which news shapers were used between 1979-1980 and 1987-1988,
as Table 1 shows. During the eight years that transpired between the end of the
Carter presidency and the end of the Reagan presidency, there was a threefold
increase in the use of news shapers by the networks. The number of news shaper
appearances in the 1979-1980 sample was only 88; this increased to 260 in the
1987-1988 sample, or more than 1 news shaper appearance per broadcast.

In the 1979-1980 sample, the 88 appearances were made by 77 individuals,
with 9 people appearing more than once. Only 1 of the 9—Henry Kissinger—

Table 1
Comparison of News Shaper Appearances in 1979–1980 and 1987–1988 Samples

	1979–1980	1987–1988
ABC	31	81
CBS	35	115
NBC	22	64
Total	88	260

appeared more than twice. President Nixon's secretary of state appeared four times. As a consequence, the 9 news shapers who appeared twice or more accounted for 20 (or 22.7 percent) of the 88 news shaper appearances.

By contrast, the 260 appearances in the 1987-1988 sample were made by 177 people. Of the 177, 143 appeared only once, while 34 were interviewed twice or more. Thus, 34 people accounted for 117, or 45 percent of all, appearances. This suggests that the networks, while increasing their use of news shapers during the last decade, have relied on proportionately fewer people to shape their news.

These findings provide support for Hess's (1990) contention that there have been changes in the way that news shapers are used by broadcast journalists, but in a different way than Hess suggests. Network reporters use more, rather than fewer, news shapers and apparently use them for a broader array of topics than in the past. Hess argues that financial cutbacks in newsrooms following takeovers in the industry have changed reporters' styles of news gathering. The findings of this study are consistent with that argument. Part of the cutbacks included the closing of news bureaus, which has made the network news reports even more dependent on "experts" for explaining breaking news events. The experts' explanations have become a substitute for on-location reporting. In 1989, for example, NBC merged its Moscow bureau with those of the British Broadcasting Corporation and Visnews, a news service partly owned by NBC. The network also closed its Paris bureau, but opened one in Barcelona, Spain (*New York Times*, August 15, 1989, C18). The Barcelona bureau was opened to improve NBC's coverage of the 1992 Summer Olympics. This move is expected to generate higher ratings and profits for the network, a policy that is consistent with Hess's thesis.

Since reporters in the later sample repeatedly used the same news shapers, it appears that the networks are using a "golden rolodex," where previously they did not. In the 1987-1988 sample, 2 individuals—Norman Ornstein and Ed Rollins—appeared ten times. No one in the 1979-1980 sample appeared this frequently. Ornstein, as previously stated, is associated with the AEI. Rollins is a longtime Republican activist and consultant, who became head of the Republican Congressional Campaign Committee in 1989. William Schneider, David Gergen,

Fouad Ajami, and Stephen Hess appeared six times, while Kevin Phillips appeared five times during 1987-1989. Schneider, like Ornstein, is associated with the AEI, while Gergen, Hess, and Phillips served under Richard Nixon and other Republican presidents. Professor Fouad Ajami, who teaches at Johns Hopkins University, appeared exclusively on the CBS network, for which he worked as a "Mideast consultant." Overall, these frequently appearing consultants did not represent very divergent political perspectives, running from center-right to far right.

Moreover, a number of news shapers who appeared in the 1979-1980 sample also appeared in the 1987-1988 sample: auto industry analyst David Healy (ABC–February 8, 1987, and NBC–August 3, 1979), conservative writer and consultant Richard Viguerie (ABC–August 12, 1987, and NBC–November 14, 1980), Free Congress Educational Foundation director Paul Weyrich (NBC–February 7, 1987, and ABC–November 10, 1980), former negotiator Paul Warnke (NBC–September 18, 1987, and ABC–November 11, 1980), Stephen Hess (ABC–November 13, 1988, and ABC–August 3, 1979), former president Nixon (ABC–November 21, 1988, and CBS–September 22, 1979), economist David Jones (CBS–May 11, 1988, and NBC–November 21, 1980), former attorney general Griffin Bell (ABC–May 18, 1988, and ABC–November 9, 1980), and *Des Moines Register* reporter James Gannon (NBC–May 15, 1988, and CBS–January 18, 1980). Only 2 of these individuals, Stephen Hess and Richard Viguerie, appeared more than once in the 1987-1988 sample. Both are identified with Republican rather than Democratic party causes.

Two of the nine people who appeared in 1979-1980 and 1987-1988 were classified as economists (i.e., David Healy and David Jones), two were associated with the Nixon administration (i.e., Richard Nixon and Stephen Hess), two were with the Carter administration (i.e., Paul Warnke and Griffin Bell), and one was with the prestige press (i.e., James Gannon).[2] Viguerie and Weyrich, regardless of how they were described by the networks, are avowed conservatives. Overall, Republicans and conservatives who appeared in both samples outnumbered Democrats by two to one, raising doubts about Sam Donaldson's (1990) assertion that the characteristics of news shapers reflect the characteristics of the Washington establishment. Moreover, the two economic analysts who appeared in both samples were associated with business firms, not universities. David Healy worked for Drexel Burnham Lambert, a brokerage firm, and David Jones was vice president and economist for the Aubrey C. Lanston Company, which specializes in securities and government bonds.

FORMER POLITICIANS AND U.S. OFFICIALS

An analysis of the party affiliations of "former officials" who appeared in the samples also casts doubt on Donaldson's assertion. The composition of the samples is presented in Table 2. The percentage of news shapers who were either former politicians or government officials increased over the years, rising from 13.6 to

Table 2
Appearances by Former Politicians and Government Officials

	1979–1980	1987–1988
Democrats	4	20
Republicans	8	33
Total	12	53
Percent of All News Shapers	13.6	20.4

over 20 percent. In the 1979-1980 sample former Republican leaders outnumbered former Democratic party leaders by a 2-to-1 margin, while in the 1987-1988 sample Republicans outnumbered Democrats by 1.65 to 1. This is the opposite of what Donaldson suggested. Regardless of the party that controlled the White House, Republicans outnumbered Democrats as news shapers. Moreover, it should be noted that two of the Democratic appearances in 1979-1980 occurred after Jimmy Carter lost the 1980 presidential election, not before. These appearances were by former Attorney General Griffin Bell (ABC–November 10) and by former defense official Paul Warnke (ABC–November 11). One Republican also appeared after the election (CBS–November 16). This was former Treasury Secretary George Shultz, who became President Reagan's secretary of state in 1982. Lastly, it should be noted that four of the eight appearances in the first sample were by Henry Kissinger, who spoke about the collapse of détente (NBC–January 28, 1980) and SALT II (ABC–September 19, 1979, and CBS and NBC–August 2, 1979).

In both samples, three of the individuals coded as "former politicians" were actually former campaign advisers, not former office seekers or holders. In the 1979-1980 sample, the appearances were by former Reagan campaign managers John Sears (NBC–May 7, 1980) and Stuart Spencer (CBS–May 12, 1980) and former McGovern adviser Frank Mankiewicz (ABC–August 2, 1979). In the 1987-1988 sample, all three were by Democrats. These appearances were by former Mondale adviser Robert Beckel (CBS–January 22, 1988), ex–Hart manager Rick Ritter (CBS–January 17, 1988), and Robert Kennedy's speech writer, Adam Walinsky (NBC–September 17, 1987).

In the 1987-1988 sample, the 50 appearances by former officials, excluding the three by speech writers and campaign advisers, were made by 34 individuals. Fourteen of the 34 were former officials of the Reagan administration. The 14 individuals accounted for 22 of the 53 (i.e., 41.5 percent) appearances attributed to former politicians and government officials. The Reagan officials included ex–undersecretary of defense Donald Hicks (CBS–November 10, 1988), former deputy assistant secretary of defense Douglas Feith (CBS–August 7, 1987), former National Security Council (NSC) member Norman Bailey (ABC–May 9, 1988), ex–labor secretary Bill Brock (ABC and CBS–November 16, 1989), former assistant secretary of defense Frank Gaffney (NBC–May 17, 1988), ex–undersecretary of state Lawrence Eagleburger (ABC–November 9, 1988), ex–White House spokesman Larry Speakes (CBS–January 24, 1988), former NSC staff member Geoffrey Kemp (ABC–February 10, 1988), and former senator John Tower (ABC–August 3, 1987), who after retiring from the Senate served as an arms negotiator. All commented on controversial issues such as the Iran/Contra arms deal, the U.S.–U.S.S.R. arms negotiations, and the budget deficit, but none were clearly identified by the networks as being former Reagan administration officials. They were described as a ''former National Security staff member'' or an ''ex–undersecretary of state'' or by another title that did not include mention of the administration that they served.

Only four officials (i.e., Sheila Tate, Dana Rohrbacher, Gary McDowell, and Ed Rollins) were clearly identified as having served in the Reagan administration. Sheila Tate (NBC–May 9, 1988) was described as an ''ex–Reagan aide,'' Dana Rohrbacher (ABC–May 9, 1988) was described as an ''ex–Reagan speech writer,'' and Gary McDowell was described as an ''ex–Justice Department official'' (NBC–May 16, 1988) and Attorney General Meese's former speech writer (e.g., ABC and CBS–May 16, 1988). Although Ed Rollins made six appearances where he was billed as a former government official (e.g., CBS–February 3, 1988, ABC–May 9, 1988, and ABC–May 19, 1988), he was clearly identified as a former Reagan aide only once (CBS–May 9, 1988). Rollins appeared on four other occasions, but was either described as a ''consultant'' (e.g., CBS–May 10, 1988) or not given a title (e.g., ABC–August 3, 1987).

Eleven of the 53 appearances were by former members of the Carter administration. Three of the 11 were by Jimmy Carter (ABC and CBS–September 22, 1987, and CBS–November 10, 1988), and two were by his director of the CIA, Stansfield Turner (CBS–February 3, 1988, and ABC–May 13, 1988). Stuart Eizenstat was described by the networks as a Carter policy ''adviser.'' He made two appearances (CBS–January 19 and November 9, 1988). The other four appearances were by former attorney general Griffin Bell (NBC–May 18, 1988), arms negotiator Paul Warnke (NBC–September 18, 1987), defense adviser Robert Komer (CBS–September 16, 1987), and Carter appointee William Oldaker (CBS–January 20, 1988), who chaired the Federal Election Commission. Oldaker commented on candidate Gary Hart's alleged violations of campaign financing laws.

Six other appearances were by former Democratic politicians. Former House speaker Thomas ''Tip'' O'Neill appeared twice (CBS–September 24, 1987, and ABC–November 9, 1988), and Stanley Brand (CBS–May 19, 1988), a former O'Neill aide who became congressional counsel, appeared once. During two appearances, Alice Rivlin (NBC–November 12 and November 16, 1988) was described as the ex–congressional budget director, so she was coded as a former government official for these appearances. Rivlin also worked for the Johnson administration. Finally, James Hamilton (NBC–February 1, 1988) appeared once. NBC described Hamilton as a "Watergate attorney," but he also served as an adviser to Sen. Edmund Muskie, so he was classified as a Democrat.

The remaining former officials served in the Nixon and Ford administrations. The appearances included ones by well-known individuals such as former president Nixon (ABC–November 21, 1988), former defense secretary James Schlesinger[3] (ABC–September 18, 1987), and Watergate defendants John Dean (ABC–May 9, 1988) and John Ehrlichman (CBS–February 10, 1988) and lesser known persons such as ex–arms negotiator John Rhinelander (ABC–February 3 and 7, 1988), former State Department intelligence director Ray Cline (NBC–February 3, 1988), ex–CIA director William Colby (ABC–February 2, 1988), and ex–solicitor general Philip Lacovara (NBC–January 22, 1988). When these and the appearances by former Reagan administration and officials are combined, it shows that Republican officials accounted for 62.3 percent (i.e., 33 of 53) of the appearances by persons described as former politicians and officials. Twenty of the appearances (i.e., 37.7 percent) were by Democrats, and three of these were by consultants who were identified as aides or advisers to leading Democrats.

The 62.3 percent does not include appearances by former Reagan officials who were described as journalists (e.g., David Gergen), think tank scholars (e.g., Richard Perle), or consultants (e.g., Ed Rollins), nor does it include individuals described as "experts," "analysts," or "economists" who worked for other Republican and Democratic administrations, such as Charles Schultze, Robert Hunter, Helmut Sonnenfeldt, William Hyland, Kevin Phillips, or Stephen Hess. When these and other individuals who are former government officials are added to those discussed above, Republicans accounted for 68.3 percent (69 of 102) of the appearances by former government officials in the 1987-1988 sample.[4] This percentage excludes individuals such as Richard Viguerie and Edward Luttwak, who are Republicans but have not been in government.

WOMEN AS NEWS SHAPERS

Of the 86 news shaper appearances in the 1979-1980 sample, only five (i.e., 5.8 percent) were by women. Moreover, three of the five appearances by women focused on stereotypical "women's" issues: Beverly Pagan spoke on the dangers of cancer and birth defects associated with exposure to contaminated areas such as Love Canal (CBS–May 17, 1980) psychologist Rosa Sanchez spoke on the effects of war on Nicaraguan children (NBC–August 8, 1979), and Center for Independent Living spokesperson Kitty Cone commented on congressional legislation concerning transportation for the handicapped (NBC–November 12, 1980). Thus over half of the female news shapers in the 1979-1980 sample spoke about birth dangers, children, and the handicapped, rather than on electoral politics or international affairs. This suggests that shaping political news is a "manly art."

In the 1987-1988 sample, women appeared with only marginally greater frequency, but they did speak on a broader range of topics. Only 16 of the 260 appearances (i.e., 6.2 percent) in this sample were made by women. The 16 appearances were made by 13 women. One woman, Alice Rivlin, was interviewed on three occasions, and another, Linda DiVall, was interviewed twice. Alice Rivlin was described once as an economist (CBS–November 16, 1988) and twice as the ex–congressional budget director (NBC–November 12 and November 16, 1988), which resulted in her being classified as a former government official for those appearances. The networks did not mention that Alice Rivlin is also associated with the Brookings Institution. Sheila Tate (NBC–May 9, 1988), a former Reagan aide, was the only other woman classified as a former government official. Linda DiVall was described as a "pollster" by the networks (ABC and CBS–September 28, 1987) and was therefore assigned to the "other" category by the coding for this study, as was one other woman. The networks did not report that Linda DiVall is a Republican pollster whose clients include the National Republican Committee, the National Republican Senatorial Committee, and the Dole '88 campaign (*Political Resource Directory*, 1989).

Three women in the 1987-1988 sample were classified as experts or consultants: Bassma Kadmani Darwish (ABC–August 5, 1987), Ann Lewis (CBS–August 14, 1987), and Connie Snapp (CBS–January 18, 1988). Bassma Kadmani Darwish was described as a "Mideast expert," Ann Lewis as a "Democratic consultant," and Connie Snapp as a "image consultant." Doris Kearns Goodwin (CBS–November 14, 1988) was billed as a "historian," while five other women were listed as spokespersons for centers, foundations, and institutions.

Overall, women appeared less frequently as news shapers than news makers. In their study of network news sources, Whitney et al. found that "86.4 percent of news sources were male and 13.6 percent" were female (1989, 170). Because these percentages include news shapers, it follows that proportionately more women appeared as news makers than shapers. Similar findings were obtained by Hoynes and Croteau (1989), who found that 10.3 percent of "Nightline" guests were women. The findings of that study are consistent with this one and show that women are strongly underrepresented on network news programs, relative to their numbers in the general population. This suggests that news shapers do not "mirror" society, as some journalists suggest. If these appearances do mirror a society, it is not that of the U.S. population, but rather that of Washinton journalists.

ECONOMISTS AND ECONOMIC ANALYSTS

Of the seven categories of news shapers, only the number of appearances by economists declined between 1979-1980 and 1987-1988, as shown in Table 3. Twenty-three news shapers in the 1979-1980 sample were described as economists or economic analysts by the networks, whereas 21 in the 1987-1988 sample were. While the absolute number of economists declined only modestly, the percentage decline was substantial, dropping from 26.1 percent to 8.1 percent.

This decline in appearances parallels an overall decline in news coverage about the economy. According to Ted J. Smith III (1988), there was less coverage

Table 3
Appearances by Economists, Economic Analysts, and Industry Analysts

	1979–1980	1987–1988
ABC	13	7
CBS	6	10
NBC	4	4
Total	23	21
Percent of All News Shapers	26.1	8.1

about the economy during the middle and late 1980s, after the economy had rebounded, than before, when the economy was inflationary and moribund. Smith's study was published by the Media Institute, a conservative organization that monitors media coverage for liberal bias. Needless to say, Smith concluded that the networks downplayed the "good news" about the economy and instead focused on problems such as homelessness, competitiveness, and the trade and budget deficits out of "liberal bias." Richard Goedkoop, who reviewed Smith's study, concluded that the different number of news stories about the economy was due to the media's tendency to cover "bad" rather than "good" news, not liberal bias (1990, 231). Goedkoop also hypothesized that the networks covered economic issues more extensively during the late 1970s when Carter was president than later because most economic news during Carter's presidency was bad.

This study offers support for Goedkoop's hypothesis—more economists and economic analysts appeared on the network news during 1979-1980, when the economy was in a recession, than during 1987-1988, when the economy was expanding. This finding provides evidence that is antithetical with Smith's argument about liberal media bias. If the media were liberally biased, they should have avoided covering the economy during the late 1970s, since such coverage was bad for Carter's presidency.

Moreover, an analysis of the individuals who shaped economic news during 1979-1980 reveals that the majority were representatives of commodities, stocks, bonds, and related business firms, which are typically more favorable to Republican than Democratic economic programs. Of the 23 individuals who discussed the economy, 16 (or 69.6 percent) were representatives of businesses. Not one economist or economic analyst was from a labor union or consumer organization.

Of the 23 economic news shapers, 10 were described as "economic or industry analysts" rather than economists. All ten represented businesses. For example, "stock market analyst" Joseph McAlinden (ABC–November 19, 1980) was with

Argus Research, "auto industry analyst" Arvid Jouppi (CBC–September 15, 1979) was with Keane Securities, "Wall Street analyst" Barry Sahgal (NBC–February 12, 1979) was with Prudential-Bache, "grain analyst" R. Conrad Leslie (ABC–January 16, 1980) had his own commodities research firm, "industry analyst" Tony Copp (ABC–January 23, 1980) was with Salomon Brothers, and "auto industry analyst" David Healy, who appeared twice (CBS–August 3, 1979, and ABC–November 21, 1980), was from Drexel Burnham Lambert. Drexel Burnham Lambert became a junk bond and takeover specialist during the 1980s. The networks never informed viewers of the business affiliations of these individuals; they were always described as "analysts."

Among the 13 economists, three were from universities (ABC–February 5, 1979; CBS–September 14, 1979, and ABC–February 10, 1979), two were foreign economists who discussed international economic issues (CBS–August 13, 1979, and ABC–November 17, 1980), two appearances were by a "healthcare economist" with a medical research organization (ABC–February 5 and 8, 1979), three were by spokesmen for industry-sponsored associations such as the Chamber of Commerce and Conference Board (CBS–August 6, 1979, ABC–September 14, 1979, and NBC–January 26, 1980), and three were from business. The three were John Schnittker (ABC–February 6, 1979) of Schnittker Associates, a consulting firm, Lawrence Kudlow (NBC–November 16, 1980) of Bear, Stearns and Company, and David Jones (NBC–November 21, 1980) of the Aubrey C. Lanston Company. Schnittker was U.S. undersecretary of agriculture from 1965 to 1969, while Kudlow became the Office of Management and Budget's director for economics and planning during President Reagan's first term. As with the "economic analysts," the business and organizational affiliations of these news shapers was never reported.

The networks' selection of economists and economic analysts was more balanced in the 1987-1988 sample than in the 1979-1980 sample. A wider political spectrum was represented. Even so, there was only one appearance by a political leftist. The appearance was by Peter Marchetti (ABC–January 26, 1988), who said that the severe shortages in Nicaragua were the result of the Contra war. Marchetti, a professor at the University of Wisconsin, has conducted research on the agrarian reforms in Nicaragua.

Robert Hormats (CBS–November 14, 1988), an assistant secretary for economic and business affairs in the Reagan administration, was described as an economist, as were Brookings Institution fellows Alice Rivlin (CBS–November 16, 1988), Barry Bosworth (NBC–November 16, 1988), and Charles Schultze (NBC–February 14, 1987). All three Brookings economists are former government officials. Alice Rivlin was director of the Congressional Budget Office, Charles Schultze was a member of the Council of Economic Advisers during the Eisenhower and Carter administrations, and Barry Bosworth was the director of the Council on Wage and Price Stability (1977-1979). Fred Bergsten, described by CBS as an economist in one appearance (November 12, 1988), worked in the Johnson, Nixon, and Carter administrations. The use of Hormats, Schultze,

Bergsten, Rivlin, and Bosworth as economists is consistent with the increased use of former officials in other news shaper categories during the late 1980s.

The economists in the 1987-1988 sample were from businesses, universities, and abroad. Four economists were from business firms, including David Jones (CBS–May 11, 1988) of the Aubrey C. Lanston Company, who appeared in the 1979-1980 sample, and Richard Hoey (CBS–November 21, 1988) of A. G. Becher Paribas, who also writes for *Forbes* magazine. The university professors were primarily from private universities such as Harvard (NBC–November 11, 1988) and Northwestern (CBS–August 7, 1987), but an economist from Georgia State University (ABC–January 20, 1988) also appeared. Anthony Thomas (CBS–November 11, 1988) and George Schopflin (ABC–May 21, 1988) are British economists. Schopflin is a professor at the London School of Economics.

Only five individuals in the 1987-1988 sample were described as "economic or industry analysts." These individuals were "retail analyst" Monroe Greenstein (CBS–May 20, 1988), insider trading "analyst" William LeFevre (CBS–February 12, 1987), "auto analyst" David Healy (ABC–February 8, 1987), and "energy analysts" Ed Krapels (ABC–August 10, 1987) and Drew Peck (CBS–February 12, 1987). Again, these individuals were primarily spokesmen for Wall Street firms. Greenstein was with Bear, Stearns and Company, Healy was with Drexel Burnham Lambert, LeFevre was with Advest, Inc., and Ed Krapels headed Energy Security Analysis, Inc. As in the 1979-1980 sample, the business associations of these "analysts" were never mentioned by the networks. But unlike the 1979-1980 sample, these representatives of businesses comprised less than half of the sample. Nine of the 21 (i.e., 42.9 percent) economists and economic analysts were from businesses.

Among the seven categories of news shapers, economists in the 1987-1988 sample exhibited the greatest diversity of viewpoints. While exhibiting the greatest diversity, economists and economic analysts were only a small percentage of this sample, as Table 4 shows. Only 21 of the 260 (i.e., 8.1 percent) news shapers discussed the economy. This is a substantial decline from 1979-1980, when over a quarter of the news shapers were economists or economic analysts. This suggests that news shapers are being used to discuss more topics than in the past, which has important implications: Network news programs are reifying social processes, such as domestic political and international affairs, that had previously been assumed to be easily understood by viewers.

While the economy has been reified by news reporters since at least the 1970s (Tuchman 1978), relatively few other social occurrences, with the possible exceptions of civil disorders and ecological disasters, have been. It is not difficult to understand why news reports about economic events, social upheavals, and ecological disasters become reified, because the theories that explain these events are themselves reified.

Since Adam Smith published *The Wealth of Nations* in 1776, economists have assumed that the impulse of self-interest would enhance public welfare. Smith's description of how a laissez-faire economy works is a reified description. It

Table 4
News Shapers by Network and Category, 1987–1988

	Former Politicians & Officials	Economists	Think Tanks	Experts, Analysts & Consultants	Journalists	Academics	Others	Total
ABC	20	7	14	15	13	8	4	81
CBS	19	10	21	33	9	19	4	115
NBC	14	4	9	17	6	13	1	64
Total	53	21	44	65	28	40	9	260

suggests individuals in pursuing their own interests are led, as if by an "invisible hand," to achieve the best for all. The economy, in this theory, functions in a godlike manner, bringing welfare to all members. When guided by this theory, it is not difficult to understand why economic news stories would become reified.

Most theories about social upheavals are also reified. Marxist theory predicts that the working class will inevitably compete with, and seize political power from, the employing class, just as the bourgeoisie seized power from the landed aristocracy. The theory of rising expectations says that revolutions are not the result of poverty, but frustrations. Individuals who have tried to better their economic standings but have made only marginal gains become frustrated and revolt, according to this theory. These and other theories describe social upheavals as inevitable and predictable occurrences. For this reason, they present a reified picture of social disorders.

The same is true of ecological disasters like oil spills, toxic dump leaks, nuclear accidents, or global warming. These appear to be "natural outgrowths" of industrialization. They are inevitable, according to both environmentalists and corporate spokesmen, even though steps can be taken to reduce the probability of their occurring. Because these are inevitable occurrences that are beyond human control, discussions and news reports concerning them become reified. Within news reports, news shapers provide background on the half-life of nuclear isotopes, projections on the effects of global warming on agriculture, or what impact oil spills have on the ocean's ecosystem. News shapers serve a similar function in reports about the economy. Economists describe the effects that a stock market crash has on the overall economy, what the relationship between national debt and taxes is, or why increased oil prices can cause recession. Economic news shapers therefore explain relationships to viewers within the context of theories.

In contrast to economics or environmental science, few theories concerning domestic politics or international affairs are reified. In fact, many political "theories," such as the domino theory of communist revolution, have turned out to be ideological arguments rather than social scientific theories. As a consequence, it is difficult to explain the reification of political news by examining political science theories.

Rather than looking at political theories for an understanding of why the reification of political affairs appears to be occurring, it is necessary to look elsewhere for explanations—at news organizations and reporters, who have either unconsciously or intentionally changed their methods of reporting during the last decade. In addition to the increased use of news shapers, other changes have occurred in the presentation of network television news. For example, Kiku Adatto found that the networks now devote about 52 percent of their reports to analyses of the theatrical aspects of presidential campaigns, such as the candidates' advertisements and images, whereas in 1968 only 6 percent of their reports focused on theatrics. In 1968, much more time was devoted to discussions of issues. Adatto also found that the duration of the "average 'sound bite' fell from 42.3 seconds in 1968 to only 9.8 seconds in 1988. Meanwhile the time the networks devoted to visuals of candidates, accompanied by their words, increased by more than 300 percent'' (1990, 20). This presents a picture of news programs constructed with visuals, quick cuts, and talking heads who pop up on the screen, squawk out a few sentences, and then disappear, just like what occurs in commercials or music videos, creating an impressionist montage, not an Edward R. Murrow report.

NETWORK TELEVISION NEWS SHAPERS: THE POPULATION

The sample of news shapers described in Table 4 provides a picture of the characteristics of news shapers, but it does not provide exact figures about the frequency with which particular news shapers appeared. For example, the sample study found that 34 individuals accounted for 45 percent of all news shaper appearances, suggesting that the networks rely heavily—and repeatedly—on a few individuals to shape their news. The sample also identified seven individuals who appeared five or more times: Norman Ornstein, Ed Rollins, William Schneider, David Gergen, Fouad Ajami, Stephen Hess, and Kevin Phillips. Because these frequencies were estimated from a sample, there is no way to know whether frequently appearing news shapers like Norman Ornstein appeared as often as the sample statistics suggest or these frequencies were due to sampling error.[5] To address the question of exactly how often certain news shapers appeared on the network news, a second study was undertaken.

The method employed in the second or population study was an extension of the method employed in the sample study: Twelve two-week intervals were randomly selected and used to generate a list of news shaper names. The names that were obtained through this sampling process were then compared to the 1987 and 1988 indexes for the *Television News Index and Abstracts* to determine how often each news shaper appeared. This procedure produced a list of each appearance made by the news shaper and, through examining the transcription of the broadcast, assured that each individual appeared as a news shaper rather than as a news maker. Only appearances by news shapers were counted.

After the list of frequently appearing news shapers was compiled, biographical information on each of these individuals was obtained and used to politically classify individuals. This was done because network news captions often failed to accurately identify news shapers' political affiliations. For example, William Hyland appeared as a news shaper 14 times during 1987 and 1988 and was described as editor of *Foreign Affairs* magazine 10 times, a Soviet analyst or foreign affairs expert three times, and a representative of the Council on Foreign Relations once. He was never identified as a former Nixon administration official, even though he worked at the State Department and NSC under Henry Kissinger from 1969 through 1977. The networks also neglected to mention that he was an analyst for the CIA between 1954 and 1969.

Table 5 contains a list of the news shapers who appeared more than 12 times on the network news during 1987 and 1988. Except for Fouad Ajami, Harrison

Table 5
The Frequently Appearing News Shapers, 1987–1988

	1987	1988	Total
William Schneider	23	35	58
Ed Rollins	21	30	51
Kevin Phillips	16	27	43
Norman Ornstein	28	14	42
Harrison Hickman	9	24	33
Robert Beckel	4	23	27
David Gergen	15	9	24
Fouad Ajami	6	15	21
Stephen Hess	6	13	19
Robert Squier	8	10	18
Richard Viguerie	12	5	17
David Jones	8	8	16
James Schlesinger	11	5	16
David Garth	7	8	15
William Hyland	8	6	14
Richard Perle	9	5	14
Judith Kipper	3	11	14
Total	194	248	442

Hickman, and David Jones, these frequently appearing news shapers appeared on all three networks. Ajami, a Middle East consultant to CBS, made all 21 appearances on CBS. Five of Hickman's appearances were on NBC; the other 28 were on CBS. Jones appeared 14 times on CBS and twice on ABC, but never on NBC.

By contrast, William Schneider made 18 appearances on ABC, 21 appearances on CBS, and 19 appearances on the NBC news. Ed Rollins appeared 11 times on ABC, 22 times on CBS, and 18 times on NBC. Stephen Hess appeared 13 times on ABC, but only 4 times on CBS and twice on NBC. Judith Kipper, the sole woman, made the fewest appearances among the individuals listed in Table 5. She appeared 7 times on ABC, 4 times on CBS, and 3 times on NBC.

The table shows that virtually all of the frequently appearing news shapers identified in the sample study were in the population of most frequently appearing news shapers, although not in the same order. This finding provides evidence that the sample study has validity. The sample study found Norman Ornstein to be the most frequently appearing news shaper, followed by Ed Rollins, William Schneider, David Gergen, Fouad Ajami, Stephen Hess, and Kevin Phillips. This population study found William Schneider to be the most frequently appearing news shaper. Schneider logged 58 appearances on the network news during 1987 and 1988. The second most frequently appearing news shaper was Ed Rollins, who appeared 51 times. Kevin Phillips was the third most frequently appearing news shaper. He made 43 appearances on the network news.

While not the most frequently appearing news shaper, Norman Ornstein did appear with regularity. He was the fourth most frequently appearing news shaper, logging 42 appearances. He was followed by Harrison Hickman and Robert Beckel, who made 33 and 27 appearances respectively. Neither Hickman nor Beckel was identified in the sample as among the most frequently appearing news shapers, but they nonetheless did appear in the sample. All of the other individuals who are listed in Table 5 were also in the sample except Judith Kipper.

Judith Kipper was a resident fellow at the AEI until 1986. She is currently with the Brookings Institution and the Council of Foreign Relations, where she is "Senior Program Associate for the Middle East Forum." During her 14 network appearances, Judith Kipper was identified four times as a Mideast expert or analyst, seven times as a representative of the Brookings Institution, and three times as a Council on Foreign Relations spokesperson.

Judith Kipper was not the only news shaper who was identified by the networks in several different ways. William Schneider was described as a political scientist, political analyst, expert, and AEI spokesman. The AEI was never described during the newscasts as a conservative think tank. Harrison Hickman was described as a political analyst three times, a political consultant twice, a consultant once, a pollster twice, a Democratic political consultant six times, a Democratic pollster 18 times, and a Simon pollster once. Hickman was therefore identified as a Democrat in 25 of his 33 (i.e., 75.8 percent) appearances. By contrast, Kevin Phillips was described as a political analyst, consultant, or columnist 31 times and a Republican or conservative analyst on just 12 occasions. His political orientation was therefore provided in only about one-fourth (i.e., 27.9 percent) of his appearances.

Based on the biographical information, the 17 news shapers listed in Table 5 were classified as think tank spokespersons, former Republican officials or activists, Democratic consultants, people with ambiguous political affiliations, university professors, or economists. Kevin Phillips, Stephen Hess, William Hyland, and James Schlesinger, who were appointees in the Nixon administration, were categorized as Republicans. Richard Perle, Ed Rollins, and David Gergen, who were members of the Reagan administration, were also coded as Republicans. Richard Viguerie, a fundraiser for numerous Republican candidates, including Jesse Helms, Phil Crane, and John Connally, was also classified as a Republican.

Only Harrison Hickman, Robert Beckel, and Robert Squier were classified as Democrats. Hickman worked as a pollster for a number of Democratic candidates, Robert Beckel was Walter Mondale's campaign adviser, and Robert Squier worked for the Hubert Humphrey and Jimmy Carter campaigns. None of the three ever held elective or appointive office. This was the opposite of the individuals classified as Republicans. All but Richard Viguerie were members of Republican administrations.

David Garth, who worked for Republicans John Heinz and John V. Lindsay and Democrat Ed Koch, was classified as having ambiguous political affiliations.

Fouad Ajami of Johns Hopkins University was the only news shaper who was coded as a professor.

Judith Kipper, William Schneider, and Norman Ornstein were coded as spokespersons for think tanks. David Jones was classified as an economist. He is the chief economist for the Aubrey C. Lanston Company, a Wall Street firm. When the political affiliations and appearances of the leading news shapers are tabulated, as is shown in Table 6, it is apparent that Republicans appear with much greater frequency than Democrats. Among the leading news shapers, 198 appearances were by Republicans, while only 78 appearances were by Democrats. This is consistent with the findings of the sample study.

The same preponderance of Republicans and conservatives is apparent when news shapers who appeared 12 or fewer times are analyzed. Dimitri Simes, an admitted political conservative, appeared on the networks 12 times. He appeared on ABC once, CBS six times, and NBC five times during 1987 and 1988. Simes is currently associated with the Carnegie Endowment, but was previously associated with the CSIS, a conservative think tank.

Also appearing 12 times was Harvard University law school professor Laurence Tribe, who shaped discussions of Supreme Court nominations and decisions. Although Tribe is certainly not a conservative, he is also not a representative of the political left. Tribe praised Anthony Kennedy's qualifications to be a Supreme Court justice (ABC–December 13, 1987), while liberal organizations such as Americans for Democratic Action and the National Organization for Women opposed Kennedy's nomination.

Gary Sick, a professor at Columbia University and "Iran expert," appeared 11 times. Before joining Columbia University, Sick was an NSC staffer in the Ford and Carter administrations.

Table 6
Affiliations and Backgrounds of Frequently Appearing News Shapers

	Number of Individuals	Number of Appearances
Think Tank Representatives	3	114
Republicans	8	198
Democrats	3	78
Indeterminate/Ambiguous	1	15
University Professors	1	21
Economists	1	16
Total	17	442

Five individuals appeared ten times as news shapers: Zbigniew Brzezinski, Robert Kupperman, Robert Hunter, Robert Legvold, and Arthur Hartman. All but Legvold and Hartman are with the CSIS, a Washington, D.C., based think tank. Robert Legvold is a Columbia University professor who spent 6 years with the Council on Foreign Relations. Arthur Hartman was President Reagan's ambassador to the Soviet Union until March 1987. He started appearing as a news shaper the month after he left his government post.

Brent Scowcroft, William Colby, George Carver, Paul Wilkinson, and James David Barber made nine appearances each on the networks news. Of the five, two (Scowcroft and Colby) are ex–Republican officials, two (i.e., Carver and Wilkinson) are with right-wing think tanks, and one (i.e., Barber) is a professor at Duke University. Colby and Carver are ex–CIA officials. At the time of his appearances, Carver was with the CSIS; Wilkinson was with the London-based Research Foundation for the Study of Terrorism. Of the five, only James David Barber is politically liberal.

By contrast, former Democratic party leaders, particularly liberals such as George McGovern and the late Michael Harrington, were excluded from the population of network news shapers. During 1988, for example, George McGovern appeared three times. In one interview he was asked whether presidential candidates get sufficient sleep. McGovern was interviewed twice at the 1988 Democratic convention, where he was asked to contrast the styles of the 1972 and 1988 conventions. He was never asked to comment about political issues.

Not only were former Democratic standard-bearers excluded from the population of news shapers, but so were representatives from liberal or Democratic think tanks such as the Institute for Policy Studies and the Economic Policy Institute. The network news teams apparently want only spokespersons from conservative think tanks to shape their news.

NOTES

1. The method used to draw the samples is provided in detail in the appendix.

2. The *Des Moines Register, Miami Herald*, and Atlanta *Constitution*, along with the *New York Times, Washington Post, Baltimore Sun*, and *Los Angeles Times*, were included in Guido Stempel III's (1965) definition of the "prestige press."

3. Although James Schlesinger served in President Carter's cabinet as the first secretary of energy, Schlesinger was chosen for this position specifically because he was a Republican. President Carter wanted this cabinet post to be nonpartisan. For this reason, Schlesinger is counted as a Republican.

4. All individuals who served in Democratic and Republican administrations, such as William Quandt and Fred Bergsten, were counted once for both parties for this calculation.

5. *Sampling error* is used synonymously with *sampling variation* and does not imply that the sample is unrepresentative or erroneous. The term *sampling error* simply means that there is a difference "between a census result and a sample result," according to Donald Plane and Edward Opperman (1981, 178).

5

THE THINK TANKS

The Roosevelt Center for American Policy Studies opened its doors in 1982 with seed money from Richard Dennis, Jr., a well-heeled Chicago commodities trader and Mondale Democrat (Kuttner 1985). The center called itself a "neoliberal" think tank, advocating a free market and smaller Washington bureaucracy, like conservative think tanks. But unlike its conservative counterparts, the Roosevelt Center wanted the federal government, not corporations, to police the environment and narrow the income gap between the wealthy and poor.

In early 1990, the Roosevelt Center closed its doors. It was unable to raise enough money to continue operating. Corporations, which have become a major source of funding for think tanks, refuse to finance any thinking that even hints at policing corporate practices.

As the doors of the Roosevelt Center were being padlocked, a conservative think tank called the Center of the American Experiment opened in Minneapolis. The center projects an income of $1.5 million annually, most of which is to be raised from corporations and conservative individual donors (Minneapolis *Star Tribune*, January 7, 1990, 1B).

The Center of the American Experiment is one of dozens of conservative think tanks that have sprung up around the United States. The AEI, Heritage Foundation, CSIS, Cato Institute, Competitive Enterprise Institute, Council for Social and Economic Studies, National Forum Foundation, and Center for Security Policy are based in Washington, D.C. Beyond the beltway are the Manhattan Institute (New York), Rockford Institute (Illinois), National Center for Policy Analysis

(Texas), Hudson Institute (Indiana), Institute for Contemporary Studies (California), National Institute for Public Policy (Virginia), Foreign Policy Research Institute (Pennsylvania), Pacific Institute (California), Institute for Foreign Policy Analysis (Massachusetts), Shavano Institute (Michigan), and Rocky Mountain Institute (Colorado).

Reagan administration appointees who have not returned to government are the stars of these conservative think tanks. Linda Chavez, former staff director for the U.S. Civil Rights Commission, joined the Manhattan Institute, former Department of Education appointee Mitch Pearlstein became president of the Center of the American Experiment, Douglas Bandow, a special assistant to President Reagan, became a senior fellow at the Cato Institute, Richard Allen, T. Kenneth Cribb, and Ed Meese went to the Heritage Foundation, former national security adviser Robert McFarlane and former State Department staffers Stephen Sestanovich and Leo Reddy were hired by the CSIS, Elliott Abrams and Frank Gaffney, Jr., are with the Center for Security Policy, and the AEI gave jobs and shelter to over two dozen high-level Reagan officials and would-be appointees like Robert Bork.

The regional think tanks attempt to do on the local level what the conservative Washington think tanks have succeeded in doing on the national level—getting attention from the mass media. These rightist "research centers" inundate the media with press releases, send thousands of op-ed pieces to newspapers, volunteer speakers for talk radio shows, and provide sound bites on any issue for television news programs. The CSIS (1989) reported that its representatives had just under 5,000 "media contacts" in 1988-1989. Of these, 357 were radio interviews, 439 were television interviews, 739 were magazine or newspaper articles, and 852 were background interviews. CSIS analysts were also quoted in over 2,500 news articles.

FAIR, which studied the guests appearing on the "MacNeil/Lehrer NewsHour," found that conservative think tanks' spokespersons appear frequently on that show and reported that two of the conservative think tanks, the CSIS and AEI, provided a disproportionately large number of "MacNeil/Lehrer" guests (1990). The CSIS provided "experts" for foreign policy discussions, while the AEI provided "experts" for domestic policy discussions.

The increased reliance by news reporters on think tank analysts as sources is apparent from a comparison of news shapers in the 1979-1980 and 1987-1988 samples of network television newscasts. In the 1979-1980 sample, 11 of the 88 news shapers (i.e., 12.5 percent) were from research centers, while 44 of the 260 (i.e., 16.9 percent) in the 1987-1988 sample were. In the 1979-1980 sample, six of the 11 appearances were by analysts from centers with highly specialized focuses, such as the Center for Independent Living (NBC–November 12, 1980), which examines issues of concern to the handicapped, the Environmental Policy Center (NBC–May 12, 1980) and Conservation Foundation (CBS–September 18, 1979), which study developmental and ecology problems, and the industry-financed Food Marketing Institute (CBS–August 13, 1979), which researches food prices and the economy. Other representatives came from less specialized institutes such as the liberal Center for National Security Studies (CBS–September 19, 1979), the Brookings Institution (ABC–August 3, 1979), and the conservative Free Congress (ABC–November 10, 1980) and Heritage foundations (ABC–November 13, 1980).

A comparison of the 1979-1980 and 1987-1988 samples shows that think tank representatives appeared more frequently in the 1987-1988 sample, but also shows that proportionately fewer think tanks were represented in the later sample. The 44 think tank spokespersons in the 1987-1988 sample came from 16 "research centers," but just six accounted for 34 of the 44 (i.e., 77.3 percent) appearances. The six think tanks were the AEI (12 appearances), Brookings Institution (eight appearances), Carnegie Endowment (seven appearances), Heritage Foundation (three appearances), Council on Foreign Relations (two appearances), and International Institute for Strategic Studies (IISS, two appearances). With the exceptions of the Council on Foreign Relations and the IISS, these think tanks are based in Washington, D.C.

Ten research centers had representatives who appeared—or were identified as coming from the think tank—only once. These include the Joint Center for Political Studies, which is concerned with black issues; Cato Institute, a libertarian think tank; CSIS; Conservative Caucus Foundation, which sponsors the Victory over Communism Project; Institute for Government and Politics, which is sponsored by the rightist Free Congress Research and Education Foundation (*Encyclopedia of Associations* 1989, 1,453); and corporate-sponsored think tanks like the Petroleum Industry Research Foundation (PIRINC) and the Employee Benefits Research Foundation. All but the New York–based PIRINC are also based in Washington. There were no appearances by representatives of liberal think tanks such as the Center for National Security Studies, Economic Policy Institute, or Roosevelt Center in the 1987-1988 sample.

The sample suggests that network reporters rely heavily on a small circle of "beltway sources" to shape the news. These Washington-based think tank analysts are frequently former government officials who, while at the think tanks, provide consultation to current officials. The think tanks appear to be part of the "revolving door" of Washington, D.C. For example, C. Fred Bergsten, the director of the Institute for International Economics, is a former economist for the U.S. Department of State (1963-1967) and assistant for international economic affairs with the NSC (1969-1971). His institute reports that it "devise[s] practical policy responses" to international economic issues and "consults with government officials" (*Research Centers Directory* 1989, 896). Bergsten was identified by CBS as an institute spokesman on one occasion (November 11, 1988), when he discussed the effects that Bush's presidency would have on the economy. When he appeared the following day, he was simply described as an "economist," as mentioned in the previous chapter.

Peter G. Peterson (CBS–May 21, 1988) and Susan Kaufman Purcell (CBS–January 16, 1988), who appeared as representatives of the Council of Foreign

Relations, are also former officials. Peterson served in the Nixon administration, Purcell in the Carter administration. And Arms Control Association spokesman Jack Mendelsohn was a senior foreign service officer who served in the U.S. Arms Control and Disarmament Agency (ACDA) during the early years of the Reagan administration (1981-1983) and as a senior ACDA representative on the Strategic Arms Reduction Talks (START) delegation. Earlier he served as a special assistant to the chief negotiator of President Nixon's SALT delegation. He appeared on CBS (May 7, 1988) to comment on the prospects of INF treaty ratification. When Mendelsohn appeared earlier on ABC (September 14, 1987), he was incorrectly identified as a former U.S. ambassador, so for that appearance was coded as a former government official. Because the think tank affiliations of many news shapers are not identified, think tank representatives undoubtedly comprise much more than 16.9 percent of the 1987-1988 sample.

Like Bergsten's institute, the Arms Control Association reports that it "provides technical advice on request to . . . appropriate officials of the Executive Branch and Congress" (*Encyclopedia of Associations* 1989, 1,366). The other think tanks also exist to counsel government officials. The AEI reports that its representatives "are extensively involved in Washington's policy debates. They are sought by congressional committees, cabinet secretaries, and the president for their advice and counsel" (AEI 1987, 2). PIRINC reports that it "has been called to testify at every session of Congress in the last decade. PIRINC briefs government officials and legislators" (PIRINC 1988). The Heritage Foundation reports that it differs from other think tanks, not just because of its extremely conservative viewpoints, but by its "ability to deliver cogent, useful information to key policy-makers in a timely fashion—not weeks before the debate has ended" (Heritage Foundation 1988, 2).

There is considerable overlap among beltway think tanks, as well as overlap with government. The Institute for International Economics' Fred Bergsten was a fellow with the Council of Foreign Relations during 1967-1968, a senior fellow at the Brookings Institution during 1972-1976, and a senior associate with the Carnegie Endowment during 1981 (*Who's Who in America*, 45th ed., 238). In addition, he sits on the editorial board of *Foreign Policy*, which is published by the Carnegie Endowment. The Arms Control Association has a "cooperative agreement" with the Carnegie Endowment and "participates in a number of joint ventures" with it (Carnegie Endowment 1989, 13). Members of the AEI are associated with other think tanks: Herbert Stein was with the Brookings Institution, Thomas W. Robinson was with the Council on Foreign Relations, and Dinesh D'Souza worked for the Heritage Foundation (*AEI Sourcebook* 1989). Peter J. Ferrara, a fellow at the Heritage Foundation, went to the Cato Institute as research director in 1988 (Cato Institute 1988, 5).

Of the 44 appearances by think tank spokespersons, 12 were described by the networks as coming from the AEI, eight from the Brookings Institution, and seven from the Carnegie Endowment. Of the 12 appearances by AEI spokespersons, 10 were by two individuals: William Schneider and Norman Ornstein. Only two other persons were identified as AEI representatives: Suzanne Garment (CBS–September 19, 1987) and Richard Perle (NBC–May 10, 1988). Garment was a *Wall Street Journal* editor and assistant to President Ford's UN ambassador, Daniel P. Moynihan. Perle was an assistant secretary of defense under President Reagan.

Of the eight appearances attributed to Brookings spokespersons, three were made by Stephen Hess. John Steinbruner, who directs Brookings' foreign policy studies program, appeared twice on CBS (November 12 and November 15, 1988). Joshua Epstein (ABC–August 13, 1987), a former Rand Corporation researcher; William Quandt (ABC–November 15, 1988), a former Rand researcher and NSC staffer under presidents Nixon and Carter; and Yahya Sadowski (CBS–September 28, 1987), a Mideast specialist, made one appearance each as Brookings spokespersons.

Of the seven appearances by persons described by the networks as Carnegie representatives, three were made by Peter Zimmerman, a physicist who specializes in defense issues and serves as an adviser to the U.S. START delegation. The other four Carnegie spokespersons appeared only once. However, three people who appeared on the networks were Carnegie representatives but were not described as such: Geoffrey Kemp, Dimitri Simes, and Charles Maynes. Geoffrey Kemp, who was a special assistant to President Reagan for national security affairs, was described by ABC (February 10, 1987) as a "former NSC staff member," not a Carnegie representative. Charles Maynes, a Democrat who worked in the U.S. State Department for Presidents Kennedy, Johnson, Nixon, and Carter, was described as the editor of *Foreign Policy* rather than a Carnegie representative. For that reason, Maynes was initially classified as a journalist using this study's coding categories. Dimitri Simes, who appeared on CBS (February 7, 1987) and NBC (September 18, 1987), was described as a "Soviet expert" rather than a Carnegie spokesman. When the appearances by Kemp, Maynes, and Simes are added to those attributed to Carnegie spokespersons, the number of appearances by Carnegie representatives increases to 11, as shown in Table 7.

AEI spokespersons also made more than their 12 attributed appearances. Norman Ornstein was described as a "political analyst" (e.g., CBS–January 21, 1988) or "political scientist" (e.g., NBC–September 14, 1987) on six occasions; William Schneider was on three occasions described as an "analyst" (CBS–September 15, 1987, and ABC–September 28, 1987) and "political scientist" (CBS–February 7, 1987); the AEI's John Makin, who writes a column for the rightist *Washington Times*, was described as a "political analyst" by NBC (May 7, 1988) rather than a think tank representative, and Frank Gaffney, Jr., a deputy assistant secretary of defense under President Reagan (1983-1987), was described by NBC (May 17, 1988) as an "ex–arms negotiator" rather than AEI spokesperson. For that reason, Gaffney was initially classified as a former government official rather than think tank spokesperson.[1] When these appearances are added to those that mentioned the AEI affiliations, the number of appearances by AEI representatives increases to 23.

Table 7
Attributed and Actual Appearances by Think Tank Representatives

	Attributed Appearances	Actual Appearances
Carnegie Endowment	7	11
Brookings Institution	8	17
American Enterprise Institute	12	23
Center for Strategic and International Studies	1	8

The same is true for the Brookings Institution and CSIS appearances. When Brookings associates who were described as "political analysts" or "experts" are included, the number of Brookings appearances increases from eight to 17. When appearances by CSIS senior counselors William Brock (ABC and CBS–November 16, 1988) and James Schlesinger (ABC–September 18, 1987), former CIA assistant director and CSIS "intelligence expert" Ray Cline (NBC–February 3, 1987), and CSIS "foreign policy experts" Robert Hunter (CBS–February 9 and 14, 1987) and Edward Luttwak (NBC–August 11, 1987) are included, the number of CSIS appearances increases to 8. When the appearances by the AEI, Brookings, Carnegie, and the CSIS are combined, representatives of the four think tanks accounted for 59 of the 260 appearances by news shapers. This is just under one-fourth (i.e., 22.7 percent) of all appearances.

The oligopolistic position that these think tanks exercise isn't limited to network television news. Representatives of the "big four" think tanks are quoted frequently by reporters for large-circulation newspapers. The opinion pages of these newspapers also carry a large number of their writings. When quotes and opinion articles are combined, spokespersons for the big four think tanks popped up 1276 times in the pages of the *New York Times* between January 1, 1987, and October 1, 1990. Six hundred and fifty (or about one-half) of these appearances were by Brookings Institution spokespersons. The next most frequently cited think tank was the AEI.

Representatives of these think tanks were also quoted frequently in the pages of the *Los Angeles Times*, as shown in Table 8. The opinions of Brookings Institution spokespersons appeared 410 times in the pages of the Los Angeles daily, while opinions of AEI representatives appeared 183 times. By contrast, spokespersons from the three largest Washington, D.C., based liberal or

Table 8
Think Tank Representatives: Quotations and Opinion Articles, 1987–1990

	New York Times[a]	Los Angeles Times[b]
Carnegie Endowment	204	83
Brookings Institution	650	410
American Enterprise Institute	296	183
Center for Strategic and International Studies	126	140
Economic Policy Institute	34	41
Institute for Policy Studies	61	27
Roosevelt Center for American Policy Studies	6	8

Sources: [a]Nexis and [b]Data Times.

Democratic party–oriented think tanks were quoted much less often. Appearances by representatives of the Economic Policy Institute, Institute for Policy Studies, and Roosevelt Center totalled only 76 in the pages of the *Los Angeles Times*. Representatives of the left-leaning think tanks did not fare any better in the *New York Times*. The three think tanks together accounted for 101 appearances in the *New York Times*, or less than the appearances by spokespersons from the CSIS. Overall, the centrist and rightist think tanks accounted for 92.2 percent of the appearances shown in Table 8. The left-leaning think tanks accounted for 7.8 percent of the appearances.

GOVERNMENT AND CORPORATE HELP

Conservative think tanks received substantial assistance from the Reagan administration, corporations, and the mass media in their bid to become the dominant voices in public policy debates. During the early 1980s, the Reagan administration withheld government grants from think tanks that were left of center, forcing them to reduce their activities, go under, or shift rightward. The Urban Institute, which was created in 1968 to conduct independent research on Great Society programs, provides an example of how the Reagan strategy worked.

Pres. Lyndon Johnson provided the Urban Institute with $6 million in federal housing funds to get it off the ground. By 1981, the institute was conducting $12 million a year of government-sponsored research. In 1982, the Reagan administration cut government funding to the Urban Institute by $9 million, forcing the institute to change its focus. After hiring Republican economists and concluding that economic growth, not federal social programs, was the key to narrowing the income gap, funding increased. By 1987, the Urban Institute was receiving about $5 million from the U.S. government and an equal amount from sources like the Ford and Rockefeller foundations. Edwin Feulner, Jr., president of the arch-conservative Heritage Foundation, describes the Urban Institute's current outlook as "Republican centrist" (*Business Week*, March 9, 1987, 116).

Another example of the rightward shift in think tank thinking is the Brookings Institution (Kuttner 1984). During the 1960s and early 1970s, this think tank developed a left-of-center label because its president, Kermit Gordon, was a supporter of the Great Society and critic of the Vietnam War. Under his leadership, Brookings developed a reputation for solid research and scholarship. Brookings' reputation is what the conservative think tanks feed off. The Heritage Foundation, the AEI, the Institute for Contemporary Studies, and others only pretend to do research.

Brookings' left-of-center stance under Gordon, however, was an aberration in the history of the think tank. Prior to the 1960s, Brookings was referred to as CBI rather than BI by Washington insiders. *CBI* referred to the Conservative Businessman's Institution, which reflected the institution's outlook and funding between 1916, when Brookings was established, and 1967, when Gordon became president (Linden 1987).

After Gordon's departure, Brookings moved steadily to the right, a trend that *Fortune* magazine (July 23, 1984) applauded. Since 1977, Brookings' president has been Bruce MacLaury, a deputy undersecretary of the treasury during the Nixon administration. In 1981, MacLaury hired Roger Semerad as the executive vice president for external affairs. Semerad's sole credential for the job was that he had served as a White House staff assistant following the Watergate scandal. Semerad became Reagan's assistant secretary of labor in 1985 (*Who's Who in America* 1988, 2795). And Brookings' most visible spokesman is Stephen Hess, a former staff assistant to President Eisenhower, deputy assistant for urban affairs to President Nixon, and editor of the 1976 Republican National Platform (Cooper and Soley 1990).

With leaders such as these, it is not difficult to understand why 160 corporate donors gave Brookings $2.2 million in 1989 (Brookings Institution 1989, 34). The gifts came from such responsible corporate citizens as Exxon, R. J. Reynolds–Nabisco, Dow Chemical, and defense contractors General Dynamics and Lockheed. Topping the list of contributors were media corporations, which drew heavily on Brookings for "liberal" opinions and sound bites: the New York Times Company; Time, Inc.; the Los Angeles Times Mirror Company; Washington Post Company; Cox Enterprises; Capital Cities/ABC; and General Electric, which owns NBC.

Brookings wasn't the largest recipient of corporate aid among think tanks. Three that are much further to the right received more. Fifty-four percent of the AEI's $10 million 1988 budget came from corporations (AEI 1989). One-third of the CSIS's $9 million budget came from corporate coffers, as did $2.5 million of the Heritage Foundation's $14.6 million budget (Heritage Foundation 1988). The largest share of Heritage's contributions came from conservative fat cats like Adolph Coors, Richard Mellon Scaife, Union Pacific chairman Drew Lewis, Amway chairman Jay Van Andel, Smith-Kline chairman Robert Dee, and investment banker Shelby Cullom Davis (Easterbrook 1986; Stone 1985). All of these contributions are used as tax write-offs, because the think tanks are nonprofit, tax-exempt organizations.

The annual budget of any one of the big conservative think tanks exceeds the combined budgets of all left-of-center think tanks. With so many resources available, the right-wing think tanks should be able to conduct very serious research, but they don't. The problem isn't that their research is highly partisan—one would expect it to be—it's that they try to pass off shopworn rhetoric as research. The difference between right-wing thought of the past and think tank output is that the former was presented at American Legion halls on Friday nights over beer, while the latter is sandwiched between well-designed covers and called research. This criticism of think tank research isn't expressed just by members of the political left; it is constantly voiced by everyone who conducts legitimate research.

In 1986, Georgetown University president Timothy S. Healy initiated an academic review of the CSIS, which at the time was affiliated with, but not under the control of, the university. The review examined the scholarship of CSIS fellows, who, like most think tank denizens, spent more time doing TV sound bites than serious thinking. The CSIS attempted to derail the review by charging that it was politically motivated and, when this was shown to be false, arguing that the review was pointless because "the university is not a top-flight university" (Muscatine 1986, 11).

Healy appointed a committee of five highly respected academics from outside the university to review the CSIS's work. The committee concluded that center fellows produced right-wing propaganda, not academic scholarship. After reviewing the committee's report, the trustees of Georgetown severed relations with the CSIS (*New York Times*, November 28, 1987, 46).

The verdict that the Georgetown trustees reached about the CSIS is repeated in almost every academic review of think tank research. For example, AEI "resident scholar" Joshua Muravchik's dissertation, which is distributed by the AEI as a book titled *The Uncertain Crusade: Jimmy Carter and the Dilemmas of Human Rights Policy*, was described by the *Journal of American History* as perplexing,

not so much its use as a doctoral dissertation but its acceptance as a piece of scholarship by the Georgetown faculty. The book can stand on its own as an essay on a first-rate subject. But despite its many footnotes it has no scholarly foundation. . . . Muravchik is reduced to a few interviews and to quoting Elizabeth Drew, Ben Wattenberg and Stanley Hoffman. (Ferrell 1986, 817).

The dissertation was written under the tutelage of the CSIS's Jeane Kirkpatrick before the think tank received its expulsion order from Georgetown. Not surprisingly, the book echoes Kirkpatrick's discredited theory about the reformability of right-wing dictatorships and the intractability of Stalinism.

Sir Alan Walters, an AEI senior fellow, wrote *Britain's Economic Renaissance: Margaret Thatcher's Reforms*. Walters was for several years an economic adviser to Thatcher. *Political Science Quarterly,* the only academic journal of note to review the book, described it as an "exercise in self-justification" containing "misrepresentation" (Alt 1987, 119). *The Media Elite*, a book coauthored by AEI "scholar" S. Robert Lichter, was panned in the *Journal of Communication*, the *Quarterly Journal of Speech, Journalism Quarterly*, and other academic journals.

Edwin J. Feulner, Jr., president of the Heritage Foundation, has not published one research article in any of the 1,000 social science journals listed in the *Social Science Citation Index* in the last 25 years. Burton Yale Pines, the Heritage Foundation's "director of research," has never published one scholarly article. Neither has Dr. Leon Aron, Heritage's "Salvatori Fellow in Soviet Studies." In fact, between 1976 and 1980 the closest that any "scholar" at the Heritage Foundation came to publishing an academic article was a letter to a journal editor.

The credentials of "scholars" at the other conservative think tanks aren't any stronger. To mask the academic anemia of their "scholars," conservative think tanks have created their own "research" journals. The journals bear names that closely resemble those of legitimate journals and are used to inflate their spokespersons' credentials. The AEI created *Public Opinion*, a counterfeit version of *Public Opinion Quarterly*, a respected social science journal that has been published since 1937. The Heritage Foundation publishes *Policy Review*, not the highly regarded *Policy Sciences*. The Institute for Contemporary Studies publishes the *Journal of Contemporary Studies*, which sounds very much like a scholarly journal but isn't. The Council for Social and Economic Studies publishes the *Journal of Social and Political Studies*, a counterfeit of the academically prestigious *Journal of Social Issues*. Other centers of rightist thought also publish "sounds like" journals. They are crammed with articles like "Bleak House: The Democrats' Doomsday Message," "The Straight Story on Homosexuality and Gay Rights," and "The Soundness of Our Structure: Confidence in the Reagan Years," which claim to be social science, but read like the Republican National Platform.

The think tank journals have produced "impressive credentials" for many of their employees. AEI "research fellow" Dinesh D'Souza has published a dozen articles in *Policy Review*, but not a single article in a legitimate scholarly journal. S. Robert Lichter, the AEI's "media expert," published ten articles on his field of expertise in *Public Opinion*, but not one in any scholarly journal devoted to mass communication research. AEI "resident fellow" William Schneider published 16 articles in *Public Opinion*, but not a single article in *Public Opinion Quarterly*. He also published four articles in the Institute for Contemporary Studies' journal, which was more than he published in political science journals during a near decade in academia.

The think tanks have also become prolific book publishers, churning out hundreds of volumes annually. Many of their books bear the names of think tank "scholars" on the covers, but are written by others. The think tank scholars edit rather than write these books. Of 12 books listed in the AEI's 1989 book catalog that bear AEI "scholar" Howard Penniman's name on the cover, 11 were edited by Penniman. Of four AEI books that have John Makin's name on the cover, three were edited, not written, by Makin. The fourth is a 54-page pamphlet containing "two essays." Makin is the AEI's "director of fiscal policy studies." Of five books attributed to AEI "resident scholar" Norman Ornstein, all were merely edited by him.

This method of publishing has allowed conservative think tanks to vastly inflate the credentials of their associates. The AEI's Norman Ornstein was described as the "author and editor of dozens of books and monographs" by the *New York Times* in 1985. While this sounds impressive, Ornstein's credentials were much more modest: In 1978 he had coauthored a book.

While the research of conservative think tanks isn't serious, their lobbying efforts on behalf of corporate contributors are. In addition to publishing endless tracts that promote capital gains tax cuts, deregulation, and unfettered corporate capitalism, the think tanks engage in some very donor-specific projects. The Heritage Foundation, which received more than $3 million of its $18 million endowment from Taiwanese corporations, has been very active in promoting issues of concern to Taiwan's businesses. Heritage escorted congressional staff members to Taiwan, sponsored conferences on U.S.–Taiwan free trade to which it invited U.S. policymakers and the media, and promoted the idea of a "Free Trade Area Agreement" with Taiwan, similar to that which the United States has with Canada. It publishes pamphlets, such as *U.S. Policy toward China's Reunification*, that promote Taiwan's positions. Heritage leaders also go on junkets to Taiwan, where they "consult" with government and business leaders (Mann 1988; Heritage Foundation 1988).

Two of the Taiwanese corporations that donate to the Heritage Foundation also give large sums to the AEI. Since receiving these donations, the AEI has sponsored conferences, seminars, and publications that promote Taiwanese positions. The AEI sponsored two large conferences to which Washington officials were invited. One praised the emergence of democracy in the capitalist East, while the second examined security in Asia. The Asian security conference was held in Taiwan. The AEI also held four seminars about Taiwan issues, such as Taiwan–U.S. relations and the People's Republic of China's military buildup. Chong-Pin Lin, the AEI's associate director for China studies, who is a Taiwan national, wrote a book that "focused attention on the People's Republic of China's arms buildup," according to AEI promotional literature (AEI 1989). Despite their apparent interest in Taiwan, AEI "scholars" have remained uncharacteristically silent about that country's political prisoners and rigged National Assembly elections, even though they expressed opinions about almost every other topic.

THE AMERICAN ENTERPRISE INSTITUTE: A CLOSER LOOK AT MacNEIL/LEHRER'S FAVORITE THINK TANK

The AEI was founded in 1943 by Lewis H. Brown, chief of the Johns-Manville Corporation, as an intellectual counterweight to New Deal philosophy. Instead of developing a reputation for research and thinking, the institute developed a reputation as a knee-jerk defender of big business. In 1954, William Baroody, Sr., left his job at the Chamber of Commerce to become the AEI's chief. Baroody attempted but failed to divest the institute of its image.

Between 1977 and 1986, the AEI was run by Baroody's son, William Jr. William Baroody, Jr., came to the AEI after a tour of duty with the Office of White House Public Liaison in the Nixon and Ford administrations. The Office of White House Liaison was part of the adminstrations' publicity apparatus, and Baroody used his acquired publicity skills to change the AEI's image from that of a procorporation lunatic fringe to that of a mainstream, albeit conservative, think tank. It was under his leadership that the AEI started its massive publicity campaigns, which included press releases concerning the AEI's seminars, forums, and policy proposals, the sending of opinion articles to newspapers, and the distributing of free radio commentaries to broadcasting stations.

While the publicity campaign helped change media perceptions of the AEI a bit, Baroody's hiring of former Ford officials after the GOP's electoral defeat in 1976 helped a lot. The big names that Baroody hired included Herbert Stein, Chairman of Nixon's Council of Economic Advisors; David Gergen, a Nixon-Ford speech writer and communications specialist; Philip Habib, Kissinger's shuttle diplomat; and former president Gerald Ford. Baroody used these big-name Republicans to promote the AEI.

An avalanche of publicity accompanied events such as "Public Policy Week," "World Forum," and the Washington seminars. "Public Policy Week" was a week-long event where corporate moguls were invited to rub shoulders and talk with former officials and foreign dignitaries. "World Forum" was a summer event hosted by Gerald Ford in Vail, Colorado, where the pockets of fat cats were picked by the Baroody bunch. The purpose of these events and the ensuing fundraising was to create and promote a conservative government-in-exile that would develop functionaries for future Republican administrations.

Baroody's strategy was immensely successful, and he succeeded in turning the AEI into a $9 million, 154-person Republican government-in-waiting. Many AEI employees eventually became high-level Reagan officials. James C. Miller became Reagan's Federal Trade Commission chairman and administrator of the Office of Management and Budget, Jeane Kirkpatrick was appointed U.S. ambassador to the United Nations, Murray Weidenbaum became chairman of President Reagan's Council of Economic Advisors, and Antonin Scalia was appointed to the Supreme Court.

Under Baroody's leadership, the AEI also grew a publishing arm that churned out books and periodicals. Most of the books were edited collections or essays by AEI scholars. The periodicals included *Public Opinion*, edited by David Gergen; the *AEI Economist*, a monthly publication edited by Herbert Stein; *AEI Foreign Policy and Defense Review*, edited by former assistant secretary of state Harold Saunders; and *Regulation*, a policy and law forum edited by Antonin Scalia. Although these publications contained few original ideas, they nevertheless created the appearance that AEI "scholars" were productive thinkers.

The AEI became sufficiently large so that even after President Reagan raided it for appointees, there were plenty of players left to keep the organization going. Some AEI associates like Michael Novak worked only briefly for the Reagan administration and then returned to the private sector, where they promoted administration goals. For example, Michael Novak and Jeane Kirkpatrick, who resigned as UN ambassador in April 1985, waged a private sector campaign to raise funds for the Nicaraguan Contras during the time that the Boland Amendment prohibited U.S. government funding for military or paramilitary activities in Nicaragua (Stone 1985). These activities and Reagan's hiring of AEI staff enhanced rather than detracted from its prestige in the eyes of the media and generated even more publicity for it.

Despite its close ties to Reagan administration appointees and policies, the AEI became a leading source of guests for the "MacNeil/Lehrer NewsHour" during the 1980s. Between January 1982 and October 1990, AEI spokesmen appeared on the "NewsHour" 142 times. This is an average of 1.4 appearances per month. By contrast, spokesmen from the Brookings Institution appeared 82 times, and spokesmen from the Carnegie Endowment appeared 72 times.[2] As a consequence, AEI representatives appeared on "MacNeil/Lehrer" almost twice as often as representatives of the Carnegie Endowment or the Brookings Institution. The AEI guests were used by "MacNeil/Lehrer" to critique the performance of the Reagan administration, which consisted of many former AEI colleagues.

During the late 1970s, the AEI looked like a very conservative organization. Its speakers were in sharp contrast to Carter administration appointees and former antiwar activists like Tom Hayden, who still commanded the press's attention. During the early years of the Reagan administration, when the political center shifted further to right, William Baroody's organization appeared less conservative than it previously had. Several other think tanks, such as the Heritage Foundation, were further to the right. These think tanks attracted the attention of conservative donors and their money. With conservative hawks such as Alexander Haig and Caspar Weinberger leading the Reagan parade, Republicans of Gerald Ford's stripe appeared to be too liberal and out of step with the new Republican ideology. As a consequence, donations to the AEI from conservatives declined, precipitating a financial and ideological crisis at the AEI. William C. Butcher, the AEI's chairman, who is also the chief executive officer of Chase Manhattan Bank, sacked Baroody. He appointed Christopher DeMuth, a former staff assistant to President Nixon and publicity man in Reagan's Office of Management and Budget, as AEI president in December 1986.

DeMuth, in turn, appointed three new "research directors" and sacked most of the AEI's foreign policy staff. For new foreign policy director, DeMuth chose Jeane Kirkpatrick. She rebuilt the foreign policy staff with anticommunist crusaders like Frank Gaffney, Jr., who was deputy assistant secretary of defense for nuclear forces and arms control under Weinberger; Richard Perle, another of Weinberger's hawkish assistant secretaries of defense; and Constantine Menges, a former special assistant for national security affairs and CIA operative.

Despite the AEI's dramatic shift to the right after DeMuth's appointment as president, spokesmen from the think tank made more appearances on network television news programs during the two years following the rightward turn (1987-1988) than the two years before (1985-1986). AEI representatives made 40 network appearances during 1985-1986, but 143 during 1987-1988. Of the 40 appearances made in 1985-1986, 15 were by Norman Ornstein, 8 were by Jeane Kirkpatrick, and 5 were by William Schneider. Ben Wattenberg appeared 3 times, and Austin Ranney, Michael Novak, and Herbert Stein each made 2 appearances.

During 1987-1988, the number of AEI appearances on network television increased to 143. Of these, 114 were made by three individuals: Norman Ornstein, William Schneider, and Richard Perle. Ben Wattenberg appeared 5 times to denounce Jesse Jackson's "light handling" by the press, Frank Gaffney, Jr., appeared 4 times, and Herbert Stein, John Makin, and Constantine Menges appeared 3 times. Other AEI representatives, including Austin Ranney, Karyln Keene, and Suzanne Garment, appeared once.

AEI spokesmen also made frequent appearances during 1989. In fact, AEI representatives appeared as often in 1989 as they had in 1985 and 1986 combined. William Schneider popped up 14 times, Norman Ornstein and Richard Perle 7 times, Robert Bork five times, and Ben Wattenberg and Herbert Stein twice.

THE HERITAGE FOUNDATION

"Advocacy tank" is a more appropriate description of the Heritage Foundation than "think tank," according to *Time* reporter Amy Wilentz (1986). Among beltway think tanks, Heritage associates have the weakest scholarly credentials, but are nonetheless the capital city's most active policy advocates. Of its 34 permanent "fellows, scholars, and staff" members, only 7 have Ph.D.'s. None are renowned scholars in their fields. The biggest names at this think tank are not thinkers, but former Republican officials. Its "distinguished scholar" for foreign policy studies is Charles M. Lichenstein, a Nixon appointee who also served under Jeane Kirkpatrick at the United Nations. Former U.S. Attorney General Ed Meese became a "distinguished fellow" at Heritage after his resignation in 1988, and Congressman Jack Kemp briefly went to the Heritage Foundation after losing his 1988 bid for the Republican presidential nomination (*Wall Street Journal*, July 15, 1988, 38, and September 14, 1988, 36).

Senior management of Heritage is also filled with former Republican partisans. Edwin Feulner, founder and president of the foundation, worked for Secretary of Defense Melvin Laird and Republican Congressman Philip Crane and was director of the House of Representatives' Republican Study Committee (RSC). During the 1980s, he held several part-time appointments in the Reagan administration. Phillip Truluck, Heritage's executive vice president, was on the staff of South Carolina Senator Strom Thurmond and was a deputy director of the RSC. Heritage vice presidents Charles Heatherly and David Hoppe were low-level Republican functionaries. Heatherly was an acting administrator of the Small Business Administration under President Reagan, and Hoppe was executive director of the House Republican Conference and an assistant to Congressman Jack Kemp (Heritage Foundation 1988). Given the backgrounds of individuals at the Heritage Foundation, there is little question as to why it is more accomplished at lobbying than research.

Heritage leaders are very open about their partisan purposes, even though it is technically a nonpartisan, tax-exempt organization. "[Our] goal is a conservative nation," says Phillip Truluck (Linden 1987, 103). Heritage Vice President Burton Pines described the foundation's purpose as "provid[ing] conservative public-policy makers with arguments to bolster our side" (Easterbrook 1986, 72). But in some cases, Heritage has done more than present arguments. In 1987, a congressional committee investigated Heritage's funneling of money to the Nicaraguan Contras. Heritage received a $100,000 donation from a wealthy Pittsburgh businessman that eventually found its way into a Contra bank account set up by Lt. Col. Oliver North. The money made its way into the bank account through Richard R. Miller, who worked with Carl R. (Spitz) Chanell as a Contra fundraiser. Miller and Chanell eventually pleaded guilty to charges of conspiring to defraud the government by raising and using tax-deductible donations for non-tax-deductible purposes providing military assistance to the Contras. Oliver North was named as a conspirator in this plot (*Washington Post*, July 14, 1987, A7).

The Heritage Foundation also lobbied for direct U.S. military aid to the Contras. On the eve of a House vote on Contra aid, the foundation held an all-day forum for congressional staff members. Top Contra officers and Nicaraguan opposition leaders were brought to the forum and later paraded through the halls of Congress. Heritage also printed and distributed an unsubstantiated report titled "Nicaragua's Terrorist Connection" that was hand-delivered to members of Congress (Wilentz 1986, 22).

The Heritage Foundation uses a similar strategy to lobby for other issues. Rather than conducting in-depth research studies, it produces brief position papers. Most contain fewer than six pages. These are hand-delivered to Congress and cabinet members by a six-person delivery staff and mailed to lower-echelon executive branch and congressional staffers (Rosenthal 1985).

The papers are produced on a production line, using recent college graduates as "researchers" and college students as "interns," who locate information for the "researchers." Needless to say, the quality of work produced by this method is sophomoric. Instead of aiming for quality, the Heritage Foundation appears to strive for quantity. In an average year, Heritage pumps out over 200 papers. These papers are also sent with press releases to journalists or rewritten as commentaries for small-circulation newspapers. The small-town papers are more politically conservative than metropolitan dailies and are also looking for free copy, which Heritage provides with their commentaries. As a consequence, small-circulation nonmetropolitan newspapers are the most frequent publishers of Heritage Foundation writings. According to sources at the Heritage Foundation, an average mailing produces 200 to 500 stories. When clips from these newspapers are obtained, they are mailed "to the congressman in whose district it appeared" in order to influence that congressman's voting (Easterbrook 1986, 73). For Washington journalists Heritage has a free delivery system. All a journalist must do is call Heritage, and it will deliver one or more of its papers that day for free.

Given Heritage's emphasis on distribution, it is easy to see why Heritage spent 36 percent of its 1988 budget on marketing. Most think tanks spend about 5 percent (Linden 1987). When Heritage's fundraising costs are added to its marketing expenses, they account for over half of the foundation's annual budget (Heritage Foundation 1988, 30). Less than half of Heritage's budget is spent on research and personnel.

Not surprisingly, the Heritage Foundation began life as a center of activism rather than thinking. It was founded by Edwin Feulner and Paul Weyrich with a quarter-million-dollar grant from Adolph Coors, a Colorado brewer and notorious antiunionist. Weyrich served as Heritage's first president until 1975, when he left to found a political action committee (PAC) called the Committee for a Free Congress. This organization became the Free Congress Research and Education Foundation (FCREF), another purported research center. The FCREF operates several other specialized centers or front groups: the Institute of Cultural Conservatism, the Institute of Government and Politics, and the Child and Family Protection Institute (*Research Centers Directory* 1990, 1453). The Child and Family Protection Institute promotes anti-abortion legislation.

These organizations have given Weyrich substantial clout, despite his extreme views. Jerry Falwell, who is also extreme in his views, described Weyrich "as pretty far out" (Bennett 1988, 393). Even so, the networks have repeatedly turned to Weyrich to shape their news. In 1987-1988, he appeared 10 times and was described as a "conservative analyst" (ABC–November 8, 1987), Free Congress Foundation spokesman (CBS–December 7, 1987), "conservative activist" (ABC–August 13, 1988), and lobbyist (NBC–February 7, 1987).

Frank Walton, who served as Gov. Ronald Reagan's secretary of transportation in California, became Heritage's president after Weyrich. When Walton returned to California in 1977, Feulner became president and William Simon was elected to the board of trustees. Simon, who served as Nixon's and Ford's secretary of treasury, is also president of the John M. Olin Foundation, which is a major funder of the Heritage Foundation. Under the stewardship of Feulner and Simon, Heritage's budget fattened. In 1978, the budget was $2.5 million. By 1980, it had climbed to over $5 million. The contributions didn't come exclusively from rich right-wingers like Richard Mellon Scaife. They also came from General Electric, Kraft, Ford, Procter & Gamble, and the General Motors foundations (*Foundation Grants Index* 1989).

Heritage's large budget and ties with Reagan aides put it in an ideal position to attract media attention after the former actor was elected U.S. president. Until Ronald Reagan became president, Heritage was a well-funded but neglected beltway institution (*New York Times*, November 21, 1988, 23).

In late 1980, following Reagan's presidential victory, the Heritage Foundation issued *Mandate for Leadership*, a thick compendium of conservative policy proposals. The proposals included funding for the B-1 bomber and MX missile programs, covert and overt intervention against pro-Soviet regimes, industry deregulation, privatization, and urban enterprise zones. The proposals were prepared with the assistance of Reagan adviser Edwin Meese.

Because *Mandate for Leadership* suggested a course that the Reagan administration might follow, it captured substantial media attention, propelling the Heritage Foundation from obscurity to center stage. The ascendancy of the Heritage Foundation is documented by the *New York Times Index*. During 1976 and 1977 the foundation didn't warrant an entry. During 1978 and 1979 it received 2 entries. During 1980 and 1981 the figure rose to 14, and during 1982 and 1983 it was referenced 24 times.

The Heritage Foundation has been less successful at shaping broadcast than print news, no doubt because Heritage spokesmen are more interested in producing a political statement than a nine-second sound bite. Between 1982 and 1989, spokesmen from the Heritage Foundation never appeared more than 11 times in any year on the three broadcast networks. The few Heritage spokesmen that did appear were Edwin Feulner, Burt Pines, Stuart Butler, and Bruce Fein. By contrast, three prestige papers—the *Washington Post, Los Angeles Times*, and *Boston Globe*—carried quotes and opinion articles by Heritage Foundation representatives a total of 102 times in 1985, 158 times in 1986, 171 times in 1987, 163 times in 1988, and 128 times in 1989.[3]

The "MacNeil/Lehrer NewsHour" used spokesmen from the Heritage Foundation much more frequently than did the networks, but not as often as the average newspaper. Between January 1, 1982, and October 1, 1990, Heritage spokesmen appeared on "MacNeil/Lehrer" 39 times. This was far less than speakers from the AEI (142 times) or the Brookings Institution (82 times), but far more than representatives from liberal or Democratic think tanks. Representatives from the Institute for Policy Studies appeared 8 times, and a representative of the Economic Policy Institute appeared 1 time.

THE CARNEGIE ENDOWMENT

The Carnegie Endowment for International Peace differs from the Brookings Institution, AEI, and Heritage Foundation in several ways. First, the endowment was established in 1910 by Andrew Carnegie as a means to promote world peace (Carnegie Endowment 1989). Because of its endowment, which began as $10 million in 1910 but has since grown to over $60 million, this think tank is not reliant on outside donors for support. As a result, it is unlikely to lobby on behalf of corporate contributors as other think tanks do.

Second, the Carnegie Endowment was created to be a forum for the expression of divergent opinions, rather than a research center. Although its associates are encouraged to conduct research, the endowment does not have a research agenda. Instead of a research staff, the endowment has a constantly rotating staff of associates with foreign policy experience who are recruited from government, universities, and the media. Because the associates are well connected before being hired, the Carnegie Endowment is essentially a policy forum for America's foreign policy elite. Academics that become Carnegie associates usually have Ivy League connections, and journalists are always from the prestige press, not community or alternative newspapers. Past and current journalists who have been Carnegie associates include Sanford Unger, who worked for the *Washington Post* and *Atlantic Monthly*; *New York Times* editor Leslie Gelb; Robin Wright of the *Los Angeles Times*; Selig Harrison of the *Washington Post*, who was also managing editor of the *New Republic*; and Andrew Nagorski, a bureau chief for *Newsweek*.

Because Carnegie associates are elite members, their views merely reflect the differences of opinion that exist among the political elite. The endowment frequently has both "mainstream" positions under its roof at the same time. For example, during the mid-1980s it had Peter Bell and Robert Leiken on board. When the issue of aid to the Nicaraguan Contras was being debated, Leiken testified for and Bell testified against aid before the Senate Foreign Relations Committee (Wilentz 1986, 22).

Ideas greatly divergent from the mainstream are not likely to be generated by Carnegie associates and, if they are, are not likely to be expressed, because Carnegie associates are not insulated with tenure like university professors. When associates leave the Carnegie Endowment after a year or two of residence, they must return to their jobs in the prestige media or government. None would want to be identified with unpopular political positions, such as supporting Nicaragua's Sandinista government. Such advocacy would only lead to being marginalized by other elites.

NOTES

1. Frank Gaffney, Jr., went from the AEI to the Center for Security Policy shortly after this appearance.

2. This figure was obtained from a data base search of the "MacNeil/Lehrer NewsHour" transcripts contained in Nexis. The search was conducted on October 3, 1990, as were other searches of the "MacNeil/Lehrer" transcripts.

3. These numbers were obtained from a data base search of these newspapers' texts using Dialogue.

6

FOREIGN AFFAIRS

The diversity of viewpoints expressed in the mass media about foreign policy is more restricted than for any other topic. The limited diversity is due to the small number of publications and institutions that legitimate foreign policy "expertise." The two periodicals that legitimate debate and establish the boundaries of acceptable discourse are *Foreign Affairs* and *Foreign Policy*. These journals have tremendous influence, despite relatively small circulations. The larger of the two, *Foreign Affairs*, has a circulation of 90,000, which is about one-half the circulation of *Mother Jones* magazine (*Writer's Market 1988*).

Foreign Affairs is edited by William Hyland and published by the Council on Foreign Relations, and *Foreign Policy* is edited by Charles Maynes and published by the Carnegie Endowment. Hyland and Maynes not only are editors who legitimate discourse, but have long been associated with other institutions that certify foreign policy expertise. Hyland was an analyst for the CIA until 1969, when he joined the NSC staff at the White House under Henry Kissinger. Between 1973 and 1976 he was director of intelligence at the State Department and deputy assistant to the president for national security. In 1977, following Jimmy Carter's presidential victory, Hyland went to CSIS, which at the time was associated with Georgetown University. A few years later, he moved to the Carnegie Endowment. In 1984, he was named editor of *Foreign Affairs*.

Maynes has a similar history. He received degrees from Harvard and Oxford universities, worked at the State Department from 1962 to 1965, was stationed in Laos and Moscow in official capacities between 1965 and 1970, became a member of the London-based IISS, and joined the Carnegie Endowment and became its secretary in 1972. He worked at the State Department again between 1977 and 1980, and then became editor of *Foreign Policy*.

All of the institutions with which Hyland and Maynes have been associated legitimate foreign affairs expertise; few other institutions do. These associations are the principal reasons why Hyland and Maynes, and not others, were selected as editors of their journals. Former CIA agents and government officials receive automatic legitimation because of their experience. Professors at private, eastern universities such as Harvard, Georgetown, Columbia, Princeton, and Johns Hopkins universities also receive automatic legitimation, as do members of big-name think tanks that specialize in foreign affairs, such as the CSIS, the Carnegie Endowment, the Brookings Institution, the California-based Rand Corporation, and the IISS. More important than these organizations is the Council on Foreign Relations, to which both Hyland and Maynes belong.

The Council on Foreign Relations is the most important source of foreign policy legitimation in the United States. The Council is a private organization of foreign policy elites, whose members include former presidents Jimmy Carter and Gerald Ford, former presidential candidates Walter Mondale and Edmund Muskie, former secretaries of state George Shultz and Henry Kissinger, and former secretaries of defense Caspar Weinberger and Harold Brown. With members such as these, it is obvious that not just anyone can join. Membership in the Council is by invitation only. Invitations are extended by the nominating committee, and entrance is approved by the membership committee. The nominating committee includes Charlayne Hunter-Gault of the "MacNeil/Lehrer NewsHour," former Secretary of State William P. Rogers, John Steinbruner of the Brookings Institution, and former Secretary of Commerce Juanita Kreps. Until he joined the Bush administration as National Security Adviser, Brent Scowcroft was chairman of the membership committee.

Members are not just current and former government officials, but captains of industry, academics, think tank fellows, and former military leaders such as retired Admiral William J. Crowe, Col. Harry Summers, and Lt. Gen. William Odon. The captains of industry have included many leaders of the news industry, including "three out of ten directors" of the *New York Times*, four of nine directors of the *Washington Post*, and William Paley of CBS (Shoup and Minter 1977, 66). Current members include Laurence Tisch of CBS, Roone Arledge of ABC, Katharine Graham of the *Washington Post*, Robert Eburu of the Times-Mirror Company, and Roger Parkinson, publisher of the Minneapolis *Star Tribune*. Overall, corporate leaders comprise 27 percent of the Council's membership (*Council on Foreign Relations* 1988).

Corporate moguls Willard Butcher, chairman of Chase Manhattan Bank; Robert Anderson, chairman of Rockwell International; Randall Meyer, former president of Exxon; Edmund T. Pratt, Jr., chairman of Pfizer, Inc.; Richard Wood, chairman of Eli Lilly and Company; and Walter Writon, former chairman of Citicorp, who serve as trustees of AEI, are Council members, as are all of the AEI's leading news shapers: Jeane Kirkpatrick, Irving Kristol, Michael Novak, Norman Ornstein, Richard Perle, William Schneider, and Ben Wattenberg. Some of these individuals, like Kristol and Ornstein, are not even listed as foreign policy experts in the AEI's directory of experts (see *AEI Sourcebook* 1989) but nevertheless have Council membership. Half of the AEI's "council of academic advisers" are also members, as are all of the CSIS's leading news shapers, as well as a good number of their lesser known savants: Barry Blechman, William Brock, Zbigniew Brzezinski, Robert Hunter, Fred Ikle, Amos Jordan, Henry Kissinger, Robert Kupperman, Walter Laqueur, Edward Luttwak, James Schlesinger, William J. Taylor, Jay Winik, and Alice Young.

The Council not only provides an imprimatur of expertise for members, but maintains a stranglehold on legitimation by its interrelationships with other legitimating institutions. Twenty-two of 33 members of Brookings' board of trustees are Council members, as are 20 of 29 Arms Control Association trustees. Fifteen of 22 Carnegie Endowment trustees are members of the Council, as are 13 of 18 members of the editorial board of *Foreign Policy*, the endowment's journal. Because these organizations have overlapping membership with the Council on Foreign Relations, they are able to act as additional gatekeepers for the Council, certifying some individuals as experts and not others.

Membership in the Council of Foreign Relations is an important prerequisite for being legitimated as a foreign policy expert, but membership in the Council is not sufficient to make an individual a nationally quoted news shaper. As of June 1988, the Council had about 2,500 members, but only a few had become leading news shapers. The most important characteristics of leading news shapers are that they have published in *Foreign Affairs* or *Foreign Policy*, have been in government, have professorships at Ivy League universities, or are fellows at one of the leading think tanks.

FOREIGN AFFAIRS

Academic journals such as the *American Political Science Review* use a "blind review" process for selecting manuscripts for publication. Blind review means that the manuscript's author isn't known to reviewers and his credentials thus cannot be used to assess the manuscript's importance. Potential articles are assessed solely on their merits. By contrast, *Foreign Affairs* asks authors who submit manuscripts to supply "his/her qualifications for writing on the topic in question (educational, past publications, relevant positions or honors)" (*Writer's Market 1988* 1987, 760). Unlike other political science journals, *Foreign Affairs* uses this biographical information to determine whether a manuscript is selected for publication.

An examination of authors in recent issues of *Foreign Affairs*, *Foreign Policy*, and several other journals supports the contention that author affiliation is an important determinant of manuscript selection for the "elite" foreign policy journals. Eight of ten articles in the spring 1990 issue of *Foreign Affairs* were authored or coauthored by Council members. The other two were authored by fellows at the IISS and Rand Corporation, two secondary legitimating institutions that are part of the Council's network. Five of ten articles in the summer 1990 issue were authored by Council members. One of the other five articles was written by George Carver, Jr., of the CSIS. The other four were written by professors at Columbia, Harvard, and Johns Hopkins universities, which are also important legitimating institutions. None were written by members of grassroots political organizations, freelance writers, or professors at public universities.

A similar concentration of Council membership is found among authors of *Foreign Policy* articles. The spring and summer 1990 issues of this journal contained 18 articles. Of these, four were written by foreign nationals: Italian Foreign Minister Gianni De Michelis, 1988 Mexican presidential candidate Cuauhtemoc Cardenas, PLO member Aby Iyad, and Japanese journalist Kan Ito. Of the remaining 14 articles, six were authored or coauthored by members of the Council on Foreign Relations. Of the remaining eight, seven were written by associates of such think tanks as the Cato Institute, Carnegie Endowment, Brookings Institution, Arms Control Association, and Rand Corporation. One article was authored by a professor from the University of Pittsburgh.

One possible explanation for why authors of articles in *Foreign Affairs* and *Foreign Policy* are almost exclusively Ivy League professors, Council members, and think tank fellows is that these individuals are better trained and better informed than other political scientists. While this argument would certainly be made by individuals who publish in the two journals, the argument isn't supported by an evaluation of articles in blind-reviewed journals such as *World Politics*, which is published at Princeton University. *World Politics* has an editorial profile and editorial board similar to the other two foreign policy journals, except that "the anonymity of the author" is maintained during the evaluation process so that manuscripts are judged on their own merits (*World Politics*, July 1990, i). In the spring (April) and summer (July) 1990 issues of this journal, not one article was penned by a member of a think tank or the Council on Foreign Relations. The articles were written by professors from private and public institutions and not just the Ivy League: the University of New Mexico, Cornell University, the University of Toronto, the University of California at Davis, Harvard University, the University of California at Irvine, the University of Michigan, Yale University, the University of Wisconsin, and the University of California at San Diego.

A similar pattern is observable among authors in the spring and summer 1990 issues of the *American Political Science Review*, the blind-reviewed journal of the American Political Science Association. Only one of the 24 articles in this journal was authored by a Council member. This was Lucian Pye, a Yale-educated professor at the Massachusetts Institute of Technology.[1] The other authors were from numerous public and private universities, not just the Ivy League. Not one article was written by a think tank "scholar."

The best explanation for why think tank and Ivy League analysts don't monopolize the pages of *World Politics* or the *American Political Science Review* is that these journals use a blind review process for selecting manuscripts. The connections and titles that individuals have do not help in the selection process, as they do with *Foreign Affairs* and *Foreign Policy*. By contrast, the "elite" journals are not blind-reviewed and use the author's affiliation to determine whether the manuscript will be accepted for publication. Since elitist organizations such as the Council on Foreign Relations and the Carnegie Endowment seek to preserve their elite stature, they close their journals' pages to all but individuals certified as experts by themselves and affiliated organizations. In the words of Robert Schulzinger, who wrote a history of the Council on Foreign Relations, these institutions "have demonstrated partiality for conventional thinking and misgivings about the legitimacy of comments by people less well (or differently) informed than themselves" (1984, xi). Because of these misgivings, they keep their list of "certified experts" as short as possible.

Despite the obvious biases in the selection of articles in *Foreign Affairs*, the journal nevertheless remains the primary legitimating publication for foreign policy expertise in the United States. The importance of the journal is demonstrated by the large number of network television news shapers published in its spring and summer 1990 issues: Harvard's Marshall Goldman (CBS–October 31, 1989), the Council on Foreign Relations' William Hyland (NBC–May 27, 1988), the IISS's Christopher Bertram (ABC–May 29, 1989), Johns Hopkins' Barry Rubin (CBS–May 12, 1987), the CSIS's George Carver (ABC–December 22, 1989), the Council on Foreign Relations' Susan Kaufman Purcell (CBS–October 28, 1989), the Institute for International Economics' Fred Bergsten (NBC–May 2, 1989), and Harvard's Jeffrey Sachs (ABC–December 18, 1989), not to mention Theodore Sorensen and Attorney General Richard Thornburgh.

These individuals also authored a large number of commentaries and opinion articles for the prestige press in the past few years. Authors of articles in the spring and summer 1990 issues of *Foreign Affairs* who also penned commentaries for the prestige press include William Hyland (*Washington Post*, September 25, 1990, A23), Marshall Goldman (*New York Times*, September 16, 1990, 11), Christopher Bertram (*New York Times*, July 20, 1989, A19), Ronald Asmus (*Los Angeles Times*, September 19, 1989, 7), Barry Rubin (*New York Times*, February 13, 1990, A21), Robert Tucker (*New York Times*, January 11, 1989, A19), George Carver (*Los Angeles Times*, January 2, 1987, 5), Susan Kaufman Purcell (*New York Times*, January 10, 1990, A19), Allen Lynch (*Christian Science Monitor*, October 13, 1987, 15), Jeffrey Sachs (*Washington Post*, December 31, 1989, C5), and Peter Tarnoff (*New York Times*, September 19, 1989, A19).

By contrast, just five of the 54 authors in the spring and summer 1990 issues of *World Politics* and *American Political Science Review* published commentaries in prestige newspapers, according to InfoTrac's *National Newspaper Index*.[2] Three of the five were Ivy League professors: Richard Lebow of Cornell (*Washington Post*, March 6, 1988, C5) and Harvard professors Marc Lindenberg (*Los Angeles Times*, October 28, 1987, 7II) and Robert Fishman (*Wall Street Journal*, October 30, 1987, 15). The other two were public university professors, who published commentaries in the *Los Angeles Times*. One of the two taught at the University of California in Los Angeles.

And not one of the authors in *World Politics* or *American Political Science Review* ever appeared on a television network news program as a news shaper. Predictably, the only people associated with either of the blind-reviewed journals who did appear as news shapers were members of the Council. These were Thomas E. Mann, John Lewis Gaddis, and Chalmers Johnson. Mann (NBC–November 4, 1988, and ABC–March 5, 1989) is a fellow at the Brookings Institution and a member of the editorial board of the *American Political Science Review*. Ohio University professor John Lewis Gaddis (CBS–December 5, 1987) is on the editorial board of *World Politics*. He was a visiting professor at Princeton University in 1987 (*Who's Who in America* 1990, 1140), the year that he first appeared as a news shaper. The other news shaper was Chalmers Johnson (CBS–August 9, 1989), a University of California professor. He is also on the editorial board of *World Politics*.

THE ORIGINS OF LEGITIMATION

When Pres. Woodrow Wilson failed to heed the advice of American aristocrats in Europe during the Paris Peace Conference of 1919, the aristocrats decided to establish an organization that would attract attention to their views and give direction to U.S. foreign policy. Morgan Bank's Thomas W. Lamont, the American Geographic Society's Isaiah Bowman, former attorney general Whitney Shepardson, Columbia University professor James T. Shotwell, and several other "leading Americans" met with a handful of British elite members in London in May 1919 to discuss the creation of a transatlantic foreign policy organization. The British and Americans decided on an Institute of International Affairs, which they hoped would "lead public opinion along the right path" on both sides of the Atlantic. The British chapter rapidly established itself and became known as the Royal Institute of International Affairs.

When Lamont's group returned to the United States, it discovered that another group composed of businessmen and lawyers was meeting regularly over dinner to discuss foreign affairs. The New York group was headed by Wall Street attorney Elihu Root, who had been Pres. Theodore Roosevelt's secretary of state. Root was approached by the returning Americans and asked whether the two groups could merge. Root and his colleagues agreed to the merger, and the Council on Foreign Relations was formed and incorporated in New York State on July 29, 1921. Root was elected honorary president of the Council, John W. Davis was elected president, Paul D. Cravath was elected vice president, and Edwin F. Gay was elected secretary.

Davis was a millionaire congressman from West Virginia who served as President Wilson's ambassador to Great Britain. He was chief counsel to the J. P. Morgan Company and became the 1924 dark horse presidential candidate of the Democratic party. Davis was picked as the Democratic candidate after convention delegates found themselves hopelessly deadlocked after 102 ballots in two weeks. He was soundly defeated by Calvin Coolidge in the general election. Cravath was a well-known Republican lawyer, while Gay was an economics professor and dean of the Harvard Business School who edited the *New York Post* following World War I.

By selecting prominent political leaders, lawyers, and academics as officers, the Council hoped that it would attract "the junkers and spokesmen of business" as members, not "the *New Republic* crowd, the cranks, the extremists and the professors" (Schulzinger 1984, 6). The "*New Republic* crowd" referred to political leftists, not members of the media.[3] From the very beginning, prominent media representatives were welcomed as Council members. These included *New York Post* owner Thomas Lamont, *New York World* editor Walter Lippmann, and *Time* founder Henry Luce.

When Council members talked of cranks and professors, they were not talking about men of the Ivy League. (Women were not allowed to join the Council until 1969.) Founding members Shotwell and Gay were professors at Columbia and Harvard universities, and many of their first recruits were also Ivy League academics. In fact, Ivy League academics and their graduates have virtually dominated the Council. Lawrence Shoup and William Minter's sociological study of the Council found that 17 percent of Council members had undergraduate degrees from Harvard. Thirteen percent attended Yale, and "if one adds Princeton and Columbia, as well, 48 percent of Council members (1969) and 42 percent of Council directors (from 1922 to 1977) attended one of these four universities" (1977, 75). The Ivy League composition of the Council is even more dramatic when graduate-level education is considered. Among members with postbaccalaureate degrees, 70 percent attended Harvard, Yale, Princeton, or Columbia. Most of the remaining members attended private universities such as Johns Hopkins, the Massachusetts Institute of Technology or the University of Chicago, not public universities.

Harvard professor Edwin Gay suggested that the Council establish a magazine that would become the country's authoritative journal of foreign affairs. Gay envisaged a journal comparable to what he had created at the *New York Post*. He transformed the *Post* from a sensationalist tabloid into a paper of sophisticated commentary and in so doing lost a quarter of the paper's circulation and $1.7 million in just a couple of years. Unlike the *Post*, the Council's journal would not have to worry about circulation or losing money, since it would be directed to a "better class" of people—lawyers, government leaders, businessmen, and men of letters.

Gay suggested that Harvard professor Archibald Carey Coolidge serve as the journal's editor and Hamilton Fish Armstrong be made assistant editor. Coolidge was director of Harvard's Widener Library and a professor of Near East studies. Armstrong was a Princeton graduate who worked under Gay at the *New York Post*. He was a member of the New York political dynasty that still gets its members elected to office. Although Coolidge was very busy, he nevertheless accepted the editorial appointment. Because of Coolidge's other responsibilities, Armstrong was left in charge of the day-to-day operations of the new journal. Armstrong officially became editor of *Foreign Affairs* in 1928, after Coolidge stepped down. He remained editor for 44 years (Council on Foreign Relations 1988).

Cass Canfield, who later became chairman of Harper and Row, became the new journal's chief fundraiser. Canfield received half of the needed $125,000 from Council board members and their associates and the rest by sending a letter of solicitation to "the thousand richest Americans" (Shoup and Minter 1977, 17). The donations that Canfield received exceeded the proposed budget, and *Foreign Affairs* went to press in September 1922.

In its first editorial statement, *Foreign Affairs* reported that it "will not devote itself to the support of any one cause, however worthy" (September 15, 1922, 1). Although the journal claimed to represent diverse viewpoints, its articles uniformly advocated "a forward United States foreign policy, interested in exploiting the world's natural resources and putting public affairs in Washington in the hands of serene, dispassionate experts who, unlike the public at large, knew what they were doing" (Schulzinger 1984, 11) This was to be expected from a journal desiring to reach "the junkers and spokesmen of business."

The early issues of *Foreign Affairs* tried to appeal to businessmen by featuring at least one article per issue on the availability of resources. These articles included "The World Oil Situation," "The Crude Rubber Supply," "Fertilizer: The World's Supply," "The Mineral Resources of the East," "The World's Crisis of Cotton," and "The Coal Question." Each issue also carried a short educational feature, complete with map and notes. These features examined the Ulster boundary, the Bessarabia dispute, the Franco-Swiss free zones, the Chinese eastern railway, and Soviet territorial divisions.

Many articles were written by prominent world leaders such as Czechoslovakian president Thomas Masaryk and Mexican president Plutarco Elias Calles and businessmen such as Price Waterhouse's George O. May and Wall Street attorney John Foster Dulles, but many more were written by members of the Royal Institute of International Affairs, Ivy League professors, and former and current government officials. Many of the Ivy League professors were former government officials or consultants, a trend that continues today. The professors included A. Lawrence Lowell, Charles H. Haskins, and William L. Langer of Harvard. Officials included William Stimson, who was Secretary of War during World Wars I and II and a law partner of Elihu Root; Alabama senator Oscar Underwood; and Secretary of State Charles E. Hughes, who became Chief Justice of the Supreme Court in 1930. Articles by members of established foreign policy associations, which are now called think tanks, Ivy League academics, and government elites have dominated the pages of *Foreign Affairs* throughout its history. It is the foreign policy journal of the "establishment."

In addition to publishing *Foreign Affairs*, the Council sponsored seminars, forums, meetings, and dinners where foreign policy issues were discussed. During the early years of the Council, these events were held at the Harvard Club, Princeton and Columbia universities, and, after 1945, the renovated Pratt mansion at 68th Street and Park Avenue in Manhattan. The Pratt mansion became the Council's headquarters after Mrs. Harold Pratt donated it to the Council. Over the years, speakers at these events included many of the world's leading dignitaries: Georges Clemenceau, Charles de Gaulle, David Ben-Gurion, Anthony Eden, and Haile Selassie. In 1987-1988, speakers at Council functions included Zambian president Kenneth Kaunda, former Korean dictator Chun Doo Hwan, Portuguese president Mario Soares, and Israeli prime minister Yitzak Shamir. Presiders and discussants at these events are invariably Ivy League professors such as Columbia University professors Gary Sick and Marshall Shulman, think tank fellows such as the Institute for International Economics' Fred Bergsten and Carnegie's Geoffrey Kemp, and former officials such as William Colby and Lawrence Eagleburger. Other discussants at Council events have been elite media personalities such as Tom Brokaw, Dan Rather, and Garrick Utley, who frequently use other Council discussants to shape their news.

Beginning in 1976, the Council started holding meetings and forums in Washington, eliminating the commute for its 400 Washington, D.C., based members. By 1987-1988, the Council was sponsoring 80 events in the capital city, including 15 general meetings and nine roundtable dinners (Council on Foreign Relations 1988, 87). These meetings also featured leading dignitaries. In 1987-1988, speakers included Israeli leader Abba Eban, Yugoslav dissident Milovan Djilas, and secretary of state George Shultz. Other speakers and discussants at these events have included the usual cast of news shapers from Columbia and Harvard universities, AEI, Brookings Institution, Carnegie Endowment, and CSIS, along with media notables such as the *Washington Post*'s Stephen Rosenfeld and Katharine Graham.

THE COUNCIL AND THE MEDIA

The Washington, D.C., and New York events are staged to keep Council members abreast of current affairs but are structured to showcase Council experts. When Alexander Zotov, a Soviet Middle East expert, spoke at a Council forum, Judith Kipper was the forum's presider. Kipper works for the Council and the Brookings Institution as a Mideast specialist. When Vitaly Zhurkin spoke about changes in the U.S.S.R., Columbia University professor Seweryn Bialer was the commentator. Council experts who have spoken at meetings include the "usual suspects": William Schneider, Edward Luttwak, Zbigniew Brzezinski, Dimitri Simes, and Susan Kaufman Purcell. Prestige reporters, who are also Council members, learn who are experts at these events, and they later contact these experts for quotes or sound bites. For example, Columbia's Seweryn Bialer spoke at a Washington, D.C., Council meeting on May 5, 1988, and was invited to appear as a news shaper on NBC the next day. Johns Hopkins University professor Riordan Roett spoke at the Council on March 14, 1988, and appeared on CBS as a news shaper the next day. Carnegie's James Chace spoke on Latin America at a Council luncheon on March 16, 1988, and appeared on ABC as a Latin American expert three days later.

Members of the press who are Council members include Public Broadcasting's Charlayne Hunter-Gault, Jim Lehrer, and William F. Buckley, Jr., and NPR's Daniel Schorr and Douglas Bennet. Network reporters who are members include CBS's Dan Rather and Marvin Kalb, NBC's Tom Brokaw and Garrick Utley and ABC's David Brinkley, Diane Sawyer, John Scali, Bob Zelnick, and Barbara Walters. *New York Times* editorial page editors Jack Rosenthal, Leon Sigal, and Leslie Gelb and *Washington Post* editorial page editors Meg Greenfield and Stephen S. Rosenfeld are also members. So are elite print reporters and columnists A. M. Rosenthal, David Ignatius, Hedrick Smith, Flora Lewis, Christopher Dickey, Harrison Salisbury, William Beecher, Robert Kleiman, Elizabeth Drew, William Safire, and George Will. *Time*'s Hedley Donovan and Kenneth Banta are Council members, as are all three *U.S. News and World Report* editors from the AEI: Richard Perle, David Gergen, and Ben Wattenberg. Journalists such as these, who are Council-legitimated experts, invariably call upon their peers when seeking foreign policy experts to shape their news.

Since 1987-1988, the Council has sought to broaden its contact with members of the press who are not Council members. Press conferences are now held to promote Council books, and book review editors are invited to these events. Council books have been reviewed in the *Washington Post*, the *New York Times*, and *Time* as a result of these press conferences, according to Council publicity. The Council, through its public affairs office, also "encourages news articles and editorials based on findings documented in Council publications" (Council on Foreign Relations 1988, 145).

The principal method that the Council uses to maintain contact with the nonmember reporters is its *News Alerts* bulletin, which draws attention to Council experts and tells reporters how to contact them for use as news shapers. In 1987-1988, after the Council stepped up its contacts with the press, Council director Peter G. Peterson and Council fellows Susan Kaufman Purcell and Paul Jabber appeared on network news programs as shapers. The three were featured in *News Alerts* that year. During 1985-1986, these individuals weren't used as news shapers by any network.

The Council also encourages members of the press to call its press office to obtain the names of Council experts that reporters can interview. The experts that the Council recommends are either Council staffers or members. And to further expand its contacts with the press, the Council has invited nonmember reporters, such as Bob Woodward, the *Washington Post*'s assistant managing editor for the investigative staff, and Susan Chira, the *New York Times*' Tokyo correspondent, to appear as presenters and discussants at Council forums.

It is contacts such as these that have made the Council on Foreign Relations the media's primary legitimator of foreign affairs expertise. Reporters, bureau chiefs, and editorial page editors learn from the Council who the "real experts" are and then call upon them to shape their news. Not only are Council experts prelegitimated, which means that no research has to be done on their credentials, but most Council-certified experts are readily available to the national press corps. All but a few live in New York and Washington, D.C., where the majority of national news originates (Dominick 1977).

Finding the experts is also easy—reporters can simply call the Council. The Council will give them the names of experts or refer them to one of the resident "fellows." Once an expert is used by a reporter, his or her name is entered into a rolodex, and when a news shaper is needed at some future time, the expert is called again.

While there is no conspiracy among elites to monopolize foreign policy debate, there are subtle sociological influences that can bar anyone but Council-certified elites from being used as news shapers. First, the Council is a legitimator of expertise. Individuals who speak at Council functions or publish in *Foreign Affairs* are Council-certified experts whose credentials will rarely be questioned, and journalists don't need to check up on the qualifications of these individuals. Journalists faced with deadlines can save time by interviewing precertified experts, rather than taking the time to locate and validate the credentials of non-Council members.

Second, the Council has a method for informing journalists about their experts. The journals, panels, forums, and lunches that the Council sponsors inform journalists about experts and their fields of expertise. Except for think tanks and universities, few other institutions sponsor events that showcase their experts.

Third, prestige journalists are frequently Council members, who use other Council members as news shapers. These prestige journalists serve as models for nonelite journalists to follow. Reporters at the bottom of the pack imitate the prestige journalists and also call upon Council members as news shapers. Simply stated, the nonelite journalists avoid highlighting their nonelite status, so they interview the elites in the Council on Foreign Relations.

Fourth, reporters need to please their bureau chiefs, editors, and publishers, and there is a high likelihood that at least one of these is a Council member, particularly if the reporter is employed by a larger newspaper. Council members would look askance at a reporter who rarely or never interviewed Council-certified experts. At the Minneapolis *Star Tribune*, for example, publisher Roger Parkinson and Washington bureau chief William Beecher are Council members. (Beecher is also a former government official. He was deputy secretary of defense for public affairs between 1973 and 1975.) *Star Tribune* correspondents are aware of the Council ties of their bosses, and this undoubtedly has a subtle influence on their selection of experts. In a typical article on the gulf crisis (August 12, 1990), *Star Tribune* reporter Steve Berg quoted the Carnegie Endowment's Geoffrey Kemp and the CSIS's Edward Luttwak, who are Council members and have been frequently used as news shapers by other reporters. Either Berg is a very dedicated pack journalist or his choices are subtly affected by his bosses' Council affiliations.

Fifth, Washington correspondents perceive themselves as the elite among news reporters, even if they do not work for prestige media. It follows that elite members interview elite members. More important, this perception promotes a self-important worldview, where the beltway is seen as the center of all that is important, in much the same way that the famous *New Yorker* map depicts Manhattan as the ganglion of the earth. Washingtonians develop a beltway-based and -biased view that excludes virtually all others, except individuals from New York City, the nation's media capital. As Pat Forceia, a political consultant and former aide to congressman James Obestar, described it: "People in Washington go to parties with other people in Washington, they talk exclusively to other people in Washington, and have little contact with anyone else. This includes congressmen and senators, who quickly lose touch with their constituents."

Washington correspondents are probably even more insular than politicians, because they have no constituency to whom they answer. This insularity cultivates a view that sees everything important—including knowledge and opinions—as originating within the beltway. Because Council experts either live within the beltway or travel there from New York City, they become this country's preeminent sources of wisdom.

Relying on Council experts has the effect of restricting the range of political opinions that are expressed, because the Council is an organization of traditional elites, who are interested in maintaining or only slightly altering the status quo. Twenty-seven percent of Council members are business executives, 25 percent are academics, 13 percent are government officials, 12 percent are with nonprofit institutions, 11 percent are journalists, and 10 percent are attorneys. Only 2 percent have other employment (Council on Foreign Relations 1988, 107). While this range of elite occupations is restricted to begin with, it is even more restrictive when one considers that the academics are from private universities, the attorneys are from corporate law firms, the nonprofit employees are from think tanks, and the business executives are from multinational corporations.

Heavy reliance on Council-certified experts has not only restricted the range of debate, but has often caused journalists to substitute the less well informed opinions of Council members for the better-informed opinions of nonmembers. This does not mean that Council-certified "experts" are completely ignorant about the subjects on which they speak; it suggests that they have far less expertise than many other people whom the media never use as news shapers.

Television network reporters turned to Council members William LeoGrande (CBS and NBC–May 6, 1989), Elliott Abrams (CBS–March 6, 1989), James Chace (ABC–March 19, 1988), Peter G. Peterson (CBS–May 21, 1988), Susan Kaufman Purcell (CBS–January 17, 1988), Pamela Falk (CBS–April 3, 1989), and Riordan Roett (NBC–February 29, 1988) to explain Central and South American events during 1988-1989. LeoGrande is a professor at American University, a private Methodist institution in Washington, D.C. Of the seven news shapers, he made the most appearances. During 1988-1989, LeoGrande popped up 18 times.

Despite being the second most frequently used news shaper on Central American events, Elliott Abrams is not a Latin America expert. He is a former Reagan administration official. His Reagan ties were disclosed in only two of the 11 appearances he made as a network television news shaper during 1989. In one of the 11 appearances, Abrams was described as a former Reagan aide (ABC–February 12, 1989). In another, he was more accurately described as "Ronald Reagan's Contra policy architect" (NBC–August 8, 1989). During the other nine appearances, he was described as a former official. The fact that he was a former Reagan, rather than Carter, official was not disclosed, even though he was commenting on policies developed by the Reagan administration.

There is no question about Abrams' partisanship, but there are questions about his expertise. Little in his record indicates a knowledge of Central America. After Abrams received his undergraduate degree from Harvard University in 1969, he went to London to study economics. He didn't go to Vietnam or Latin America. When Abrams returned to the United States, he resumed his studies at Harvard. Abrams received a law degree in 1973 and then went to work for a Wall Street law firm. He later became an aide to Sens. Henry (Scoop) Jackson and Daniel Patrick Moynihan. In 1981, Abrams went to work at the State Department under Alexander Haig. In 1985, he was promoted to undersecretary of state for inter-American affairs, having worked himself up from the division of human rights and humanitarian affairs (*Who's Who in America* 1990, 8). He received the inter-American affairs appointment without ever having written a monograph or book about Latin America. Although Abrams was involved in private efforts to fund the Nicaraguan Contras and lobbied Congress in their behalf, this does not make him a Central America expert.

The credentials of James Chace and Peter G. Peterson are hardly better than those of Abrams. Harvard graduate James Chace is a journalist turned think tank fellow. He was an editor of the *New York Review of Books*, assistant editor of *Foreign Affairs*, and editor of *East Europe* magazine. *East Europe* was published by the Free Europe Committee, an organization that was covertly funded by the CIA between 1958 and 1964, the years that Chace was with the committee (Marchetti and Marks 1975). He wrote *The Rules of the Game* (1960), *Conflict in the Middle East* (1969) and *A World Elsewhere* (1973), none of which focused on Central or South America.

While serving as an editor of the *New York Review of Books* during the 1980s, Chace turned his attention to Central America, where the United States had already become heavily involved. In 1984, he penned a 137-page, mass-market paperback titled *Endless War* that examined the conflicts in Central America. The book was based, in part, on articles he wrote for the *New York Review of Books*.

Peter G. Peterson, the Council's president, received his undergraduate degree at Northwestern University and his master of business administration at the University of Chicago. He worked at the McCann-Erickson advertising agency during the 1950s and headed Bell & Howell during the 1960s. In 1971, Peterson was appointed secretary of commerce by President Nixon (*Current Biography* 1972, 349). After leaving government, he became the chairman of Lehman Brothers, and then head of the Blackstone Group, an investment company (*Who's Who in America* 1990, 2578). Peterson is not a Latin America expert, even though CBS turned to him for expert commentary on Panama (May 21, 1988). CBS reporters also turned to Peterson when they needed an economic expert. As an economic expert, he was asked to comment on the declining dollar (CBS–January 3, 1988) and inflation (October 21, 1988). During the January appearance, he was described as a representative of the Blackstone Group, during the May appearance he was described as a spokesman for the Council on Foreign Relations, and during the October appearance he was described as the ex–secretary of commerce.

Columbia-educated Susan Kaufman Purcell taught at UCLA during the late 1970s. While there, she wrote *The Mexican Profit-sharing Decision* (1975). She worked at the U.S. State Department during 1980-1981, and then went to the Council on Foreign Relations, where she became a senior fellow and head of the Latin American studies project. During the early 1980s, she edited books for the Academy of Political Science and the Council and wrote pamphlets for Central American Peace and Democracy Watch and the Cuban-American National Foundation, an organization of anti-Castro Cubans. Paula Falk is a Columbia University professor; Roett is a Johns Hopkins University professor. Falk authored one book, *Cuban Foreign Policy* (1986), and edited several anthologies on Latin America. Roett is the author or coauthor of three books and editor of four others. Roett and Purcell appeared four times during 1988-1989, and Falk appeared five times.

While the networks and other prestige media turned to these Council members as news shapers, they shunned many other Latin America experts who have far more impressive credentials. The shunned experts invariably came from outside the beltway, from public universities, or from the political left. James Petras, Maurice Zeitlin, and Irving Louis Horowitz are three scholars to whom the networks did not turn for "expert opinion," but whose credentials can be contrasted with those of Council "experts." State University of New York professor James Petras is the author or editor of fifteen books on Latin America. Among those he authored are *Politics and Social Forces in Chilean Development* (1969), *Politics and Social Structure in Latin America* (1970), *The Nationalization of Venezuelan Oil* (1977), *Latin America: Bankers, Generals and the Struggle for Social Justice* (1986), and *U.S. Hegemony under Seige* (1990). A comparison of citations in the *Social Science Citation Index* shows that Petras was cited as an expert by other Latin America scholars more frequently than any of the Council experts during the 1970s and 1980s.

UCLA professor Maurice Zeitlin is the author or editor of over a dozen books, including *Cuba, Tragedy in Our Hemisphere* (1963), *Revolutionary Politics and the Cuban Working Class* (1967), *Latin America: Reform or Revolution?* (1968), and *The Civil Wars in Chile* (1984). Rutgers University professor and *Society* magazine editor Irving Louis Horowitz is one of America's leading political sociologists. He has written extensively on Latin American politics and society.

His books include *Revolution in Brazil* (1964), *Latin American Radicalism* (1969), *Masses in Latin America* (1970), and *Cuban Communism* (1984).

When the topic is the Middle East, the prestige media turn to Brookings' Judith Kipper, Johns Hopkins university professor Fouad Ajami, and Columbia University professor Gary Sick for expert opinion. Kipper appeared 14 times as a network news shaper during 1987-1988 and was a consultant to ABC during the 1990 Middle East crisis (*USA Today,* August 30, 1990, 3D). Ajami appeared on CBS 21 times during 1987-1988. He has been CBS's paid consultant on the Mideast since 1986 (Magner 1991). Sick, an ex–NSC staffer in the Ford and Carter administrations, appeared on the networks ten times in 1988.

While the three Council members have shaped network television news about Iran, UCLA professor Nikki Keddie has not. Keddie is one of the leading U.S. experts on Iran, but she is not a Council member, think tank denizen, or Ivy League professor. Her research in Iran was funded by grants from the Social Science Research Council, American Council of Learned Societies, American Philosophical Society, and John Simon Guggenheim Foundation, not the Council on Foreign Relations. She speaks Farsi and is the author or editor of eleven books on the non-Arab Middle East, including *Religion and Rebellion in Iran* (1966), *Iran, Religion, Politics, and Society* (1980), and *Roots of Revolution* (1981).

Of the three Council experts, only Gary Sick is a bona fide Iranian expert and author. He wrote *All Fall Down: America's Tragic Encounter with Iran* (1985), a study of the Iranian hostage crisis. Ajami is an expert on Lebanon, not Iran. Kipper has undergraduate and master's degrees in psychology (Gamarekian 1985). She has never written a book or monograph about the Middle East. Her expertise is derived from her travels and work at the AEI, Brookings Institution, and Council of Foreign Relations.

When network reporters shaped news about the Soviet Union and Eastern Europe, they almost always turned to Council spokespersons or members of think tanks that are closely tied to the Council for analysis. During 1987-88, the networks most frequently turned to *Foreign Affairs* editor William Hyland and Columbia University professor Robert Legvold, who heads the Harriman Institute. Hyland appeared 14 times during 1987-1988; Legvold appeared 10 times. During 1987-1988, network reporters also turned to a group of analysts who have been closely associated with Henry Kissinger for almost two decades. This informal group includes Helmut Sonnenfeldt, Dimitri Simes, and Brent Scowcroft. Hyland, who served under Kissinger in the Nixon and Ford administrations, is also a member of the group.

In 1989, as major changes occurred in the Eastern bloc, the networks increasingly turned to news shapers from the Council who were not closely associated with the cold war, as were Hyland, Kissinger, and Legvold. The most frequently appearing of these new faces was Princeton University professor Stephen F. Cohen. During 1989, he appeared 14 times on CBS, which employed him as a consultant. During 1987-1988, Cohen appeared only once. In those years, cold warriors like Henry Kissinger (CBS–December 7, 1988) were still suggesting that Soviet president Gorbachev's policies "were consistent with an attempt to split Europe" away from the United States and did not reflect substantive changes in policy. When it became apparent to all but a few diehard conservatives that Gorbachev was different from his predecessors and intent on changing the Soviet system, only then did the networks turn to analysts who had been saying this all along.

Another Soviet expert who appeared with increasing frequency during 1989 was Edward Hewett, a fellow at the Brookings Institution. Hewett appeared as a news shaper once in 1987, twice in 1988, and 11 times in 1989. Like Cohen, he is not identified with the cold war. Another Brookings fellow, Jerry Hough, made five appearances during 1989.

The networks' reliance on the analyses of old cold warriors during 1987-1988 presented news consumers with a very distorted picture of what was happening in the Soviet Union and Eastern bloc. The traditional views about Gorbachev that were expressed by Kissinger and his associates left many in the United States unprepared for what soon transpired in Eastern Europe. After events there discredited the traditional cold war view of Soviet leaders, the networks and other prestige media still turned to the same old set of cold warriors to shape their news, even as they added Cohen, Hewett, and a few others with somewhat different views to their roster of news shapers. For example, "This Week with David Brinkley" (December 23, 1990) turned to Brookings' Ed Hewett, the CSIS's Stephen Sestanovich, Harvard's Marshall Goldman, former secretary of defense Caspar Weinberger, and Dimitri Simes to provide a background report on Soviet Foreign Minister Eduard Shevardnadze's resignation. Brinkley's guests were William Hyland and former secretary of state George Shultz, who discussed the implications of the resignation on U.S. foreign policy. On the same day, the guest on "Meet the Press" was Zbigniew Brzezinski, who also discussed Shevardnadze's departure. (Brzezinski appeared on "Meet the Press" with Jeane Kirkpatrick three weeks earlier.) "Face the Nation" used Council fellow Michael Mandelbaum as its discussant of Shevardnadze. *Los Angeles Times* reporter Norman Kempster turned to CSIS's George Carver and Carnegie's Dimitri Simes for comments on the resignation. Simes continued to express skepticism about whether there were really major differences between Gorbachev and party conservatives, as Shevardnadze intimated in his resignation speech. Simes said, "If Shevardnadze's desperation is justified, if indeed there is a profound crisis in the Soviet Union, then all relations with the Soviet Union are in doubt" (*Los Angeles Times*, December 21, 1990, A1, A12).

NON-COUNCIL EXPERTS

Council members claim expertise in the traditional fields of foreign policy—U.S.-Soviet relations, international trade, military hardware, regional conflicts, and the like. The media turn to Council members when they need news shapers on these topics, but not when the topics are highly technical, as with space technology. Another time when the news media turn to non–Council members is when reporters are originating stories from abroad and quickly need quotes or sound bites from "experts." Because foreign affairs stories usually originate outside the United States—and since Council members must be U.S. rather than foreign citizens—reporters do find themselves turning to non-Council foreign experts as news shapers. These foreign experts are almost always "red-brick" university professors, European journalists, and members of policy institutes, such as the London-based IISS, that have fraternal relations with the Council on Foreign Relations.

U.S. experts who are not Council members also shape foreign affairs news, but not very often. Of the 17 most frequently appearing news shapers of 1987-1988 (see Table 5), eight were Council members and nine were not. The nine non–Council members never commented on foreign affairs. They always shaped domestic news. The nine non–Council members were campaign analysts Ed Rollins, Kevin Phillips, Harrison Hickman, Bob Beckel, Stephen Hess, Robert Squier, and David Garth, economist David Jones, and conservative publisher Richard Viguerie. While the non-Council experts never spoke about foreign affairs, some Council members shaped both domestic and foreign affairs news. David Gergen, Norman Ornstein, James Schlesinger, and William Schneider commented on domestic and foreign affairs. Council members Fouad Ajami, William Hyland, Richard Perle, and Judith Kipper commented exclusively on foreign affairs news.

Twenty-five of the 44 appearances by think tank analysts in the 1987-1989 sample were made by Council members (see Table 4). The 19 non-Council appearances were primarily made by analysts from foreign research centers or by spokespersons for U.S.-based think tanks that are concerned with domestic issues. Don Kerr (CBS–August 11, 1987) and Hans Binnendijk (ABC–May 10, 1988) commented on foreign affairs but are not Council members. They are with the IISS. The domestic-issue think tanks that fielded non-Council spokespersons included the Cato Institute (NBC–November 16, 1988), Joint Center for Political Studies (CBS–November 9, 1988), Employee Benefits Research Institute (ABC–November 16, 1988), and Environmental Policy Institute (ABC–November 11, 1988). Five representatives from Washington's leading think tanks (the CSIS's George Carver, the AEI's Suzanne Garment, and three Heritage Foundation spokesmen) were also not Council members, but they were the exceptions.

Of the 65 appearances by "experts, analysts, and consultants" who appeared in the 1987-1988 network television sample (see Table 4), 37 appearances concerned domestic political stories. Twenty-eight concerned foreign news stories. Of the 28 appearances by foreign affairs analysts, nine were by Council members, four were by technology experts and 15 were by foreigners—experts residing outside the United States.

The nine appearances by Council members who were described as experts, analysts, or consultants were by Marshall Goldman (CBS–May 15, 1988), Fouad

Ajami (CBS–September 22, 1987), Helmut Sonnenfeldt (NBC–September 14, 1987), Dimitri Simes (CBS–February 6, 1987, and NBC–September 18, 1987), Edward Luttwak (NBC–August 11, 1987), David Denoon (CBS–September 22, 1987), and Robert Hunter (CBS–February 9 and February 14, 1987). Goldman was called a "Russian expert," Ajami was described as a "consultant," Sonnenfeldt and Simes were described as "Soviet expert[s]," Luttwak was called a "military analyst," Denoon was described as an "analyst" of Iranian affairs, and Hunter was described as a "terrorism expert" during one appearance and a "foreign affairs expert" during another. Sonnenfeldt, Simes, Luttwak, and Hunter are associated with Washington, D.C., think tanks, Goldman and Ajami are professors at Harvard and Johns Hopkins universities, and Denoon is a former deputy secretary of defense in the Reagan administration and New York University professor.

The four technology experts were Saunders Kramer (ABC–May 11, 1988), who was described as a "Soviet space expert"; Byron Ristevst (NBC–September 26, 1987), a "consultant" who specializes in nuclear testing; Stan Norris (NBC–May 17, 1988), a "missile expert"; and James Oberg (ABC–November 15, 1988), a "Soviet space expert." None are Council members. Of the four, Oberg is the best known. He works at NASA's Mission Control in Houston and is the author of numerous articles and books about the Soviet space program. His books include *Red Star in Orbit* (1981), *Pioneering Space* (1986), and *Uncovering Soviet Disasters* (1988).

Of the 15 appearances by foreigners who were described by the networks as "experts, analysts, and consultants," eight were by journalists, two were by think tank spokespersons, and two were by government officials. The actual occupations of these individuals were not disclosed to viewers. Another appearance was by University of Essex professor Peter Frank (ABC–May 7, 1988), and another was by Paris-based "terrorism expert" Kenneth Timmermann (CBS–May 20, 1988). Other media (e.g., Minneapolis *Star Tribune*, January 14, 1991, 9A) have described Timmermann as a "defense expert." Lastly, NBC described Lord Bethell (NBC–May 10, 1988) as a "Polish expert."

The journalists who were described as "experts, analysts, and consultants" were Olivier Todd (NBC–May 7, 1988), a conservative French journalist and author of *Cruel April* (1990), a book about Vietnam; former Fleet Street writer Ronald Payne (CBS–February 4, 1987); author Anthony Sampson (CBS–September 23, 1987), who once worked at the London *Observer*; Vahe Petrossian (CBS–September 24, 1987) and David Butter (CBS–August 3, 1987), who write for the *Middle East Economic Digest*; and George Joffe of the *Economist*. Joffe made three appearances during August 1987 and was described in each as a "Mideast expert." Todd was described as an "analyst." His sound bite concerned the French elections. Ronald Payne was described as a "terrorism expert," and Anthony Sampson was dubbed an "arms expert." Sampson is the author of several books, including one titled *The Arms Bazaar* (1977). His best-selling books, however, are travel guides (*Contemporary Authors*, 1981 New

Revision, 3: 483). Butter was described as a "Mideast expert," and Petrossian was described as an "Iran expert" during his 1987 appearance. Petrossian made three more network appearances in 1988, and four appearances in 1989.

The two think tank spokespersons who were described as "experts" were with the IISS (CBS–May 8, 1988) and the French Institute of International Affairs (ABC–August 5, 1987). The French institute spokesperson was Bassma Kadmani Darwish, whom NBC and CBS also used as a Mideast expert during 1986 (see CBS–October 30, 1986, and NBC–November 11, 1986).

The two foreign government officials who were described as "analysts" were Gennadi Gerasimov (ABC–August 7, 1987) and Meron Benvenisti (NBC–November 15, 1988). Gennadi Gerasimov is a familar news maker to television viewers. He is usually, and more accurately, described as a Soviet Foreign Ministry spokesman. Meron Bevenisti is relatively unknown. He was the longtime deputy mayor of Jerusalem. Benvenisti was described as Jerusalem's deputy mayor in only one appearance (ABC–April 10, 1988). In other appearances, Benvenisti was described as a "political analyst" (CBS–June 6, 1988), "Palestinian expert" (NBC–August 7, 1988), "Arab expert" (ABC–June 5, 1987), "West Bank Data Base Project spokesman" (ABC–December 30, 1987), and "sociologist" (CBS–December 21, 1987). He appeared on the news 11 times in 1987-1988. During nine of these appearances, he was used as a news shaper.

To describe Benvenisti as anything other than an Israeli official verges on mendacity. He was the director of economics and development for the Ministry of Tourism between 1960 and 1965. After that, he was the administrator of the Old City and East Jerusalem and, beginning in 1978, was deputy mayor of Jerusalem (Karpman 1978, 77).

The networks' descriptions of Benvenisti provide a graphic example of what is wrong with the media's use of news shapers. News shapers are too frequently given prestigious-sounding but inaccurate titles, such as "Palestinian expert" or "political analyst," that mask the true political identity of the individual. If news viewers were aware that Benvenisti was an Israeli politician, not a university sociologist, it would undoubtedly affect the way that they react to his analysis. Unfortunately, the truth is too frequently held from the public.

NOTES

1. Pye was not just a member of the Council, but one of its directors from 1966 to 1982 (Council on Foreign Relations 1988).

2. The CD-ROM InfoTrac search was conducted on December 10, 1990, and covered the *Washington Post, New York Times, Christian Science Monitor, Los Angeles Times,* and *Wall Street Journal* back to July 1987.

3. The *New Republic* was a left-wing publication until 1974, when it was purchased by Martin Peretz. After the purchase it moved sharply to the right on foreign policy and to the center on domestic issues (see Perrin 1990).

7

KISSINGER AND COMPANY

Among foreign affairs news shapers, none is more important than former secretary of state Henry Kissinger. Kissinger was the pioneer in news shaping, even though he now shuns nine-second news appearances. He much prefers the ten minute or longer appearances accorded him on programs such as "Nightline" and "This Week with David Brinkley." Between January 1985 and April 1988, the former secretary of state made a record 14 appearances on "Nightline" (Hoynes and Croteau 1989). During the "Nightline" appearances, Ted Koppel respectfully referred to him as "Dr. Kissinger," as though he were a renowned brain surgeon rather than the architect of the failed U.S. program of "Vietnamization." No other guest was treated with this deference. David Brinkley, George Will, and Sam Donaldson also pay homage to "Dr. Kissinger" whenever he appears on "This Week with David Brinkley," as during his appearances on May 1, June 4, and August 6, 1989.

Kissinger's influence on news shaping comes from his employment as an on-air analyst for NBC and ABC and from his connections with think tanks, businesses, and government officials. The think tanks include the CSIS, the Aspen Institute, and the Council on Foreign Relations. The businesses include Union Carbide, International Telephone and Telegraph (ITT), American Express, and Coca-Cola, which are clients of the former secretary of state's company, Kissinger Associates, Inc. The government officials include current national security adviser Brent Scowcroft and deputy secretary of state Lawrence Eagleburger, who not only were partners in Kissinger Associates, but have secretly briefed Kissinger about President Bush's foreign policy. During 1989, for example, private citizen Kissinger was secretly informed by Brent Scowcroft of covert U.S. contacts with Chinese Communist leaders following the massacre at Tiananmen Square.

After leaving government in 1977, Kissinger became a businessman, best-selling author, lecturer, academic, think tank scholar, and journalist—all at the same time. He was hired by Chase Manhattan Bank and the Wall Street firm of Goldman Sachs and Company as an adviser. Kissinger also became a leading lecturer on the corporate circuit, getting $10,000 for every speech that he delivered to corporate managers. Georgetown University hired him as a professor, and the Center for Strategic Studies made him a "senior counselor." He also became a fellow at the Aspen Institute and a director of the Council on Foreign Relations. He served in the latter capacity for free. Kissinger signed a lucrative contract with Time, Inc.'s book publishing subsidiary, Little, Brown, and a five-year million-dollar contract with NBC. These contracts netted Kissinger an estimated $400,000 in 1977 (Kalb 1978, 58). The $400,000 was small potatoes compared to what Kissinger netted in following years.

In 1977, former CBS lawyer Marvin Josephson negotiated a book contract with Little, Brown for his client, Henry Kissinger. Little, Brown paid Kissinger $2 million for the hardcover, book club, and paperback rights for his memoirs. The memoirs were eventually published as *The White House Years* (1979). The book stirred considerable controversy upon its appearance, because Kissinger secretly changed sections of the book dealing with Cambodia after British author William Shawcross's book, *Sideshow: Kissinger, Nixon and the Destruction of Cambodia*, appeared. Shawcross's book, which relied heavily on documents obtained under the Freedom of Information Act, argued that the decision by Nixon and Kissinger to enter Cambodia resulted in Prince Norodom Sihanouk's overthrow and the resulting Khmer civil war. Kissinger rewrote parts of his book immediately prior to its publication to refute Shawcross's assertions. The former secretary of state denied having rewritten the portions, instead claiming that he had added at most a paragraph and a few footnotes (*New York Times*, October 31, 1979, 10). A comparison of the original galley proofs and the published book, however, revealed substantial changes. All of the changes were designed to strengthen Kissinger's version of events.

The book was also controversial because Kissinger relied heavily on classified documents to write the book, apparently without government approval. While Shawcross and others had to use the Freedom of Information Act to get information about Kissinger's activities, the former secretary used whatever documents he wished in writing the book. Even though the book's foreword claims that use of "classified materials in this book had been worked out with the office of the national security advisor, Dr. Zbigniew Brzezinski," Brzezinski's office claimed that only a "very small part" of the manuscript was submitted for review. After reviewing that part of the book, Brzezinski sent the manuscript back to Kissinger, advising him that clearance of the book would have to await a review of the total manuscript. Kissinger never submitted the finished manuscript for review (Lewis 1980).

Although Kissinger relied on classified materials for his book, he tried to pro-
hibit others from gaining access to the documents that he used. He appealed to
the courts to maintain control of transcripts of telephone conversations he had
while in the White House and State Department. Kissinger took the transcripts
with him when he left office, claiming that they were personal, not government,
property (*New York Times*, November 1, 1979, 22).

All of these controversies arose as the government was suing former CIA
operative Frank Snepp for publishing *Decent Interval* without first obtaining
government approval. The book was highly critical of U.S. government and CIA
policies prior to the Communist victory in Vietnam. In Snepp's case, there was
no claim that he had revealed classified information. On the contrary, the government conceded that there was nothing in the book that had not been declassified.
The Justice Department filed a civil suit against Snepp because it claimed that
he had violated his employment contract with the CIA, which stated that employees
must clear their writings with the agency before they are published. The courts
eventually ruled that Snepp had violated his contractual obligations with the CIA
and ordered him to turn his book royalties over to the government (*Newsweek*,
May 8, 1978, 37; Snepp 1978). While the government took on Frank Snepp,
it did nothing about Kissinger's breaches.

These controversies, along with Kissinger's frequent appearances on NBC, made
the book an even bigger seller than had been anticipated. When the earnings from
the serial and foreign rights to the book were added to his domestic earnings,
Kissinger reportedly made $6 million for the effort (*New York Times*, January
6, 1980 15III).

KISSINGER AS JOURNALIST

None of Kissinger's contracts, while stirring controversy, were as contentious
as his contract with NBC. In 1977, Josephson helped negotiate a unique contract
with the network, which made Kissinger a "special consultant on foreign affairs."
The contract was approved by NBC president Herbert Schlosser, a personal friend
of Kissinger. The five-year contract apparently cost the network $1 million; some
reports claimed the contract was for $2 million (McDowell 1979). It required
Kissinger to do one special broadcast each year for the network, as well as appear on news programs to provide analysis. The contract gave Kissinger much
needed publicity, enhancing the sales of his book, as well as an audience for his
criticisms of President Carter's policies.

Kissinger's first special aired in early January 1978 and consisted of a conver-
sation with David Brinkley, mixed with old news footage and interviews with
foreign dignitaries. The program was not a typical news interview. Brinkley never
challenged Kissinger, even when the former secretary's statements were clearly
false. Columnist Anthony Lewis (1978) observed that Kissinger frequently
distorted the truth during the program and Brinkley abetted the distortions. The
former secretary of state claimed that Portugal was very close to being taken over

by communists during 1974-1975. "It was a very close thing," Kissinger told Brinkley. The communist threat was averted only because the Portuguese were "determined to fight the communists" and because "a united Western policy" supported "the democratic forces." The reality, which Brinkley never pursued, was that the United States refused to give Portuguese democrats any assistance; the assistance that they did obtain came from Western Europe. Moreover, Kissinger accused Portuguese foreign minister Mario Soares, a socialist, of being a "Kerensky—the Russian whose brief 1917 government led to the Bolshevik revolution" during this "critical period" in Portuguese history (Lewis 1978).

Kissinger also distorted his record on promoting democracy in the world and his efforts to prop up the South African government. After the former secretary of state declared that the promotion of democracy was the best way to defeat communism, Brinkley should have, but didn't, ask Kissinger why he supported the overthrow of the democratic government of Chile, if this were the case. Fortunately, most viewers were not misled by Kissinger and Brinkley, because they were watching other programs that night. Kissinger's special was the lowest rated program that week—65th in a field of 65 (Kalb 1978).

David Brinkley's disgraceful deference to Kissinger raised questions in the minds of some journalists about NBC's dedication to truth in news. One question, as Lewis (1978) posed it, was whether a television network that has $1 million invested in a political figure "will let its reporters ask him real questions. Or will the network be inclined to give him a kind of immunity to protect its investment?"

The answer to this question came the following year, when NBC hired David Frost to interview Kissinger for another program. Frost was unaware when he was hired that NBC had a separate agreement with the ex–secretary of state. That agreement allowed Kissinger to supplement the original interview with additional material, "adding to, subtracting from, or supplementing answers that he gave." According to Frost, the agreement "trangressed fundamental journalistic ethics, and it was quite improper." Unlike most other public figures, "Dr. Kissinger is to be allowed a second opportunity to answer questions first put to him three days earlier, a clear breach of our understanding to each other and the press," Frost wrote in a letter to NBC. Because of this breach of ethics, Frost resigned from the project (*New York Times*, October 7, 1979, 1).

NBC News president William Small denied that the network had compromised any of its principles. Just as Kissinger and his publisher denied making any substantial changes in *The White House Years* before publication, Small denied that Kissinger was allowed to substantially alter his answers to Frost's questions. Only ten additional minutes with Kissinger were recorded after the original interview, NBC executives noted. What they failed to note was that ten minutes amounted to one-fifth of the program's total length.

At the time that Frost withdrew from the interview project, he also disclosed that an NBC executive scolded him for asking questions that were "too tough, almost as rude." One NBC executive reportedly told Frost that "you don't interrupt a former secretary of state, even if he interrupts you" (*New York Times*,

October 7, 1979, 33). Overall, these events suggested that NBC was more interested in protecting its investment in Kissinger than the truth, as Lewis (1978) had suspected.

Kissinger's contract called for his appearing on the network news as a "foreign affairs analyst" in addition to appearing on specials. Kissinger frequently appeared as an analyst on NBC, criticizing Carter's foreign policy, offering the "correct" solution to foreign policy problems, endorsing political candidates, and eulogizing deceased dignitaries, including Nelson Rockefeller and Golda Meir.[1] Needless to say, Kissinger's analyses were usually highly partisan.

NBC (October 26, 1978) provided Kissinger with time on the network evening news just prior to the November election to campaign for Republican senator Edward Brooke of Massachusetts. Brooke was not only up for reelection, but was being investigated by the Senate Ethics Committee for his financial dealings. Kissinger praised Brooke as a man of "integrity."

Kissinger also used his on-air appearances to tell viewers what the Carter administration should be, but wasn't, doing to halt the spread of communism in Italy (NBC–January 13, 1978), why the United States needed to keep the Shah of Iran in power (NBC–November 6, 1978), and why the United States needed to provide additional weaponry to Israel (NBC–May 8, 1978). Although he publicly endorsed the SALT II treaty that Carter had negotiated, Kissinger also cautioned that the United States also needed to increase its defense spending, something that Carter wasn't doing (NBC–August 2, 1979). A few of Kissinger's appearances were somewhat less partisan, as when he praised Golda Meir's accomplishments upon her death (NBC–December 8, 1978), and denounced the Palestine Liberation Organization (PLO) threat to attack Israeli citizens (NBC–March 15, 1978).

Because Kissinger's contract with NBC was not an exclusive contract, he was also able to appear as a news shaper on ABC and CBS. And appear he did. During 1979-1980, the last two years of Carter's presidency, Kissinger made twenty appearances on these networks. During the appearances, Kissinger usually criticized the Carter administration's policies. After UN ambassador Andrew Young's contacts with the PLO became public, Kissinger appeared on ABC (August 24, 1979) stating that the United States should have no discussions with the PLO. After Cyrus Vance, Carter's secretary of state, claimed that Soviet troops in Cuba had apparently been stationed there since the 1960s, Kissinger appeared on CBS (September 5, 1979) to deny the claim. In another appearance (ABC–April 10, 1980), Kissinger stated that the administration needed to make its intentions concerning Iran and Afghanistan clear to allies and adversaries, something the Carter administration was failing to do.

By the end of the Carter years, Kissinger was dominating the shaping of network news about foreign affairs. A small cadre of people associated with him in government and at the CSIS also started popping up on the networks as news shapers in 1980. More of his cronies appeared in 1981, and even more appeared in 1982. By the late 1980s, they had become fixtures on the network news, shaping foreign policy news almost every week.

Kissinger's cronies include William Hyland, Edward Luttwak, Helmut Sonnenfeldt, Dimitri Simes, and Robert Kupperman. Hyland, who helped Kissinger write *The White House Years* and served under him at the State Department, made his network debut on ABC on April 24, 1980. CSIS "defense analyst" Luttwak made his inaugural appearance on CBS on February 7, 1980. Luttwak worked as a consultant to Kissinger's State Department during the 1970s. Helmut Sonnenfeldt, another Kissinger underling in the Nixon administration, made his debut as a news shaper on ABC on November 14, 1980. CSIS fellows Dimitri Simes and Robert Kupperman made their network premieres in 1981. The appearances by these and other associates of Kissinger increased throughout the 1980s. During 1987 and 1988, for example, Kissinger's associates appeared more than 100 times as network news shapers. This averages out to one network news appearance every week during the two year period.

All of Kissinger's associates are members of the Council on Foreign Relations and are active in Council affairs. However, Kissinger's friends and protégés represent an extremely narrow range of perspectives, even by Council standards. Until just recently, they advocated distrust of the Soviet Union, believed that groups and governments that receive Soviet support are Soviet pawns, and contended that the U.S.S.R. is one of the principal sponsors of international terrorism. Simes, Kupperman, and the others viewed the Sandinista government of Nicaragua as a communist threat, the Contras as freedom fighters, not terrorists, and the African National Congress (ANC) as a communist-backed terrorist group. They invariably endorsed the views expressed by one another when they appeared as news shapers.

ABC AND AFTER

When Kissinger's contract with NBC expired, he moved to ABC, where he was hired as a "contributing analyst" for the news. Kissinger's agreement with ABC gave the network "first call on his services for breaking news" (*Wall Street Journal*, September 15, 1989, 1). The contract allowed Kissinger to appear on other networks as a news shaper when ABC wasn't using him. Another service Kissinger provided for ABC was advice about which "experts" should be interviewed. While admitting that Kissinger had a role in selecting news shapers, the network has denied that Kissinger had any voice in editorial decisions (Cooper and Soley 1990).

By 1983, when Kissinger joined ABC, he had already started his consulting firm, Kissinger Associates, Inc. Kissinger Associates charges corporate clients $200,000 or more for "geopolitical insight, advice and entree" (*New York Times*, April 30, 1989, 1). The clients are usually multinational firms such as ITT, Union Carbide, and Daewoo Corporation, which are looking for advice on contracts or for contacts with government officials. The specific arrangements that Kissinger Associates makes with each company and the services it provides are not known because clients are required to "declare in writing that they won't make public consulting arrangements" (*Washington Post*, March 9, 1989, A3).

Kissinger stated that he did not use his government connections to establish the consulting firm or secure clients (*Washington Post*, January 18, 1989, E13), but many of his clients had contact with him during the Nixon–Ford years. ITT, for example, was actively involved in covert activities to depose Chilean president Salvador Allende. In 1970, John McCone, a director of ITT and former head, offered the CIA $1 million to help prevent Socialist party candidate Allende from being elected. The CIA, which was heavily involved in the previous Chilean presidential election, turned down ITT's offer because it felt that the ITT plan would not succeed. In addition, the agency concluded that Allende's electoral victory was not assured and that, even if he were elected, it would not affect the global balance of power (Barnet and Muller 1974).

Kissinger opposed the CIA's position and sided with ITT. In a secret government meeting concerning the Chilean elections, Kissinger stated: "I don't see why we need to stand by and watch a country go Communist due to the irresponsibility of its own people" (Prados 1986, 317). Even though the Nixon administration did not block Allende's becoming president, it nevertheless had a hand in destabilizing his government—a strategy that ITT supported. Despite the continuity between his government activities and consulting contracts, Kissinger nevertheless insists that he is a new Horatio Alger, who never used his government contacts to make money.

Not only are Kissinger's clients multinational firms with which he had contact while in government, but his employees and partners are also former government officials. A month after Lawrence Eagleburger resigned from his post as President Reagan's undersecretary of state for political affairs, he joined Kissinger Associates. He became a principal in the firm, as well as president. By 1988, Eagleburger was making $660,000 yearly in salary and bonuses and an additional quarter million dollars in severance pay, which he received after quitting the firm to become President Bush's deputy secretary of state (*Washington Post*, March 9, 1989, A3). Another principal and high-paid employee of Kissinger Associates was Brent Scowcroft, who worked with Kissinger in the Nixon administration and later became President Reagan's national security adviser. When Scowcroft resigned from his government post, he also joined Kissinger's company. Like Eagleburger, he returned to government in 1989, after having made a small fortune as a partner in Kissinger Associates. Scowcroft became President Bush's national security adviser that year.

During the years that Scowcroft was with Kissinger Associates, he frequently appeared as a network television news shaper. During 1987-1988, Scowcroft made nine network news appearances. Eagleburger made only three news shaper appearances during 1987-1988, but he was a regular on "Nightline." Hoynes and Croteau (1989) reported that Eagleburger appeared 10 times on Ted Koppel's late-night news program. During these appearances, it was never disclosed that Scowcroft and Eagleburger were partners in Kissinger Associates and were advising corporate clients about some of the topics that they shaped.

The potential conflicts of interest arising from work with Kissinger Associates were so extensive that Eagleburger told the Senate Foreign Relations Committee that he would excuse himself from dealing with specific companies and industries operating in more than a dozen countries if he were confirmed as President Bush's undersecretary of state. The network newscasts also failed to disclose Scowcroft's and Eagleburger's ties to the Reagan administration, even though they commented on Reagan administration policies. Scowcroft was always described as a retired general (ABC–January 14, 1987) or "ex–national security adviser" (ABC–July 4, 1988), even when he commented on policies that he helped develop. For example, Scowcroft (ABC–November 16, 1987) criticized Democratic House Speaker Jim Wright's Central America initiative, claiming that foreign policy was the prerogative of the executive branch. Scowcroft helped develop President Reagan's Central America policy, which was at odds with the one that Wright was pursuing.

While there is no evidence that Scowcroft and Eagleburger shaped news in a way that was economically advantageous to their business clients, there is evidence that they blurred the line between their private dealings and government service after joining the Bush administration. There is also evidence that Henry Kissinger's business interests conflicted with the news shaping that he did while serving as ABC's "contributing analyst." The evidence concerning Scowcroft and Eagleburger is that they briefed Kissinger about their secret contacts with the Chinese government following the Tiananmen massacre. Scowcroft telephoned Kissinger in Europe to tell him about a scheduled trip to China. Kissinger characterized the call as "a courtesy" rather than a breach of public trust. The former secretary of state said that the call was made so that he would not be taken by surprise if a reporter were to ask him about it sometime in the future (*Washington Post*, December 14, 1989, A52).

At the time of the phone call, Kissinger was a partner in China Ventures, a Delaware-registered limited partnership for investing in China. The company sought to raise $75 million from U.S. investors for joint ventures with China International Trust and Investment Corporation, (CITIC), an arm of the Chinese government. China Ventures was a secret until September 1989, when its existence was revealed by *Wall Street Journal* reporter John Fialka (1989). The revelation came three months after the Tiananmen crackdown. When asked about the secrecy surrounding the partnership by *Washington Post* reporter Walter Pincus, Kissinger said that he planned to unveil the firm during June 1989 but canceled the plan because of the Tiananmen incidents (Pincus 1989).

Rather than revealing his financial interests in good relations with Communist China, Kissinger opted to appear as a "detached" foreign policy analyst on an ABC News special and "This Week with David Brinkley." He actually discussed the Tiananmen incidents on Brinkley's program twice—once shortly before the massacre (May 21, 1989) and once after (June 4, 1989). During the news special and the second Brinkley appearance, Kissinger spoke against imposing economic and diplomatic sanctions on the Communist regime. On the ABC News special "Worlds in Turmoil" (June 4, 1989), Peter Jennings reverentially asked Kissinger, "So what should America do, Dr. Kissinger?" "I wouldn't do any sanctions," the partner in China Ventures replied. Kissinger continued with a lecture on the importance of a close relationship between the United States and the Deng Xiaoping regime. Why a close relationship was necessary he never fully explained. By the time of Tiananmen, glasnost had already come to the Soviet Union and Solidarity had won the elections in Poland. If the Soviet Union remained a threat to the United States, it was a very weak one.

Kissinger provided a more in-depth exposition of his views in a syndicated *Washington Post* column titled "The Caricature of Deng as a Tyrant Is Unfair" (August 1, 1989, A21). Kissinger wrote: "China remains too important for America's national security to risk the relationship on the emotions of the moment." In the column, Kissinger asserted that the Soviet Union needed to be countered in Asia and only a strong China could do this. While revealing his complete misunderstanding of what was transpiring in the Soviet Union and Eastern Europe, Kissinger did not reveal his business ties with the Chinese government. The column also justified the crackdown, claiming: "No government in the world would have tolerated having the main square of its capital occupied for eight weeks by tens of thousands of demonstrators." In this instance, Kissinger was speaking out of empathy with the Communist regime. During the Vietnam era, Kissinger and other Nixon officials used everything except tanks to stop antiwar protests.

For example, the Nixon administration mobilized 5,000 metropolitan police, 1,500 national guardsmen, 500 national park police, and several thousand troops to squelch Vietnam War demonstrations scheduled for May 3-5, 1971. Armed with tear gas and clubs rather than tanks, these forces arrested almost every demonstrator in sight. Over the three-day period, over 12,000 antiwar demonstrators and bystanders were arrested. Those arrested were confined in a practice field used by the Washington Redskins and the Washington Coliseum, a hockey arena. Conditions in these places were similar to those in Chinese prisons: there was no running water or toilets and no shade in the field, forcing the confined demonstrators to "broil in the sun" (Zaroulis and Sullivan 1985, 362). Because of the improprieties in the arrests and incarcerations, a federal judge ordered the demonstrators released, over the objections of Nixon officials.

ABC News executives contend that they did not know about Kissinger's business interests in China at the time when he appeared as a news shaper. "If I knew then what I know now, I would not have wanted him on the broadcast, plain and simple," Peter Jennings told John Fialka (1989) about Kissinger's appearance. "And I think my management would have understood that perfectly," he contended.

Jennings' cloaked criticism of Kissinger occurred after the former secretary of state resigned from ABC. Jennings' comments appeared on September 15; Kissinger was elected to the CBS board of directors on September 13. Kissinger's election immediately ended his relationship with ABC. Kissinger became one of 14 CBS board members, but the only one who previously worked for NBC and ABC. That was about the only dissimilarity that Kissinger had to other board members. At the time that Kissinger joined CBS, 10 of the 13 directors were members of the Council on Foreign Relations. The three who were not were retired news anchor Walter Cronkite, former Revlon chairman Michael Bergerac, and Preston Tisch, the brother of CBS president Laurence Tisch. Laurence Tisch, William Paley, Harold Brown, Roswell Gilpatric, James Houghton, Newton Minnow, Henry Schacht, Edson Spenser, Marietta Tree, and James Wolfesohn were Council members. All were also directors of other corporations, as was Kissinger. Former secretary of defense Harold Brown was on the boards of Cummins Engine, IBM, and Philip Morris; James Houghton was chairman of Corning Glass and a board member of Metropolitan Life and J. P. Morgan & Company; and Newton Minnow, the former Federal Communications Commission chairman, was on the boards of Sarah Lee, Aetna, and Foote Cone & Belding.

The CBS directors also sat on the boards of many of the think tanks and research centers that fielded "experts" for the CBS news. Schacht and Wolfesohn sat on the board of the Brookings Institution; Spenser and Minnow were on the board of the Carnegie Endowment; Brown and Kissinger were directors, not just members, of the Council on Foreign Relations; Minnow and Brown were on the board of the Rand Corporation; Wolfesohn was on the board of the Institute for Advanced Study at Princeton University; Paley was on the board of the Harriman Institute for Soviet Studies at Columbia University; and Kissinger was a senior counselor at the CSIS, the conservative think tank that produces a large number of the foreign affairs experts interviewed by reporters. Unlike other CBS board members who were minor players at the think tanks where they were directors, Kissinger was a major player at the CSIS.

THE CENTER FOR STRATEGIC AND INTERNATIONAL STUDIES

Although Henry Kissinger is now a leading guru of the CSIS, he was not a founder of the think tank. Its founders were Adm. Arleigh Burke, Rev. James Horigan, and David Abshire. Burke was a hardline conservative who served as chief of naval operations from 1955 to 1961. He was the first head of the CSIS. Horigan was a member of the Georgetown faculty and gave the think tank its direct link with the Jesuit university. Abshire was the CSIS's first executive director and later became President Nixon's assistant secretary of state for congressional relations (Dickson 1971). Abshire returned to the CSIS after this stint in government. It was he who recruited Henry Kissinger to the center after President Ford's defeat. A few years after he recruited Kissinger, Abshire returned to government. President Reagan appointed him ambassador to NATO. Abshire again returned to the CSIS after this tour of government (Herman and O'Sullivan 1989). He is currently president of the think tank.

Burke, Horigan, and Abshire founded the CSIS in 1962, the year that Henry Kissinger was promoted to professor at Harvard University. The think tank was created with the ideological and financial assistance of the AEI, which at the time focused exclusively on economic issues (Linden 1987). The CSIS was created to give conservatives a think tank specializing in foreign policy, in addition to one specializing in economics. The CSIS grew rapidly and, four years after its founding, severed ties with the AEI.

The CSIS began life with a $120,000 budget, which has grown over the years to more than $9 million. Unlike other think tanks, the CSIS does not publicize its donors. The *Foundations Grants Index* (1990) shows that its supporters include corporate and right-wing foundations and the mass media. These are also the AEI's primary donors. The CSIS's corporate donors include ARCO, R. J. Reynolds–Nabisco, Prudential, Chase Manhattan, Texaco, and Rockwell International. Each of these corporate foundations donated $10,000 or more to the think tank in 1988. The CSIS received its largest donations from the ultraconservative John M. Olin Foundation, which gave $259,000; the Lynde and Harry Bradley Foundation, which gave $250,000; and the Sarah Scaife Foundation, which gave $225,000. Other donors include media such as the *New York Times* and NBC News (Easterbrook 1986).

When the CSIS's budget grew to over six figures, it moved from the modest Georgetown townhouse where it began to lavish accommodations in downtown Washington, D.C. The new accommodations are equipped with suites for its big-name "scholars"—Henry Kissinger, James Schlesinger, William Brock, and Zbigniew Brzezinski. These big names are important to the CSIS's fundraising. They appear at think tank functions where corporate executives pay big bucks to shake hands and listen to these former officials.

The think tank does not deny its conservative label, but it does deny that it is partisan in outlook. This is because former Democratic appointees like Zbigniew Brzezinski, Robert Hunter, Joyce Starr, Jay Winik, and Barry Blechman are among its fellows. However, the Democrats at the CSIS tend to be hawks rather than doves, and the few doves that are at the CSIS never appear in the mass media as news shapers.

Almost everyone except the news media admit that the views of Democratic officials such as Brzezinski and Republican officials such as Kissinger are similar. In *Mortal Rivals*, William Hyland wrote that the differences between Kissinger and Brzezinski were primarily personal, not political. The two former national security advisers agreed more than they disagreed about foreign policy, particularly when it concerned the Soviet Union. They were both "conservative anticommunists," according to Hyland (1987, 184). Hyland served under Kissinger in the State Department, and worked with Brzezinksi in 1977 as part of a foreign policy transition team. Some reporters have recently, but begrudgingly, admitted that the CSIS's Democrats represent conservative, rather than "liberal," viewpoints. On December 4, 1990, the "MacNeil/Lehrer NewsHour" used Robert Hunter to represent the hawkish point of view on the hostages in Iraq and former attorney general Ramsey Clark to represent the dovish view. "MacNeil/Lehrer" had previously used Hunter, a one-time foreign policy adviser to Sen. Edward Kennedy and a Carter administration official, to represent the liberal viewpoint in foreign policy debates.

Even though Democrats are CSIS fellows, Republicans dominate the think tank. Former Republican appointees who are at the CSIS include Henry Kissinger, William Brock, James Schlesinger, Diana Lady Dougan, Fred Ickle, Amos Jordan, Robert Kupperman, Michael Moody, Leo Reddie, Paul Craig Roberts, Stephen Sestanovich, and Murray Weidenbaum. Jeane Kirkpatrick is a member of the CSIS's international research council. Military men such as James Blackwell, William J. Taylor, Harlan Ullman, and David van Esselstyn are also CSIS fellows.

Kissinger might not have founded the CSIS or placed it on a conservative track, but his presence at the think tank has had a profound impact on its evolution. A large number of Nixon officials followed Kissinger into the CSIS. Former Nixon officials who joined the CSIS were William Hyland and Amos Jordan, who joined shortly after Kissinger in 1977; Edward Luttwak, a consultant to the NSC and State Department, who joined in 1978; and Robert Kupperman, James Schlesinger, and George Carver, Jr., who joined in 1979. Former CIA deputy director Ray S. Cline, who was director of intelligence and research in Nixon's State Department from 1969 to 1973, was already a CSIS fellow when Kissinger came aboard. Cline joined the CSIS immediately after leaving the State Department. Dimitri Simes, a conservative Soviet émigré, was also at the CSIS when the ex-secretary of state arrived. In 1980, Simes left the CSIS for Johns Hopkins University; in 1983, he joined the Carnegie Endowment. He was a paid political analyst for CBS News during 1985-1987 and in 1987 was hired by NBC. Helmut Sonnenfeldt, another Nixon State Department official, also stayed in Washington, but went to the Brookings Institution rather than the CSIS. While at Brookings, Sonnenfeldt collaborated with his CSIS colleagues. With William Hyland he wrote a 24-page essay titled *Soviet Perspectives of Security* (1979) that was published by the IISS.

The think tank "scholars" who congregate around Kissinger are extraordinarily similar in their perceptions and analyses. What one think tank denizen says to a reporter another repeats to the press a few days or weeks later. By this method, their analyses become conventional wisdom, regardless of the accuracy of the statements. For example, William Hyland (ABC–March 31, 1982) predicted that there would be political chaos in the Soviet Union if Leonid Brezhnev died. His conclusions were repeated by Helmut Sonnenfeldt (NBC–November 7, 1982), who predicted a "drawn out" succession struggle following Brezhnev's death. When Brezhnev died on November 10, there was neither political chaos nor a drawn out succession. Yuri Andropov was quickly selected as general secretary, and his appointment was made public on November 12.

Sonnenfeldt (NBC–October 3, 1985) contended that Soviet proposals on arms control were for propaganda purposes, rather than genuine negotiations. Simes (CBS–January 15, 1986) also contended that Mikhail Gorbachev was conducting propaganda rather than seriously negotiating about arms control. As it turned out, the United States, not the U.S.S.R., was stalling on an arms control treaty. A year later, Dimitri Simes (CBS–April 14, 1987) explained to viewers that a

Soviet–U.S. agreement is important for political reasons rather than its ability to limit arms. Two months later, Hyland (CBS–July 28, 1987) said that arms control was politically important for the United States and the Soviet Union.

Not only do these individuals have similar viewpoints, but they share common histories as news shapers. Hyland, Sonnenfeldt, and Luttwak appeared as news shapers for the first time in 1980. Kupperman, Simes, and Schlesinger first appeared in 1981. These appearances parallel the networks' increased reliance on news shapers during the 1980s.

Table 9 presents the network news appearances of Hyland, Sonnenfeldt, Simes, and Kupperman from 1980 through 1986. As the table shows, appearances by the news shapers increased slowly between 1980 and 1983, increasing from just two appearances in 1980 to eight appearances in 1983. This was followed by a rapid increase in appearances during 1984. The frequency of their appearances increased slightly in 1985 and again in 1986. By 1986, these news shapers were appearing on the network news more than once every two weeks.

During 1987-1988, the four appeared 46 times. When the appearances by Kissinger, Hyland, Sonnenfeldt, Simes, Kupperman, and their associates are combined, they made over 100 appearances during 1987-1988, or approximately one network appearance each week over the two-year period. The other Kissinger associates who accounted for these appearances were Ray S. Cline (8 appearances), George Carver (9 appearances), Brent Scowcroft (9 appearances), James Schlesinger (16 appearances), Edward Luttwak (4 appearances), Lawrence Eagleburger (3 appearances), and Amos Jordan (2 appearances). (Jordan was described as a "Mideast expert" in his first 1987 appearance [NBC–July 24, 1987] and as a "Korea specialist" in the second [NBC–December 16, 1987].) The 109

Table 9
Network Appearances by Four Foreign Policy News Shapers, 1980–1986

	William Hyland	Helmut Sonnenfeldt	Dimitri Simes	Robert Kupperman	Totals
1980	1	1	0	0	2
1981	0	1	2	4	7
1982	3	3	0	1	7
1983	3	2	2	1	8
1984	7	4	9	2	22
1985	11	4	5	7	27
1986	6	9	14	8	37

appearances by Kissinger and his cronies excludes appearances by Democrats such as Zbigniew Brzezinski and Reagan appointees such as Stephen Sestanovich, who are also at the CSIS but have less direct connections to Kissinger than the others.

The appearances by these news shapers increased over time, despite the inaccuracy of their predictions. For example, Hyland (ABC–March 31, 1982) predicted political chaos in the Soviet Union following Brezhnev's death, which was highly inaccurate. Hyland (ABC–November 15, 1982) then claimed that the U.S. conflict with Iran presented a "major opportunity" for the Soviet Union to advance its interests in the Middle East, which also didn't occur. As a result of these insights, Hyland became a guest analyst on "This Week with David Brinkley" (November 14, 1982). The next month, he appeared on the ABC news (December 16, 1982), predicting that the cruise missile would be a "nightmare" for the Soviet Union. Hyland disappeared, then reappeared four months later (ABC–April 8, 1983), warning about the seriousness of the Soviet arms buildup. As it turned out, the Soviets were looking for a way to cut defense spending to concentrate on rebuilding the civilian economy.

Hyland's appearances also illustrate the way that networks use, and change, the titles that they apply to news shapers. During Hyland's first appearance (ABC–April 24, 1980), he was described as a State Department official under Kissinger. He was never again described as a former official. During his next appearance (ABC–March 31, 1982), he was described as a "Soviet intelligence analyst." On December 16, 1982, ABC described him as a "defense analyst." During 1984, he was usually described as the editor of *Foreign Affairs*, following his appointment as editor of that journal, but he was also described as a Council on Foreign Relations representative (CBS–May 23, 1984). On other occasions, he was described as a foreign policy "analyst" (ABC–March 17, 1986) and "expert" (NBC–October 11, 1986).

The same evolution was true with Helmut Sonnenfeldt. Early on (ABC–January 3, 1982), he was described as a former State Department aide, but the administration for which he worked was never disclosed. Later Sonnenfeldt was described as a "Soviet expert" (NBC–November 7, 1982), "strategist" (NBC–January 10, 1982), "Soviet analyst" (NBC–January 18, 1984), and Brookings Institution spokesman (CBS–May 23, 1984). Simes was initially described as a Johns Hopkins University professor (CBS–December 26, 1981), a Carnegie representative (NBC–August 4, 1984), and "Soviet analyst." After being hired as an analyst by CBS, he was promoted to "Soviet expert."

KUPPERMAN AND TERRORISM

William Hyland, Helmut Sonnenfeldt, and Dimitri Simes usually shape news about the Soviet Union and Eastern Europe, while Robert Kupperman usually shapes news about terrorism. Kupperman is one of a handful of terrorism "experts" called upon by the media for analysis. Just as Sonnenfeldt, Hyland, and

Simes have remarkably similar views about the Soviet Union, these analysts have remarkably similar views about terrorism. They sit on the editorial boards of each other's journals, "review and write forewords for their colleagues' books, and cite one another copiously" (Herman and O'Sullivan 1989). Edward Herman and Gerry O'Sullivan claim that these individuals have developed a "terrorism industry," which provides consultation to government and businesses, sells security services, and publishes books and periodicals. The news media are important components of the industry, because they publicize the experts and their abilities.

Like the Soviet analysts, the views of this small group of "terrorism experts" are expressed so often in the mass media that their views become conventional wisdom. And like the Soviet "experts," the terrorism "experts" are usually associates of conservative think tanks, ex–government and military officials, or professors at private, eastern universities.

The terrorism experts are typified by Kupperman, who made his debut as a news shaper in a series on terrorism that aired on the ABC nightly news during March 1981. Like other terrorism experts, Kupperman is with a think tank. He is a fellow at the CSIS. Like other terrorism experts, Kupperman operates a consulting firm, Robert Kupperman Associates. Kupperman started the firm almost immediately after leaving the U.S. Arms Control and Disarmament Agency. He is also the author and editor of several terrorism books, including *Terrorism: Threat, Reality, Response* (1979), which was published by the Hoover Institution, and *Low-Intensity Conflict* (1983), which was published by Kupperman's firm for the U.S. Army.

Kupperman also typifies the television terrorism expert by subscribing to the theory that terrorism is part of a worldwide conspiracy, rather than the work of small, fanatical cadres. In Kupperman's case, he sees terrorism as the handiwork of the Soviet Union. He shares this view with Richard Pipes, Yonah Alexander, and Ray Cline, who also shape news about terrorism. Other analysts, such as former CIA officer Harry Rositzke, consider this view of terrorism to be "horseshit" (Stein 1980). Kupperman nonetheless told ABC viewers on March 12, 1981, that the U.S.S.R. was the backer of the terrorist Red Brigade. He presented the view as though it were documented fact rather than conjecture. Kupperman also asserted that the Soviet Union was behind the attempted assassination of Pope John Paul II (CBS–May 27, 1985). At a conference of the American Academy of Political and Social Science, he asserted that "there is incontrovertible evidence of Soviet involvement" in terrorism, which was used as a "low-cost, low-risk means of engaging the West in low-intensity conflict" (Kupperman, Opstal and Williamson 1982, 32-33). However, Kupperman conceded that terrorism was a complex issue that would certainly continue "even if the Soviet Union withdrew all patronage" (1982, 33).

In most other network television appearances, Kupperman presented his opinions as though they were fact. Kupperman, who has a Ph.D. in applied mathematics, not physics or climatology, dismissed the theory of nuclear winter as "purely propaganda" (ABC–October 31, 1983) after the National Academy of Sciences issued a report stating that the theory had scientific validity. He also asserted that the news media were largely responsible for a rash of plane hijackings (ABC–June 14, 1985). On CBS the same day, Kupperman called for the United States to retaliate against Iran for the hijacking of TWA flight 847 by Lebanese Shiites. On the CBS news on January 19, 1987, he predicted that terrorist attacks on U.S. citizens would increase. Kupperman repeated his prediction six months later (CBS–June 17, 1987). In August, the State Department reported that, after subtracting the bombings in Pakistan by agents of the Afghan intelligence service, the number of international terrorist attacks actually decreased between 1986 and 1987 (*New York Times*, August 23, 1988, 13).

Richard Pipes is a Harvard University professor who served as an NSC adviser to President Reagan during 1981-1982. Pipes has also been associated with the rightist Foreign Policy Research Institute and U.S. Global Strategy Council (USGSC) which is headed by Ray Cline. Although the Polish-born Pipes has asserted in books and newspapers that the U.S.S.R. is behind international terrorism, he has never had the opportunity to express this view on network television. His views about terrorism are so outlandish that, while the networks have turned to him for analysis about President Reagan's policies (ABC–September 28, 1984) and Soviet policy (ABC–January 5, 1985 and NBC–September 30, 1986), they have never sought his comments on terrorism. Pipes was one of the promoters of the theory that Korean Airlines flight 007 was diverted from its original flight path by a secret electronic ray emitted by the Soviet Union, which then shot down the airliner (Johnson 1986).

Another terrorism expert who believes that the U.S.S.R. is a principal sponsor of terrorism is Yonah Alexander. Like Kupperman, Alexander made his debut as a network news shaper on ABC's special series on terrorism during March 1981. Alexander is head of the Institute for Studies in International Terrorism, a think tank based at the State University of New York (Oneonta). The think tank publishes a journal, *Terrorism*, which Alexander edits. He has also been a visiting fellow at the CSIS and is a member of the IISS. Alexander has worked closely with Ray Cline on books and consulting projects for businesses. He and Cline coauthored *State-sponsored Terrorism* (1985), which was published by the CSIS, and *Terrorism: The Soviet Connection*, which was published by Crane Russak & Company and distributed by the U.S. government. Alexander has coauthored or edited over a dozen other books on terrorism, making him this nation's most prolific author on the topic. Alexander and Cline also conduct "risk analysis" for a number of corporations, including General Dynamics and Hewlett-Packard (Herman and O'Sullivan 1989).

Although Herman and O'Sullivan report that he is one of the terrorism experts most frequently quoted by the news media, Alexander hasn't made a network news appearance since June 26, 1985, when he appeared on ABC. The few appearances cannot be due to his extreme viewpoints. Others, like Kupperman and Cline, have similar views, but are still used as news shapers. A more likely explanation is that Alexander lacks the legitimacy of Cline and Kupperman because he teaches at a public rather than private university, has never been in government, and is not a member of the Council on Foreign Relations.

Ray Cline, by contrast, is Harvard-educated, a former official, a think tank dweller, and a member of the Council on Foreign Relations. He appears frequently on network news shows as a terrorism and intelligence expert. Cline was a deputy director of the CIA and director of the State Department's Bureau of Intelligence and Research. After leaving the State Department in 1973, he went to the CSIS. In 1989, Cline left the CSIS to head the USGSC.

Shortly after joining the CSIS, Cline appeared as a network news shaper for the first time. During his first appearances (CBS–October 17 and 18, 1974), Cline shaped news concerning the CIA. In both appearances, he defended CIA covert actions. In later appearances, Cline contended that U.S. legislators and the press were misinterpreting the agency's role in domestic spying (NBC–December 22, 1974), defended the CIA's payments to Jordanian King Hussein as money well spent (NBC–February 18, 1977), and voiced support for the agency's covert operations against Fidel Castro (CBS–June 9, 1977). Although Cline is the most vigorous defender of the CIA to appear on network television, he is just one of many former CIA operatives and officials who have shaped network television news. Others include George Carver, William Colby, William Hyland, Robert Komer, Stansfield Turner, James Schlesinger, Raymond Garthoff, and Graham Fuller, who currently works for the Rand Corporation.

In 1983, Cline shifted from being an intelligence "expert" to being a terrorism "expert." Cline made his debut as a terrorism expert on ABC on September 14, 1983, when he commented on the Soviet shootdown of Korean Airlines flight 007. He subsequently discussed U.S. ability to retaliate in reponse to a Kuwaiti jet hijacking (CBS–December 6, 1984), possible repercussions of extraditing Marwan Hamadei (CBS–January 16, 1987), the kidnapping of Lt. Col. William Higgins in Lebanon (CBS–February 22, 1988), and the role of education in the fight against terrorism (CBS–January 10, 1989). Even after becoming a terrorism expert, Cline continued to shape news about the CIA. On NBC (February 2, 1987), he disagreed with William Casey's decision to resign as CIA director because of ill health. Casey died four months later. Cline also accused Bob Woodward of lying about having interviewed Casey for the book *Veil* (ABC–September 28, 1987). Cline's accusations, while sensational, were based on speculation, not knowledge.

Another frequently appearing terrorism expert is Brian Jenkins, who also worked at the Rand Corporation before starting his own consulting firm. The Rand Corporation is a California-based think tank that was established by the air force in 1948 to conduct a "program of study and research on the broad subject of intercontinental warfare, other than surface, with the object of recommending to the Army Air Force preferred techniques and instrumentalities for this purpose" (Dickson 1971, 53). Based on this mandate, Rand conducts research on counterinsurgency and terrorism. Brian Jenkins is one of Rand's resident experts on these topics. Before joining Rand, Jenkins served in the Dominican Republic and Vietnam with the Green Berets (Jenkins 1982).

Jenkins' credentials are like most other terrorism experts—in addition to working for a think tank, he is the editor of the *TVI Journal*, which examines terrorism, violence, and insurgency. Jenkins differs from experts like Kupperman, Alexander, and Cline in that he does not accept the theory that the U.S.S.R. is behind international terrorism. He sees terrorism as an outgrowth of domestic or regional conflicts, rather than something that is controlled from Moscow (Jenkins 1982). Jenkins appeared first as a news shaper in 1981, as did Kupperman and Alexander. In his first appearance (CBS–May 26, 1981), Jenkins was described as a Rand spokesman. This title eventually gave way to the generic title of "terrorism expert" in 1985 (CBS–October 8, 1985, and NBC–November 26, 1985).

Other terrorism experts called upon by the networks are also associated with think tanks. Joseph Churba (NBC–November 26, 1985) is with the International Security Council, a think tank that was established with the assistance of Rev. Sun Myung Moon (Herman and O'Sullivan 1989, 94). Churba worked for air force intelligence before becoming a "terrorism expert." He has close ties to many other rightists, including retired general John Singlaub; the now-dead head of the Jewish Defense League, Meier Kahane; and John Rees of the John Birch Society.

Two other terrorism experts used by the news media are Ariel Merari and Jillian Becker. Of the two, Merari is the most frequently appearing. He appeared five times in 1987–1988 and twice in each of the two preceding years. Unlike Kupperman, Alexander, and Cline, Merari sees the hand of Yasser Arafat in almost every act of terrorism, rather than the hand of Mikhail Gorbachev. Merari heads the Jaffee Center for Strategic Studies at Tel Aviv University.

Jillian Becker is director of the London-based Institute for the Study of Terrorism, which was founded in 1986. Almost immediately after the institute was founded, Becker started popping up as a news shaper (NBC–September 5, 1986). In her inaugural appearance, Becker suggested that Yasser Arafat was involved in the Pan Am flight 73 hijacking, a theme she would repeat whenever a terrorist incident occurred. While Becker believes that Arafat is involved in much of the world's terrorism, she has also stated that the Soviet Union is a major sponsor of terrorism, particularly in southern Africa. Becker described the Southwest African People's Organization (SWAPO) as a "Soviet-aided terrorist organization" and asserted that the ANC is "the only terrorist organization in the world which is actually controlled by the Communist Party of the Soviet Union" (Herman and O'Sullivan 1989, 114). Following SWAPO's victory at the polls in UN-supervised elections in Namibia, the freeing of Nelson Mandela, and the legalization of the ANC in South Africa, Becker disappeared from the network television news. She has not appeared since April 10, 1988. Thank goodness.

NOTE

1. Between 1978 and 1980, most of Henry Kissinger's appearances as a news shaper were "location shots" rather than studio appearances, giving viewers the feeling that his comments constituted news rather than mere opinion. Kissinger's on-air endorsement of Senator Edward Brooke (NBC–October 26, 1978) was given while the ex-secretary of state was travelling in Massachusetts. His assertion that the United States needed to increase defense spending (NBC–December 8, 1978) was made before a congressional committee. Both appearances seemed as though they were "real news events," but they were not. (One Republican endorsing another Republican is not news.)

Although the news shapers of the late 1980s still testify at congressional hearings (for example, see U.S. Senate 1990), their testimony at hearings no longer appears in newscasts. Instead, news shapers now give the networks separate sound-bites that were either shot in the network studios or in the news shapers' offices (invariably filled with books). This produces "talking head" segments clearly discernible from real news segments. The appearances by news shapers during the late 1970s were not as discernible.

8

DOMESTIC DRAMAS

SIDESHOWS, PSEUDOEVENTS, AND GAMES

Melodramas such as "Miami Vice," "Dallas," and "L.A. Law" have set the standards for reporters on the campaign trail. In primetime television programs, drama is produced by sex, unexpected twists, and violent conflicts. In journalism, drama is produced by sideshows, pseudoevents, and games.

Sideshows at circuses usually have sword swallowers, fire eaters, and geeks—performers who are irrelevant to what's happening under the big top. Since the media, with the help of the candidates, have turned the presidential campaign into a circus, it is not surprising that we find similar sideshow spectacles here. These sideshows are irrelevant to the real purpose of the campaign, which is to debate the policies that the candidates advocate.

Sideshow performances in the 1988 presidential campaign are memorable: the spectacle of reporters jousting with Dan Quayle in his hometown of Huntington, as an angry crowd booed and hissed (headline: "Quayle Hunt Provokes Public Wrath"[1]), a few hecklers in a crowd of hundreds who stole the show (headline: "Hecklers Make Tough Day for Both Candidates"), or the Federal Aviation Agency and a plane upstaging Dukakis's speech (headline: "FAA Adds Its Own Disruption"). The greatest sideshows involved reports on what convention delegates were doing in Atlanta and New Orleans—sideshows about pseudoevents (headline: "Cholesterol, Humidity, Humor Run High in New Orleans").

Pseudoevents are news events that have been fabricated by candidates and their consultants. They are staged events that have been planned for the sole purpose of getting press coverage. The candidates and media euphemistically describe them as "photo ops."

During the 1988 campaign, almost everything that wasn't a sideshow or game was a pseudoevent: George Bush's visit to a flag factory, a helmeted Dukakis on a tank, the debates, Bush posing in the cockpit of a World War II bomber. Television reporters love pseudoevents because they produce good visuals.

The ultimate pseudoevents are the national conventions. They are scripted, staged, choreographed, rehearsed, and carefully timed. The candidates are nominated so that their acceptance speeches can be given at 10 P.M. Eastern Standard Time, producing the maximum television audience. There are no longer slipups as in 1972, when George McGovern gave his acceptance speech after half of America had gone to sleep. Given their predictability, one has to wonder why 12,500 members of the press, twice the number of delegates and alternates, are needed to cover the national conventions.

While sideshows and pseudoevents produce the best visuals, game stories— which are also referred to as "horserace stories" (Berkman and Kitch 1986; Patterson 1980)—are the media's main fare. Game stories produce drama by presenting the campaign as a sporting event, complete with front-runners and long-shots and winners and losers. Issues, if they are discussed at all, are merely the fodder for the horserace story. Instead of covering issues, the media focus on election strategies, polls, and political commercials. Sports metaphors that more appropriately describe bigtime boxing (headline: "Debaters Jab without a Knockout"), baseball (headline: "Pitching the Issues Will Be a Complex Task"), or the Kentucky Derby (headline: "Stretch Run—Bush Is Confident but Plans to Hustle") dominate this reporting.

Thomas Patterson (1980) studied news reports during four presidential elections and concluded that almost two-thirds of network news reports were game stories. Newspapers didn't perform any better. During the 1980 primary, Douglass Lowenstein (1980) found that the *Washington Post* emphasized game stories over issue stories by a three-to-one margin, while the *New York Times* preferred game reports by a two-to-one margin.

The most important sources in game stories are the candidates' campaign strategists and aides. Between May and October 1988, more than a Baker's dozen of Bush strategists gave spin to network news stories about the election. Collectively, these spin doctors appeared more frequently than the candidate. Some, like Lee Atwater, appeared more frequently and generated more publicity than the vice-presidential candidate. The Bush strategists who marched across the television screens of the news-watching public included media consultant Roger Ailes (CBS–September 6), campaign manager Lee Atwater (NBC–May 19), campaign chairman James Baker (CBS–September 8), adviser Richard Bond (NBC–May 11), campaign spokesman Fred Bush (CBS–June 17), campaign aide Ceci Cole-McInterff (CBS–June 8), Bush economic adviser Martin Feldstein (CBS–September 27), chief of staff Craig Fuller (CBS–September 22), Bush adviser Thaddeus Garrett (CBS–May 19), campaign spokesman Stuart Gerson (NBC–June 22), Bush aide Mark Goodin (ABC–October

10), campaign finance chairman Robert Mosbacher (ABC–September 29), Bush aide Eileen Padberg (CBS–May 11), economic adviser Rich Rahn (CBS–September 27), Bush media adviser Sig Roglich (CBS–October 25), Bush adviser Dennis Ross (CBS–October 20), Bush consultant Karl Rove (ABC–October 28), and foreign policy adviser Brent Scowcroft (CBS–September 8).

Bush campaign advisers weren't the only ones to appear. The Dukakis campaign also fielded a large number of on-screen analysts. They included adviser Madeleine Albright (CBS–September 8), campaign spokesman Michael Barnes (CBS–June 10), Dukakis aide Donna Brazile (CBS–September 15), adviser Paul Brountas (CBS–July 11), media adviser David D'Alessandro (CBS–October 25), Dukakis issue director Chris Edley (ABC–September 25), campaign manager Susan Estrich (CBS–June 8), campaign treasurer Robert Farmer (ABC–September 29), adviser Ann Lewis (NBC–October 10), adviser Kirk O'Donnell (CBS–June 9), adviser Paul Parks (ABC–June 11), strategist John Sasso (NBC–October 25), campaign adviser Alice Travis (CBS–May 21), and campaign spokesman Joe Warren (CBS–August 7). As was the job of the Bush campaign representatives, the Dukakis advisers were to insulate the candidate from the press corps, provide spin that was favorable to their candidate, and explain to viewers what he was trying to communicate to voters that day.

The media's reliance on spin doctors wasn't restricted to the general election. Each candidate in the presidential primaries had campaign representatives who provided analysis for the ubiquitous television cameras. For example, seven advisers to Jesse Jackson appeared on network newscasts. They were campaign manager Gerald Austin (CBS–July 8), campaign adviser Jim Hightower (CBS–June 8), campaign adviser Ann Lewis (ABC–May 10), campaign representative Eleanor Holmes Norton (CBS–June 10), adviser Ron Walters (CBS–June 22), adviser Maxine Waters (CBS–June 22), and campaign spokesman John White (ABC–July 16). The vice-presidential candidates had their own spin doctors. Dan Quayle had Mitch Daniels (CBS–September 3), and Lloyd Bentsen had Joseph O'Neill (ABC–September 19).

Because the spin doctors represent political candidates and do not claim to be objective analysts, they cannot be called news shapers. They are, however, only a step away from becoming news shapers. Political consultants such as Ed Rollins were used as news shapers by the networks before they went to work for candidates and after their candidates dropped out of the race. Rollins was an adviser to Rep. Jack Kemp during the early primaries.

When working for a candidate, these consultants are described as all-knowing insiders rather than the spin doctors they are; if not part of the campaign, they become detached "analysts." As a result, spin doctors whose candidates are trounced in the primaries can still make a bundle of money by becoming consultants to the news media instead of politicians. They are transfigured from being partisans to analysts by the news media. Longtime Democratic consultant Bob Squier was transfigured in 1988. He served as a paid political analyst for NBC's "Today Show."

After political consultants, pollsters like Peter Hart, Mervin Field, and Harrison Hickman are the most important sources in game stories. While consultants discuss strategy in game stories, pollsters pontificate about the meaning of the previous day's survey (headline: "Polls Show Neither Bush nor Dukakis Is Liked Very Well") or suggest what issues the candidate should or shouldn't emphasize (headline: "Vision of a Declining America Won't Sell in New Hampshire"). Pollsters have also sold their "expertise" to the media. Harrison Hickman was one of CBS's paid analysts during 1988 and one of the most frequently appearing network news shapers.

Spin doctors, "analysts," and pollsters allow the networks to present *Rocky*-like minidramas that play out during a news segment. While all *Rocky* films feature contenders, trainers, promoters, and oddsmakers, as do real boxing events, the political minidramas feature candidates, their advisers, analysts, and pollsters. The candidates play the same roles in game stories that the contenders play in *Rocky* films. The advisers play the same roles as trainers, explaining the strategy that the candidate will use to win the election bout. The analysts are like promoters, claiming that the contest will be a good one if both candidates are in shape. Just as fight promoter Gil Clancy does on boxing matches that CBS telecasts, the political analyst describes the strategies that each candidate must follow to win. The pollsters play the role of Jimmy the Greek in the political game dramas: they inform the viewer of the odds. In addition, other politicians, those who were whipped by the candidate in a primary or who ran for office in the state where the candidate is campaigning, play the role that sparring partners play in bigtime boxing. Based on firsthand experience, they explain to viewers how candidates are shaping up and what types of errors the candidates need to avoid.

CBS's May 11, 1988, report on the upcoming California primary typifies these minidramas. In that report, former contender Pat Robertson reported that he was helping Bush get votes from conservatives. In other words, the sparring partner was helping Bush avoid getting KO'd by a strong right. Reagan's campaign manager, Stuart Spencer, then compared Bush to Reagan, just as every heavyweight contender is compared to Joe Louis, Rocky Marciano, and Muhammad Ali. The newscast featured a brief discussion of voting patterns in California, then cut to Jimmy the Greek (Mervin Field), who explained why the polls weren't as favorable to Bush as they might be. California Governor George Deukmejian, another veteran of California's primary wars, then explained the difficulties of entering the ring in California. After that, trainers Eileen Padberg and Lee Atwater appeared. They explained how Bush planned to get past Dukakis's left—the women and Hispanics, who might KO their candidate. Mervin the Greek reappeared, and then Stuart Spencer resurfaced. He suggested that Bush needed to step out of Reagan's shadow but still ride on the president's coattails if he wanted to win. In other words, he suggested that Bush move slightly to the left, while throwing a hard right.

Night after night, these minidramas unfolded on the network newscasts. In some instances, as on CBS's May 11 newscast, the candidate never appeared. In others, as on CBS's June 8 newscast, the candidate, spin doctors, pollsters, and politicians were present, but the analysts were absent. In that minidrama, the newscast began with a poll-based report claiming that women preferred Dukakis to Bush. Bush, appearing on camera, denied that a "gender gap" existed, just as George Foreman denied that he was overweight for his 1990 bout with heavyweight champion Evander Holyfield. Gov. Jim Thompson then appeared, saying that Bush needed to add day care centers to his list of campaign stops. Bush campaign aide Ceci Cole-McInturff appeared next. She described Bush's strategy for overcoming the problems detected by the polls. The little drama ended with pollster Linda DiVall setting new odds on a Bush victory.

On some nights, the candidate was present, but the spin doctors were absent (CBS–June 7). On other nights, the spin doctors were present, but the pollsters were absent (CBS–May 9). Sometimes the analysts were present, but the pollsters weren't (CBS–May 12). Even without one or two of the characters, the dramas nevertheless unfolded in predictable, game-like fashion.

Within these minidramas, the news shapers are the "pollsters," "analysts," and "consultants," who purport to be feeding viewers objective information. The media present pollsters as though they are scientists, who objectively measure public attitudes, just as physicists measure radiation, temperature, and force. The analysts are usually former government officials or advisers, journalists, professors, or think tank denizens. The former officials are perceived as objective sources because they are no longer in office or are no longer giving advice to politicians. Journalists are definitionally objective, and since journalists have written about the campaign, they are considered experts on it. Professors are presumably objective, because they have been taught to leave their political baggage behind when they walk into the classroom. Think tank fellows pretend to be professors without universities. The media invariably show them sitting in front of bookcases overloaded with books, which, by implication, they have surely read. In the case of political consultants, their objectivity is based on the fact that they aren't being paid by any of the candidates. Their expertise is based on their mastery of the thirty-second television spot.

Although news programs fail to mention it, the thirty-second spots that the political consultants exalt in their sound bites are what have denuded U.S. politics of grassroots citizen involvement. The spots have replaced political activism with passive television viewing. The networks use political consultants to describe and sanctify the tactics that have undermined political parties and grassroots political participation.

During the six months that preceded the November election, 40 different individuals paraded across the network newscasts, shaping game stories about the presidential election. Most of these individuals appeared more than once. Some, like Kevin Phillips, Ed Rollins, and William Schneider, appeared several times each month. These presidential horserace callers were described as "analysts," "consultants," "pollsters," "strategists," "advisers," "briefers," "presidential historians," or "political scientists" or by other names that denoted expertise.

During May 1988, there were 39 appearances by news shapers in horserace stories. During June, there were 42 appearances. That is more than 1 appearance every three days per network. More horserace stories would probably have been produced during May had it not been for the Reagan-Gorbachev summit in Moscow. During the last week in May, when the summit was taking place, there was little coverage of the presidential campaign. More game stories would probably have been aired during June had the primary season not ended with the California primary on June 7.

The 39 May and 42 June appearances exclude those by news shapers who discussed domestic news stories other than the election, and there were many during those two months. Other domestic news stories focused on the investigation of Attorney General Ed Meese (CBS–May 6), the strength of the U.S. economy (NBC–May 6), Nancy and Ronald Reagan's use of an astrologer (ABC, CBS, and NBC–May 9), and the war against drugs (CBS–May 14). All of these stories used news shapers. Not surprisingly, many of the news shapers who appeared in game stories also appeared in the other domestic news reports. Norman Ornstein (ABC–May 11), Ed Rollins (NBC–June 7), and William Schneider (CBS–May 23) helped shape election news, but they also discussed other topics, such as the war on drugs (CBS–June 15), President Reagan's Teflon coating (CBS–May 10), and James Baker's resignation (NBC–June 14).

The titles that the networks conferred on individual news shapers frequently changed, depending on the story. For example, Harrison Hickman was described on some occasions as an analyst (CBS–April 26 and NBC–July 11), on other occasions as a consultant, (NBC–April 26 and CBS–August 11), and on still others as a pollster (CBS–June 7 and July 12). The titles that were used conveyed different meanings. "Analyst" was used to imply nonpartisanship or forewarn viewers of a forthcoming profundity, such as William Schneider's (ABC–September 28, 1987) observation about Rep. Pat Schroeder's bid for the presidency: "I think it's risky to nominate a woman for the top of the ticket and the Democrats are probably aware of that." Analysts, unlike consultants, also commented about domestic policy, not just campaign tactics. The term *consultant* was used to convey that the news shaper had worked in a previous presidential campaign or was employed by the network. The term *pollster* was used whenever survey results were discussed.

The "analysts" used to call the presidential horserace during 1988 were Republicans Haley Barbour (NBC–October 3), John Buckley (CBS–July 9), John Deardourff (NBC–February 15), Kevin Phillips (NBC–May 4), and Ed Rollins (NBC–June 7), think tank denizens Stephen Hess (ABC–May 12), John Makin (NBC–May 7), Norman Ornstein (NBC–June 11), William Schneider (NBC–September 10), and Ben Wattenberg (NBC–July 14), and Democrats Bob Beckel (ABC–June 11), Harrison Hickman (NBC–July 11), and Paul Maslin (CBS–October 22). Overall, Republicans and representatives from conservative think tanks were ten times more likely to be called analyst than were Democrats. For example, Kevin Phillips was described as an "analyst" in 36 of the 43 network appearances that he made during 1987-1988. By contrast, Bob Beckel was described as an "analyst" in just eight of his 27 appearances and Harrison Hickman was described as an "analyst" in just three of his 33 appearances. Democrat Robert Squier was described as an "analyst" in only two of his 18 appearances. Squier's two appearances as an "analyst" were in 1987. During 1988, he was always described as a "consultant."

When Democrats appeared, they were much more likely to be described as "consultants" than "analysts," but many Republicans were also described as "consultants." The Democrats who were called "consultants" during the last six months of the 1988 presidential campaign were David Axelrod (CBS–October 24), Bob Beckel (CBS–May 4), George Christian (CBS–August 4), Tom Donilon (CBS–July 15), Bill Hamilton (CBS–August 11), Harrison Hickman (CBS–June 22), David Sawyer (CBS–July 11), Greg Schnieders (CBS–June 9), Tony Schwartz (CBS–October 25), Robert Shrum (CBS–May 12), Robert Squier (CBS–September 6), and Bill Sweeney (CBS–August 7). The Republicans who were described as "consultants" were Douglas Bailey (CBS–October 22), John Buckley (CBS–June 12), John Deardourff (CBS–August 19), Eddie Mahe (CBS–May 7), Ed Rollins (CBS–August 6), Stuart Spencer (CBS–June 6), and Roger Stone (ABC–August 12). David Garth (NBC–September 21, 1987), who has worked for Democratic and Republican candidates, was also described as a "consultant."

When news shapers were described as "consultants," their party affiliations were frequently disclosed. They were described as "Democratic consultants" or "Republican consultants." This was not true of individuals who were described as "analysts." The political affiliations of "analysts" were rarely disclosed. As a consequence, the party affiliations of Democrats were almost always revealed, but the affiliations of conservatives and Republicans were not. For example, Kevin Phillips, who was almost always described as an "analyst," was called a conservative or Republican in just 12 of his 36 appearances. John Deardourff was described as a Republican in only two of his eight appearances. By contrast, Bob Beckel was described as a Democrat or "ex–Mondale campaign manager" during 14 of his 27 appearances. Harrison Hickman was described as a Democratic partisan during 25 of his 33 appearances. Six of the seven appearances when Hickman wasn't described as a Democrat occurred prior to October 1987, during the preprimary stage of the presidential campaign. During the general election, he was always described as a Democrat, as were Beckel and Squier.

The networks' propensity to describe Democrats as "consultants" was not confined to the six months leading up to the presidential election or to horserace stories. In the 1987-1988 sample (see Table 4), 37 of the 65 "experts, analysts, and consultants" discussed domestic issues. Of the 37 domestic news shapers, 21 were described as "analysts" and 16 were described as "consultants." None were called experts. Of the 21 analysts, 18 were Republicans or fellows at conservative think tanks and one was a Democrat. Two of the analysts were nonpartisan. By contrast, 8 of the 16 "consultants" were Democrats. Five "consultants" were Republicans or think tank denizens, and three were nonpartisan. "Security consultant'' Jack McGeorge (CBS–August 14, 1987) typified the nonpartisan analysts and consultants. He discussed air safety after President Reagan's helicopter had a near miss with a private plane.

Thirteen individuals were used as "pollsters" or "poll directors" by network reporters between May and the end of October. They were Clairborne Darden (ABC–June 16), Linda DiVall (CBS–June 8), Mervin Field (NBC–June 7), Peter Hart (NBC–May 19), Harrison Hickman (CBS–June 7), I. A. Lewis (NBC–August 9), Paul Maslin (CBS–August 8), Rich Maullin (CBS–July 9), Ed Rollins (NBC–August 5), Rob Schroth (CBS–August 6), Lance Tarrance (CBS–August 4), Steve Teichner (ABC–June 6), and Richard Wirthlin (CBS–July 11). Others who shaped horserace coverage were described as "strategists" (NBC–June 8 and CBS–September 2), "advisers" (CBS–September 17), and "briefers" (ABC–September 23).

LEADING THE PACK

Of the ten news shapers who appeared most frequently on network newscasts during 1987-1988 (see Table 5), three were Democratic consultants, four were ex–Republican officials, two were fellows at the AEI, and one was a university professor. The Democratic consultants were Harrison Hickman (33 appearances), Robert Beckel (27 appearances), and Robert Squier (18 appearances). The ex–Republican officials were Ed Rollins (51 appearances), Kevin Phillips (43 appearances), David Gergen (24 appearances), and Stephen Hess (19 appearances). The AEI analysts were William Schneider (58 appearances) and Norman Ornstein (42 appearances). Fouad Ajami was the only professor in the group and the only one who spoke exclusively on foreign affairs. Therefore, nine of the ten most frequently appearing news shapers primarily addressed domestic issues and six of the nine were associated with conservative policy organizations—the Republican party and the AEI. The ex-officials accounted for 137 appearances, and the AEI spokesmen made 100 appearances, so that the six accounted for 237 appearances. By contrast, Democratic consultants accounted for 78 appearances. Not only were Democratic consultants vastly outnumbered by their conservative counterparts, but unlike the conservatives, *they never shaped news about public policy*. The Democrats were used solely as news shapers during game stories about the primary and general elections. By contrast, William Schneider (CBS–January 22, 1988, and CBS–July 5, 1988), Ed Rollins (e.g. CBS–July 7, 1987, and ABC–October 7, 1987), Kevin Phillips (CBS–September 8, 1987, and CBS–May 13, 1987), Norman Ornstein (CBS–June 15, 1988, and CBS–January 30, 1988), David Gergen (NBC–November 7, 1987, and NBC–May 6, 1988), and Stephen Hess (ABC–December 4, 1987, and CBS–May 9, 1988) shaped a variety of reports about domestic and foreign policy issues, including the U.S.–U.S.S.R. summits, the antiabortion movement, Reagan's presidency, Supreme Court nominees, and the federal budget.

The most frequently appearing pundit was AEI "resident fellow" William Schneider, who Sam Donaldson said could always be depended upon to "deliver the goods'' (Donaldson 1990, 25). The goods that Schneider delivered were attacks on Democrats and happy talk for his friends and associates. When Sen. Gary Hart reentered the Democratic primary race, saying that voters, not reporters, should judge his candidacy, Schneider asserted that Hart's message to the American people was "screw you" (ABC–December 20, 1987). When Democrats rallied around Mike Dukakis, Schneider asserted that it was really an expression of fear of Jesse Jackson (NBC–March 26, 1988). By contrast, Schneider asserted that his friend Mexican presidential candidate Carlos Salinas de Gortari "wants to reform the ruling party of Mexico that won every election for sixty years" (CBS–July 5, 1988). In reality, Salina's Institutional Revolutionary party rigged the presidential election (*New York Times*, July 10, 1988, 1) and used violence to deal with its political and labor foes (*New York Times*, November 5, 1989, 13, and March 7, 1990, A6).

Schneider was given an assortment of titles during his network appearances. He was described as a "political scientist" (CBS–February 7, 1987), an "analyst" (CBS–September 15, 1987), and an AEI fellow (NBC–November 13, 1988), although the AEI's conservative bent was never disclosed. The title of analyst was misleading not just because of Schneider's biases, but because terms such as *analyst, expert,* and *economist* allow reporters to present a narrow range of political opinions while appearing to present "objective" reports. For example, NBC (September 10, 1988) used AEI fellows Schneider and Marvin Kosters in a newscast about the presidential election. Schneider was described as an "analyst," and his colleague Marvin Kosters was described as an "economist." Viewers were never informed that the two news shapers were members of the same conservative policy organization.

The next most frequently appearing pundit was Ed Rollins, a former Nixon-Ford-Reagan appointee and adviser, who made 51 network news appearances during 1987-1988. Network correspondents were addicted to Rollins' analyses. During the two years preceding the 1988 presidential election, Rollins was on two networks on the same night seven times. He was on one network or another for two or more consecutive nights four times. Rollins made six appearances during two separate 30-day periods. In one four-month period (May–August 1988), he appeared 19 times. CBS reporter Bill Plante and NBC reporter Lisa Meyers used Rollins seven times to shape their reports, while ABC's Sam Donaldson went to Rollins five times. He was described as a "political analyst" (NBC–June 7, 1988), "political consultant" (CBS–May 10, 1988), "Republican pollster" (NBC–August 5, 1988), "ex–White House political director" (ABC–May 11, 1988), "ex–Reagan campaign aide" (CBS–April 12, 1988), and "ex–Reagan-Bush campaign manager" (NBC–April 22, 1988).

Although network reporters described Rollins in a variety of ways, they never once described him as a "lobbyist," which was his chief occupation after leaving government in 1985. Rollins became a partner in Russo, Watts & Rollins, a Washington-based lobbying firm, which has Tenneco and the Norfolk Southern Corporation for clients. Rollins' firm specialized in "double-dipping," according to the *Washington Post* (October 27, 1985, 17). Double-dippers are lobbyists who get "huge fees to help elect members of the House and Senate, and then get huge fees to lobby the members they helped elect on behalf of corporations and trade associations." Rollins tried to make double-dipping even more corrupt than the *Washington Post*'s description of it. Rollins tried to become an adviser to PACs, including the Teamsters' PAC, which donate large sums of money to political candidates. As a PAC adviser, political consultant, and lobbyist, Rollins sought to become the ultimate political kingmaker, directing and funding politicians' campaigns and then, after making them dependent on his funding and advice, recommending how they should vote on legislation. When asked about the ethics of this double-dipping, Rollins told the *Washington Post*, "I don't know what the response is. Actually, I guess I do: I'm going to continue lobbying anyone I can." These ethics probably helped Rollins get appointed chairman of the Republican Congressional Committee in 1988.

Not only did network reporters fail to describe Rollins as a "lobbyist" or ask him about his double-dipping—which was the real story in 1987-1988—but they usually failed to identify him as presidential contender Jack Kemp's campaign adviser. Only three times between October 1987 and March 1988, after which Kemp dropped out of the presidential race, did network reporters describe Rollins as a Kemp man. Instead, they described him as an ex–White House aide, allowing him to undermine whenever possible the credibility of the Reagan-Bush administration, which included Kemp's chief political rival, George Bush. For example, CBS used Rollins to shape news about Reagan's Supreme Court nominee Douglas Ginsburg. On Ginsburg's nomination and marijuana use, Rollins said, "It is a terrible embarrassment. I think it makes the Reagan administration look a little hypocritical" (November 6, 1987). Rollins was back on the air three more times during November 1987. Two of these appearances were on NBC.

"Rollins was one of my favorites during the campaign," admitted NBC's Washington correspondent Lisa Meyers. "He was used so heavily because he was in no way affiliated with the Bush campaign. He's also very candid, he has a lot of experience, not likely to spin his answers in any strange way, and you know who his client list is," Meyers asserted (Cooper and Soley 1990, 25). Despite Meyers' assertions, Rollins was neither open about his client list nor objective. He refused to identify his list of lobbying clients for the *Washington Post*, and he has a long history of playing politics in a "dastardly fashion," according to former Democratic party leader Charles Manatt (*Los Angeles Times*, March 24, 1983, 20). About the only thing that Rollins was open about was his political client list, which is essentially public information under the disclosure provisions of the Federal Election Campaign Act.

David Gergen was the most sought after news shaper when it came to presidential affairs. This former Nixon-Ford-Reagan aide shaped White House news in 20 of his 24 appearances during 1987-1988. He appeared only four times in horserace stories.

During February 1987, Gergen appeared on every network to discuss the impact of the Iran-Contra arms deal on Reagan's presidency. On NBC (February

6, 1987), he dismissed stories concerning Ronald Reagan's lack of knowledge about goings-on in the White House. If there were a problem, Gergen asserted, it rested with White House staffers, not the president. Described only as a *U.S. News and World Report* editor, Gergen told viewers that "the staff is the one who helps him understand the world around him. If the staff isn't up to that, he's not going to have the acute sense he needs to be president." A couple weeks later on ABC (February 27, 1987), Gergen told viewers that the Iran-Contra scandal had reduced Reagan's stature, but that "he can bounce back, he can regain some of his stature."

During his network appearances, Gergen was most frequently described as a journalist with the *U.S. News and World Report*, and this was particularly true during the 1988 election year. Among the networks, NBC was the only one to accurately and consistently describe Gergen as an "ex–Reagan aide" (see NBC– March 30 and May 6, 1988). ABC (January 25, February 25, and August 14, 1988) and CBS (May 14 and August 13, 1988) described Gergen as a journalist, even when he was plugging his longtime colleague George Bush. During an appearance on CBS, Gergen stated that Bush was already running the government (August 13, 1988), which contributed to the image that Bush, not Dukakis, was the experienced statesman. The only time that ABC or CBS didn't call Gergen a journalist was when another description added more drama to the horserace story. For example, on the eve of the Bush-Dukakis debate (September 23, 1988), ABC described Gergen as a debate "briefer of Ronald Reagan."

Another Republican stalwart who helped assure that network news was shaped in a conservative fashion was Kevin Phillips, the architect of the GOP's race-based electoral strategy. Phillip's political career began in 1964, when he became an aide to Bronx congressman Paul Fino. Fino, a representative from the largest Irish-Italian district in the United States, learned that he could get votes by attacking Great Society programs, which he did with relish. He branded such programs as urban renewal as programs that would benefit "black power" activists (*New York Times*, October 14, 1966, 26).

In 1968, Phillips joined Richard Nixon's campaign team, and after the election he was appointed special assistant to attorney general John Mitchell. In 1969, he wrote *The Emerging Republican Majority*, which argued that Democratic party support for equal rights would turn blue-collar, ethnic voters against the Democratic party. Phillips suggested that the GOP capitalize on this resentment. According to Phillips,

From now on, the Republicans are never going to get more than 10 to 20 percent of the Negro vote and they don't need any more than that . . . but Republicans would be short-sighted if they weakened enforcement of the Voting Rights Act. The more Negroes who register as Democrats in the South, the sooner the Negrophobe whites will quit the Democrats and become Republicans. That's where the votes are. Without that prodding from the blacks, the whites will blackslide into their old comfortable arrangements with the local Democrats. (*New York Times Magazine*, May 17, 1970, 107).

Because of his advocacy of race-based politics, Phillips earned a reputation as a cynical and contemptible political strategist. Joe McGinniss, who wrote *The Selling of the President* (1968), a book about Richard Nixon's 1968 presidential campaign, considered Phillips to be "a quack, an absurdly misprogrammed human computer filled with sawdust." Author Richard Harris described him as a "bumptious ass, an insensitive Neanderthal with almost sadistic social concepts" (*New York Times Magazine*, May 17, 1970, 107). These endorsements earned Phillips a job as a columnist with King Features in 1970. He remained with King Features until 1983.

During 1987-1988, network reporters went to Phillips 43 times for analysis. Among those seeking Phillips' wisdom were Lesley Stahl, Jeff Greenfield, John Martin, Bill Plante, and Lisa Meyers. Phillips was most frequently described as a "political analyst" (ABC–February 16 and 26, 1988, CBS–May 5 and 13, 1988, and NBC–May 4, 1988). However, he was described as a "political consultant" when asked to comment about Gary Hart (CBS–May 4, 1987), an "analyst" when he stated that the AIDS issue would help Republican presidential aspirant Pat Robertson (CBS–June 22, 1987), and a "columnist" when he asserted that presidential candidates could make it difficult for the administration to negotiate an arms treaty (CBS–September 19, 1987).

Phillips was described as a "conservative" only when his political viewpoints were so blatant that they couldn't be passed off as anything but far right or when the moniker made a horserace story seem more interesting. For example, Bill Plante aired a sound bite from Phillips on September 8, 1987, where Phillips was described as a "conservative commentator." In that segment, Phillips accused the Reagan administration of weakening the NATO alliance with arms negotiations. After that assertion, Bill Plante would have had an extremely difficult time convincing even the most gullible viewer that Phillips was simply a detached "political analyst." On October 27, 1987, CBS described Phillips as a "conservative analyst" when he added drama to a horserace story by stating that Jack Kemp was a conservative candidate at a time when voters were moving toward the middle. When asked why Phillips was identified as a conservative or Republican in only eight of the 23 appearances that he made on the CBS network during 1987-1988, "CBS Evening News" senior producer Rome Hartman stated that "we consider Phillips to be a political analyst and don't feel it necessary to give someone's complete background each time he appears" (Cooper and Soley 1990, 46).

Despite Hartman's contention that Phillips was nonpartisan, Phillips' comments concerning Democrats have been consistently partisan and pejorative. He suggested to CBS (January 24, 1988) viewers that Democrats lost their base among blue-collar workers because they had turned their backs on nationalist sentiments. Phillips suggested that Democrats, by opposing the free trade policy supported by Republicans, had finally discovered an issue that would allow the Democratic party to portray itself as nationalist. "To be able to portray yourself as economic nationalists means at least you're one type of nationalist and that's a kind of hormone infusion,'' Phillips contended. On November 7, 1988, Phillips explained to CBS viewers why voters had rejected the Democratic party. Arguing that the Democratic party is dominated by the heritage of sixties radicalism, Phillips said, ''It was disorder in the streets, on the campuses, [liberals] didn't have the stomach to finish the job in Vietnam, just weak, they weren't patriotic, they didn't defend the country against criminals. I think people had the sense that there was a big change in liberalism and people haven't lost that sense.''

THE FOURTH ESTATE AND THE IVORY TOWER

David Gergen and Kevin Phillips weren't the only former officials described as journalists by the networks. Ex–Nixon administration official William Hyland was described as the editor of *Foreign Affairs* (CBS–September 15, 1987) and ex–Johnson administration official Charles Maynes (ABC–January 15, 1988) was described as the editor of *Foreign Policy*. When the appearances by Gergen, Phillips, Hyland, Maynes, and a few other ex-officials are counted, just under 11 percent of the news shapers used by the networks during 1987-1988 were journalists. When these individuals are excluded, journalists comprised just under 8 percent of the news shapers who appeared during 1987-1988 evening newscasts.

The bona fide journalists consisted of columnists, editors, reporters, and publishers. Of these, columnists were the most frequently appearing. Unlike reporters and editors, the columnists were free to express their opinions and partisanships, which represented a much broader range than did the views of the ex–government officials, think tank fellows, or experts. The diversity of viewpoints among journalists existed because a small group did not monopolize discourse, as occurred among think tank denizens and consultants. Among the bona fide journalists, none appeared more than eight times. Almost all discussed domestic rather than foreign affairs.

The journalists who popped up most on the networks were columnists. CNN ''Crossfire'' host and syndicated columnist Patrick Buchanan appeared eight times as a news shaper following his resignation in 1987 as White House communications director. During most of his appearances, the well-known conservative was accurately described as an ''ex–White House aide'' (NBC–November 7, 1987) or ''ex–White House communications director'' (ABC–December 10, 1987). *Boston Globe* columnist Ellen Goodman appeared eight times, *Washington Post* columnists David Broder and Mark Shields appeared five times, and *Washington Post* reporter Lou Cannon appeared three times. A large number of journalists, including *Baltimore Sun* columnist Jack Germond, *Newsweek* reporter Eleanor Clift, then–*New York Times* reporter Hedrick Smith, *Des Moines Register* reporter James Gannon, and *Washington Post* editor Ben Bradlee, appeared twice. There were no Norman Ornsteins among the ranks of journalists.

Almost every other prestige newspaper and weekly news magazine fielded news shapers. They came from the *Atlanta Constitution* (NBC–December 18, 1987), the *Dallas News* (ABC–January 25, 1988), the *Miami Herald* (CBS–May 14,

1988), the *Los Angeles Times* (ABC–August 3, 1987), the *San Francisco Examiner* (CBS–November 8, 1988), *Time* (CBS–September 23, 1987), and *Forbes* (CBS–May 5, 1988). The reliance on members of the prestige press produced many elite, but few nonelite interpretations of political events, despite the political differences among the journalists. When "liberal" columnists such as Radcliffe College–educated Ellen Goodman shaped news, they shaped it from an elite, upper-class perspective, not from the perspective of the working and poor classes.

The networks' reliance on journalists from the prestige press effectively barred representatives from local, specialized, or alternative media from shaping news. The few times that reporters from nonprestige local media appeared, they discussed local, not national, issues. Rob Davis, a KCTI-TV editor in Des Moines, was used by CBS (January 17, 1988) to comment on the Iowa presidential caucuses. Local reporters such as Davis were never used to shape news about national or regional issues. This was left to members of the prestige press. When editors of small-circulation publications appeared, they usually spoke about highly specialized issues that lacked direct policy implications. For example, *Investment* magazine editor Michael Morrow (ABC–September 23, 1987) discussed the climate for U.S. investments in China. Members of politically liberal and alternative publications were almost never used as news shapers. The one alternative journalist who did appear was *Village Voice* writer Nat Hentoff (NBC–June 27, 1988), who is also (and not coincidentally) a fellow at the Cato Institute (Cato Institute 1988).

While journalists from the *Nation, In These Times*, and *Mother Jones* were never used as news shapers, spokesmen from many conservative publications were. Richard Viguerie, billed occasionally as the editor of *Conservative Digest* (ABC–August 12, 1987), appeared 17 times during 1987-1988. During most of his appearances, Viguerie was accurately described as a "conservative lobbyist" (CBS–October 6, 1987), "conservative analyst" (ABC–January 25, 1988), "conservative fundraiser" (CBS–March 28, 1988), or "conservative activist" (ABC–June 3, 1988). Editor Wesley Pruden (ABC–September 27, 1987) and writer Jeremiah O'Leary (ABC–April 12, 1988) of the far right *Washington Times, Human Events* editor Thomas Winter (CBS–June 17, 1988), and a bevy of pundits from the center-right *New Republic* also shaped news. The news-shaping *New Republicans* were Michael Kinsely (ABC–September 13 1988, and NBC–February 9 and October 13, 1988), Fred Barnes (ABC–October 14,1987, and NBC–August 21, 1987), and Charles Krauthammer (ABC–March 20, 1987).

If presidential game stories provided local, nonelite reporters with opportunities to serve as news shapers on the network news, these game stories also provided the same opportunities to professors at public universities. University of Massachusetts professor Ralph Whitehead (CBS–September 19, 1988) spoke about Mike Dukakis, Ohio University professor Herbert Asher (CBS–May 1, 1988, and ABC–May 3, 1988) described attitudes of Ohio voters on the eve of that state's primary, University of Texas professor Kathleen Jamieson (CBS–August 6, 1988) discussed the problems that George Bush had in projecting an image, Cleveland

State University professor Sidney Kraus (NBC–September 21, 1988) added a little drama to the upcoming presidential debates, and UCLA professor John Petrocik (CBS–May 3, 1988) provided a sound bite about George Bush.

With the exception of these presidential game stories, professors at public universities were rarely used as news shapers. Instead, network reporters turned time and again to professors from a small number of private universities located in the Trump Shuttle corridor, running from Washington, D.C., to Boston. The Trump Shuttle universities include Harvard, Columbia, Princeton, Johns Hopkins, Georgetown, and American universities. Although numerous well-known public universities such as the University of Maryland, Temple University, Rutgers University, and the City University of New York are located within the Trump Shuttle corridor, professors from these universities were virtually absent from the television screen.[2]

Even when news reports originated outside the Trump Shuttle corridor, network reporters invariably turned to private universities for news shapers. When stories originated in the Midwest, professors from the University of Chicago (CBS–November 11, 1988) or Northwestern University (NBC–September 22, 1987) appeared; professors from Purdue University, the University of Wisconsin, or the University of Illinois did not. When reports originated from the west coast, professors from Stanford University (CBS–February 11, 1987) and the University of Southern California (CBS–August 2, 1987) were used. On just a few occasions—and these always dealt with highly technical topics—University of California professors were called upon for expertise. An example of the exception was when network reporters interviewed UCLA professor of atmospheric science Richard Turco about the theory of nuclear winter (ABC–November 11, 1988).

The use of news shapers from private, east coast universities was particularly prevalent when the news story concerned foreign, rather than domestic, affairs. Every news shaper who discussed the Soviet Union, the Middle East, or Latin America was from Princeton, Harvard, Columbia, Georgetown, American, or Johns Hopkins. The one exception to the private universities' monopoly on foreign affairs discourse concerned news coverage of the People's Republic of China. Since John King Fairbank retired from Harvard University, foreign affairs reporters have turned to University of Michigan professors, including Michael Oksenberg (CBS–May 13, 1989) and Kenneth Lieberthal (ABC–May 21, 1989), for expertise.

The University of Michigan differs from other public universities because it fields news shapers for the national media, but it is different in several other respects. Its student body is disproportionately drawn from east coast, upper-income families rather than from the state of Michigan, it has close academic ties to private, east coast universities rather than to other Big Ten universities, and it has produced a considerable number of Washington, D.C. based news shapers, including journalist Robin Wright, the AEI's Norman Ornstein, and Brookings' Ed Hewett.

The bias toward private universities is observable by analyzing the affiliations of the "academics" listed in Table 4. The table lists forty appearances by individuals described by the networks as political scientists, historians, sociologists, or professors. These individuals were classified as academics, but five had no university affiliations. The five were AEI spokesmen Norman Ornstein (NBC–September 14, 1987) and William Schneider (CBS–February 7, 1988), who were billed as "political scientists"; authors Stanley Karnow (CBS–November 11, 1988) and Frank Braynard (ABC–January 19, 1988), who were described as "historians" but are journalists by profession; and former Harvard University professor Doris Kearns Goodwin (CBS–November 14, 1988), whom CBS called a "Kennedy historian." Although no longer teaching, Ornstein and Schneider are also former professors. Ornstein taught at Johns Hopkins and Catholic universities and Schneider at Harvard University.

Of the 35 appearances by "active" professors, 3 were from public universities, 27 from private universities, and 5 from foreign universities. Consequently, professors at private universities accounted for 77.1 percent of all appearances by university faculty. This percent excludes the appearances of former professors Goodwin, Ornstein, and Schneider and appearances by academicians who were described as "analysts," "economists," or "former officials." If these appearances were included, the percent of appearances by professors from private universities would increase.

Two of the three appearances by academicians at public institutions were by University of California professors (ABC–November 11, 1988, and NBC–May 19, 1988). The other appearance was by an Iowa State University professor (ABC–November 15, 1988), who discussed farm foreclosures. By contrast, there were seven appearances by Johns Hopkins professors and five by Harvard professors. Five of the seven Johns Hopkins appearances were by Fouad Ajami. All of his appearances were on the CBS network, as was an appearance by Johns Hopkins professor Barry Rubin (CBS–February 4, 1987). The other Johns Hopkins professor was Riordan Roett, who appeared on the NBC network (January 19, 1988). Other private universities that had news shapers appear more than once were Columbia (CBS–September 23, 1987, CBS–May 15, 1988, and NBC–August 3, 1987), Northwestern (NBC–September 22 and 23, 1987), and American (ABC–September 18, 1987, and NBC–August 14, 1987) universities.

NOTES

1. This headline ran in the August 26, 1988, issue of the Minneapolis *Star Tribune*. All other headlines listed in parentheses also appeared as heads or subheads in 1988 issues of the *Star Tribune*.

2. The exceptions to this were former officials, such as Winston Lord, Jr., who have received academic appointments at public universities. However, when these news shapers appear, their public university affiliations are never disclosed.

9

THE CONFLICT WITH
IRAQ: A CASE STUDY

Even before the Bush administration created news pools and censored reports about the war with Iraq, the public was getting much of its information from a gaggle of "experts," to whom the media turned for analysis, commentary, and opinion. These individuals speculated about military strategy, provided psychological evaluations of Iraqi dictator Saddam Hussein, and discussed the rifts between Iraq, Kuwait, and other nations of the region. Their opinions became a substitute for hard news, which trickled out of the Middle East.

These spin doctors of war are typified by Edward Luttwak. Until Iraq invaded Kuwait on August 1, 1990, few people had seen or heard of him. During the early and mid-1980s, the Romanian-born Luttwak was touted as a NATO defense specialist by the CSIS, where he is a senior fellow. He garnered some attention from his 1979 article in *Commentary* magazine, which alleged that Cuba threatened U.S. national interests in the Middle East. According to Luttwak, Soviet-armed Cuban troops in South Yemen were prepared to strike Oman from a base in South Yemen, creating a domino effect in the Arabian peninsula. He wrote:

A Cuban intervention force is being trained in armored warfare. The appropriate equipment is being stocked in South Yemen—the entry point. And the traditional-moderate Sultanate [of Oman] is a ready initial target, itself the perfect platform for a wider offensive that can be more ambitious. The pieces are on the chessboard; the operation can unfold at any time. (1979, 65)

After presidential candidate Ronald Reagan used Luttwak's allegations to attack President Carter's defense posture (CBS–February 7, 1980), Luttwak started popping up as a news shaper on network television. Luttwak's error in predicting what was unfolding in the Middle East apparently helped rather than hindered his career as an expert.

Luttwak appeared as a news shaper three times in the first year following Reagan's assertions. He commented on U.S. and Soviet troop strengths (ABC–October 7, 1980), the Phoenix missile (ABC–October 9, 1980), and the U.S.S.R.'s "killer" satellites (ABC–October 10, 1980). Luttwak appeared on network newscasts with greater frequency as the years went by, reaching a peak in 1986. He made six network news appearances that year.

As the cold war started thawing, the television networks started giving Luttwak the cold shoulder. He made three appearances in 1987, one appearance in 1988, and zero appearances in 1989. As East European communism and the Warsaw Pact faded into oblivion, so did Edward Luttwak's career as a defense expert.

But impending war and death in the Middle East gave Luttwak's career new life. Reporters flocked around Luttwak like vultures around carrion, eagerly eating up his opinions and comments. In the thirty days following Iraq's August 1 invasion of Kuwait, Luttwak logged three appearances on "Nightline" and penned commentaries for the New York Times (August 9, 1990, A23) and the Los Angeles Times (August 12, 1990, M7). The Minneapolis Star Tribune (August 12, 1990, 17A) dubbed Luttwak a "Middle East expert" and proceeded to ask him about the Iraqi government. Iraq has "a highly efficient dictatorship. Bloodthirsty, but very efficient," Luttwak explained. Four days later, a commentary by Luttwak appeared in that newspaper's pages (August 12, 1990, 31A).

As tensions in the Middle East increased, so did Luttwak's appearances as a news shaper. The opinions and analyses of Luttwak popped up 78 times between September 1 and December 31, 1990 in the Los Angeles Times, St. Louis Post-Dispatch, Boston Globe, Rocky Mountain News, and 13 other newspapers with full texts included in the Data Times computer system. He wrote additional commentaries for the Los Angeles Times (September 2, 1990, E19), the Washington Post (September 9, 1990, D1), and the New York Times (November 1, 1990, E19). By the time that the United States and Iraq went to war on January 16, 1991, Luttwak had become one of the media's most frequently cited experts on Mideast military strategy, even though his résumé fails to list any military duty (Who's Who in America 1990, 2058).

The "MacNeil/Lehrer NewsHour" turned to Luttwak for analysis on January 15, the night of the UN deadline for an Iraqi withdrawal from Kuwait, and again on January 16, the night that war began. That night, Luttwak popped up as an "analyst" on two network newscasts. A Los Angeles Times analysis (January 17, 1991, A8) on the outbreak of war described Luttwak as "a prominent defense expert" and interviewed him about the sudden U.S. attack on Iraq. "If this decision had been delayed," Luttwak explained, "you would have seen an amazingly rapid unraveling of the coalition." The CSIS "expert" appeared on the "MacNeil/Lehrer

NewsHour'' again on January 30, arguing that U.S. ground commanders in Iraq were interfering with the correct waging of the war. He asserted that President Bush had chosen ''gardeners to be his cooks'' by selecting Gen. H. Norman Schwarzkopf and other army commanders to wage the Persian gulf war. The same day, another commentary by Luttwak appeared in the *Los Angeles Times* (p. B7). The commentary was reprinted in other newspapers, including the Minneapolis *Star Tribune* (p. 19A), on the following day. The next day Luttwak appeared as an analyst on NPR, and five days later (February 7, 1991) he was back on ''MacNeil/Lehrer,'' claiming that the United States was not properly conducting the air war.

Luttwak is just one of the retreads to whom the media turned for expertise following the Iraqi invasion of Kuwait. Almost every former government official, think tank denizen, and Ivy League academic previously used by the media as a news shaper resurfaced after the August 1 invasion. These familiar ''experts'' not only shaped television discourse about the crisis, but filled the pages of the prestige press with their opinions. Former national security adviser-turned-Columbia University professor Gary Sick appeared on ''Nightline'' (August 1), ABC's special coverage of President Bush's August 20 address, and CNN (August 23). His commentary entitled ''Hussein Must Be Stopped'' appeared in the *New York Times* (August 3, 1990, A11). Former CIA director Stansfield Turner appeared on ''Nightline'' (August 7) and CNN (August 24). He wrote a commentary that appeared in the *Christian Science Monitor* on August 30, 1990 (p. 18). Zbigniew Brzezinski shaped news for CBS (August 19) and published a commentary in the *Washington Post* (August 16, 1990, A23). Brookings' John Steinbruner appeared on the NBC ''Nightly News'' (August 31) and penned a column for the *Los Angeles Times* (August 25, 1990, B7).

Henry Kissinger appeared on ''Nightline'' (August 24), PBS's ''American Interests'' (August 24), and CNN (August 24). His commentaries appeared in the *Washington Post* (August 19, 1990, C7) and the *Los Angeles Times* (August 19, 1990, M1). James Schlesinger appeared on CNN (August 24). He wrote an opinion article for the *Washington Post* (August 5, 1990, D7). Former assistant secretary of defense turned Brookings scholar Lawrence Korb appeared on ''Nightline'' (August 29), the NBC ''Nightly News'' (August 19), and the CBS ''Evening News'' (August 26). He wrote ''We Can Afford to Fight Iraq'' for the *New York Times* (August 21, 1990, A15). Former Nixon-Carter adviser turned Brookings scholar William Quandt shaped news for Peter Jennings (ABC–August 17) and wrote a commentary for the *New York Times* (August 30, 1990, A23). CSIS fellow turned Johns Hopkins University professor Barry Rubin appeared on ''Nightline'' (August 22) and penned two opinion articles for the *Wall Street Journal* (August 3, 1990, A10, and August 24, 1990, A10) and the *Los Angeles Times* (August 8, 1990, B7, and August 19, 1990, M2).

Many other ''usual suspects'' also popped up in August. Former undersecretary of state Joseph Sisco shaped news on ABC (August 16) and CBS (August 10) and wrote a column for the *Washington Post* (August 15, 1990, A21). Ex–Reagan official Robert Hormats appeared on "Nightline" (August 23) and penned a commentary for the *Washington Post* (August 28, 1990, A17). Former CIA staffer turned Rand researcher Graham Fuller appeared on ABC (August 31) and wrote "It's More Than Hussein Can Chew" for the *Los Angeles Times* (August 7, 1990, B7). Brookings' Elisa Harris appeared on ABC and NBC on August 8 and wrote a commentary for the *Los Angeles Times* (August 17, 1990, B7). Fred Bergsten, director of the Institute for International Economics, appeared on NBC on August 8. The ubiquitous Norman Ornstein showed up on "Nightline" on August 23, and Brookings' Joshua Epstein was on ABC's "World News Tonight" on August 28. Bergsten, Ornstein, and Epstein were about the only familiar faces who shaped television news in August but didn't write a commentary for one of the country's leading dailies.

Former Reagan adviser Geoffrey Kemp wrote commentaries for the *Los Angeles Times* (August 12, 1990, M2), and *New York Times* (August 4, 1990, 15) and appeared on ABC (August 6). He appeared on CNN on September 1, 3, and 7. As events in the Middle East heated up, Kemp appeared with increasing frequency on the "MacNeil/Lehrer NewsHour." He appeared on "MacNeil/Lehrer" on December 14, January 8, January 9, January 15, and January 16.

Some of the usual experts appeared on television during the first month of the crisis but didn't publish commentaries until the second month. This was the case with CSIS fellows Robert Kupperman and Shireen Hunter. Kupperman appeared on NBC's "Nightly News" on August 18, but his commentary in the *Christian Science Monitor* didn't appear until September 24 (p. 18). Hunter appeared on CBS on August 30 and published an opinion article a few days later in the *Los Angeles Times* (September 7, 1990, B7).

Other usual "experts" followed an opposite course from Kupperman and Hunter—appearing in print in August, but not appearing on television until September. Truman-era cold warrior Paul Nitze published a commentary in the *Washington Post* (August 26, 1990, C7) before appearing on CNN (September 7). Former Reagan appointee Frank Gaffney wrote columns for the *Los Angeles Times* (September 3, 1990, B5) and *Wall Street Journal* (September 6, 1990, A14) and appeared a few weeks later on the CBS "Evening News" (September 30).

In August, economists also came out of their closets and onto the network newscasts. Among these were former Reagan economic adviser Lawrence Kudlow, described as "Bear Stearns' chief economist," who appeared on ABC (August 4). He was joined by the perennially appearing David Jones (CBS–August 6) and David Healy (ABC–August 4), who speculated about the impact of the crisis on the U.S. economy.

AUGUST 2–31: A SYSTEMATIC EVALUATION

The above-mentioned individuals were not the only news shapers who appeared on network newscasts during August. Between August 2, when reports about the

Iraqi invasion of Kuwait were first aired, and August 31, the last day of the month, there were 194 appearances by "Middle East experts," "defense analysts," "oil industry experts," and "economists" on the network evening newscasts. This averages out to about 6 appearances each evening, or approximately two news shapers per network newscast. The 194 appearances do not include individuals who shaped news about other events, such as women's rights (CBS–August 26), District of Columbia mayor Marion Barry's drug-use trial (NBC–August 11), South African violence (ABC–August 22), or the Federal Deposit Insurance Corporation's financial woes (ABC–August 14).

Of the 194 appearances, 83 (or 42.8 percent) were by individuals who appeared only once. Twenty-two people appeared twice during August, and 17 people appeared three or more times. The 17 most frequently appearing individuals accounted for 67 (or 34.5 percent) of the 197 appearances.

Among news shapers, the largest number of appearances was by economists, industry analysts, and business consultants, who discussed the sharp rise in oil prices, worldwide demand for oil, and possible effects of the gulf crisis on the economy. These economists and industry analysts appeared 42 times, accounting for 21.6 percent of all appearances by Gulf crisis news shapers who appeared in August. This was approximately the same percentage observed in the 1979-1980 sample, where 26.1 percent of the news shapers were described as economists or industry analysts (see Table 3). The two percentages provide support for Goedkoop's (1990) hypothesis that "bad" economic news produces an increase in the number of economic stories covered by the news media. The month of August not only saw the steepest one-month increase in the price of oil, but a drop in the stock market and an increased belief that the United States was in the midst of a recession. The United States was also suffering economic woes in 1979-1980, when a large number of economists and industry analysts also appeared. By contrast, only 8.1 percent of the news shapers in the 1987-1988 sample discussed the economy. In 1987-1988, the U.S. economy was expanding rather than receding. When the economy is doing well, the media pay little attention to it.

Nine of the 42 economists and industry analysts who shaped news in August 1990 were from abroad. Four appearances were by Jordanian economists Ahmed Amani (CBS–August 7), Jawar Anani (CBS–August 14), and Fahed Fanek (CBS–August 6 and ABC–August 13). One appearance was by a Soviet economist (ABC–August 25), who discussed Soviet oil production, and one appearance was by an Iranian oil analyst (NBC–August 21). Three appearances were by London-based "oil analysts" Peter Gignoux (CBS–August 2 and August 13) and David Bowers (ABC–August 6). Gignoux works at Shearson Lehman Brothers (London), and Bowers works for Barclays. Shearson and Barclays are investment firms. Neither Gignoux nor Bowers was described as a stock or investment analyst; each was simply described as an "oil analyst."

Twenty-eight of the 33 appearances by U.S.-based economists and industry analysts were made by representatives of brokerage firms, banks, or oil companies. Nine of the 28 were by people described as "economists" or "analysts" for the firms where they were employed; the others were simply described as "economists" or "industry analysts." Ted Eck (CBS–August 8) was described as "Amoco chief economist," Bill Herman (ABC–August 3) was described as a "Chevron oil economist," Irwin Kellner (NBC–August 6 and ABC–August 7) was described as a "Manufacturers Hanover economist," and Michael Lauer (CBS–August 25) was described as a "Kidder, Peabody defense analyst." By contrast, Susan Lakatos, who also works at Kidder, Peabody, was described as an "economist," as was David Jones (CBS–August 2) of the Aubrey C. Lanston investment firm. Allen Brooks (CBS–August 3) of Rotan Mosle in Houston was described as an "oil industry analyst," and Jack Aydin of McDonald & Company, who appeared twice on CBS, was called a "Middle East oil analyst." Adam Sieminski of County NatWest USA was described in one appearance as an "oil analyst" (CBS–August 24) and in another as a "Washington analyst" (ABC–August 6).

Five appearances were made by economists and analysts who were not associated with Wall Street firms, banks, or oil companies. The 5 appearances were made by four individuals: Henry Schuler, Bernard Weinstein, Philip Verleger, and Ernest Preeg. Schuler appeared four times in August. He was described once as an "energy analyst" (NBC–August 23) and once as an "economist" (CBS–August 4), even though he has a law degree, not a Ph.D. in economics. In other appearances he was described as a CSIS analyst. Weinstein (CBS–August 8) was the only economist who appeared in August who was affiliated with a university. He teaches at Southern Methodist University (SMU) and is head of the Center for Enterprising, a campus-based research institute (*Research Centers Directory* 1990). Weinstein appeared in a news report that originated in Dallas, where SMU is located. Verleger was described once as an "oil economist" (NBC–August 9). During two other appearances in August, he was identified as a spokesman for the Institute for International Economics. Preeg was described in one appearance as an "international business specialist" (NBC–August 29). During an appearance on ABC the day before, he was described as a representative of the CSIS, where he is a senior fellow.

Overall, only one of the economists came from a private university; none came from public universities. There were also no appearances by economists associated with Democratic or liberal think tanks, such as the Economic Policy Institute, Center for National Policy, or Center for Budget and Policy Priorities. The economists who shaped network newscasts came primarily from the corporate world, which can be expected to be probusiness and pro-Republican, or conservative think tanks. This is an even higher concentration of corporate or business voices than observed in the 1987-88 sample.

While representatives of Democratic or liberal think tanks were as scarce as hens' teeth, spokesmen from the CSIS appeared frequently. Henry Schuler and Ernest Preeg, who collectively appeared six times in August, were not the only CSIS news shapers. James Schlesinger, Zbigniew Brzezinski, Shireen Hunter, Robert Kupperman, and William J. Taylor also made obligatory appearances, running the CSIS's tally up to to 13 appearances. Brookings Institution fellows were also ubiquitous. Network news shapers from Brookings included Judith Kipper (ABC–August 2, 9, 15, 23, and 24), Elisa Harris (ABC and NBC–August 8), Lawrence Korb (NBC–August 19 and CBS–August 26), Joshua Epstein (ABC–August 28), Robert Litan (NBC–August 9), John Steinbruner (NBC–August 31), and William Quandt, who appeared in two different stories during one newscast (ABC–August 17). Brookings' tally for August was 14 appearances. Together, Brookings and CSIS representatives made 27 appearances in August, or almost 1 network appearance each day. This number excludes appearances by former Brookings and CSIS fellows, such as Georgetown University's Robert Lieber (NBC–August 6).

Brookings and CSIS were not the only think tanks that fielded news shapers in August. As Table 10 shows, nine of the 17 most frequently appearing news shapers were affiliated with think tanks. If the Council on Foreign Relations is counted as a think tank, a function it also fills, ten of the 17 news shapers were think tank analysts. Two were professors at private, beltway-area universities, and four were retired military officers. Two of the news shapers, Anthony Cordesman and Richard Murphy, were also ex–Republican administration appointees, and two of the retired military officers were advisers to Republican presidents. Overall, the most frequently appearing Middle East news shapers match the profiles of most news shapers: former Republican officials, think tank analysts, corporate economists, and professors at private universities.

Typical of these news shapers were the spokesmen for the Institute for International Economics (IIE), who appeared six times in August. The IIE is Washington's leading advocate of "free trade." Its spokesmen oppose the "protectionism" advocated by many Democrats and unionists, although viewers were never apprised of this. The spokesmen for this think tank were Philip Verleger (NBC–August 9 and 15 and CBS–August 15), Jeffrey Schott (ABC–August 9 and 28), and Fred Bergsten (NBC–August 8). Schott and Bergsten are former government officials, but viewers were never informed of their backgrounds.

Many of the other oft called upon think tanks also fielded news shapers. The industry-supported American Petroleum Institute fielded Charles DiBona (NBC–August 7 and CBS–August 9) and William O'Keefe (NBC–August 29); the other oil industry–funded think tank, the PIRINC, fielded John Lichtblau (CBS–August 2) and Lawrence Goldstein (CBS–August 15); Geoffrey Kemp (ABC–August 6) appeared as a representative of the Carnegie Endowment (ABC–August 6); and Rand Corporation analysts Graham Fuller (ABC–August 31) and David Grissmer (CBS–August 15) also made appearances. Fuller was identified as a Rand analyst, whereas Grissmer was identified as a "defense analyst." In neither appearance were Rand's ties to the U.S. government disclosed.

Several of the less frequently heard from "research centers" also produced news shapers. Patrick Clawson (NBC–August 6) appeared as a representative of the Foreign Policy Research Institute, a conservative Philadelphia-based think tank. Peter Schweizer (ABC–August 22) appeared as a representative of the

Table 10

The Leading Mideast News Shapers: Network TV News Appearances, August 1990

News Shaper	Appearances	Affiliation
George Crist	10	Retired military officer
Anthony Cordesman	5	Georgetown University/former official
Judith Kipper	5	Council on Foreign Relations/Brookings Institution
Richard Murphy	5	Council on Foreign Relations/former official
William Crowe	4	Retired military officer
Kamel Abu Jaber	4	Jordan Center for Mideast Studies (University of Jordan)
Henry Schuler	4	Center for Strategic and International Studies
Mohammed Ahmed	3	Center for Strategic Studies (Cairo)
Fouad Ajami	3	Johns Hopkins University
Joseph Alpher	3	Jaffee Center for Strategic Studies (Tel Aviv)
Michael Dewar	3	International Institute for Strategic Studies
Fred Halliday	3	London School of Economics
Saad Eddin Abrahim	3	Center for Political and Strategic Studies (Cairo)
William Odom	3	Retired military officer
Allen Sinai	3	First Boston Bank (economist)
William J. Taylor	3	CSIS/retired military officer
Philip Verleger	3	Institute for International Economics

newly created right-wing American Foreign Policy Council. Schweizer previously worked at the National Forum Foundation, another rightist organization in Washington. His credentials as an "expert" consist of his holding a B.A. from George Washington University, having written a few articles for such publications as *National Review*, and having coauthored a "book" titled *The Soviet Concepts of Peace, Peaceful Coexistence and Détente* (1989). The book is an overlong list of statements made by Soviet authorities that have been taken out of context. The few words that were actually written by Schweizer are shopworn anticommunist slogans, such as these explanations of what peace means to the Soviets: "[In] Soviet logic it is axiomatic that 'world peace' necessarily means 'world socialism'; a 'peace offensive' is by its very nature a 'socialist offensive' " (p. 2) and "This [Soviet] view of 'peace' conveniently ignores the Gulag, the purges under Stalin, the suppression of Eastern Europe, and the torture of Soviet dissidents" (p. 3).

A few representatives of think tanks that are not on the far right of the political spectrum also appeared. These analysts came from the Center for Defense Information (CDI) and two think tanks that specialize in environmental issues. The CDI, a think tank headed by retired Admiral Gene La Rocque, opposed the "excessive expenditures for weapons" during the 1980s (Smith 1991, 275). It fielded retired Admiral Eugene Carroll, who made two network appearances on ABC during August. As the war marched on, the CDI's Gene La Rocque and David Johnson were also used as "military analysts" by the media. The two environmental research centers that fielded news shapers were the Worldwatch Institute (CBS–August 25) and the World Resources Institute (ABC–August 9). Both are Washington-based and are funded by foundations, international agencies, and corporations (*Research Centers Directory* 1991).

Another think tank that fielded news shapers in August was the Washington Institute for Near East Policy, which is essentially a pro-Israel lobby group. Its director is Martin Indyk (CBS–August 3), who oversees the institute's annual "George Shultz Lecture in Middle East Diplomacy." Indyk was formerly associated with the American-Israel Public Affairs Committee (AIPAC). His credentials as a researcher consist of his having penned a few opinion articles denouncing Yasser Arafat and praising Israeli prime minister Yitzak Shamir and having coauthored two pamphlets, one of which was published by AIPAC.

The Washington Institute has fielded several other "experts," to whom the media have also turned for analysis. These experts are Hirsch Goodman (ABC–August 11), Seth Carus, and Michael Eisenstadt. Goodman is coauthor with Carus of a book titled *The Future Battlefield and the Arab-Israeli Conflict* (1990), which was published by the institute and Transaction Books. Goodman previously worked for the *Jerusalem Post*, and Carus worked for AIPAC. Their appearances as "experts" demonstrate how easily political partisans are palmed off on the media when they carry the moniker of a "research center." If Indyk, Carus, and the others were still spokesmen for AIPAC, which is essentially what they are, reporters would have had much greater difficulty describing them as detached "analysts" instead of pressure group spokesmen.

The Washington Institute was not the only pro-Israel think tank to produce news shapers. Network reporters based in Israel turned for analysis to Mark Heller (CBS–August 3) and Joseph Alpher (NBC–August 3 and 11 and ABC–August 8) of the Jaffee Center for Strategic Studies. Alpher was consistently described as a representative of the Jaffee Center, whereas Heller was simply described as a "Middle East analyst." Ron Ben-Yishai (CBS–August 9) was also used as a news shaper. Ben-Yishai spent quite a few years in Washington, D.C., while serving as a correspondent for *Yedioth Ahronot*, Israel's largest daily. He too has ties with the Jaffee Center (see Ben-Yishai 1981). In his appearance, Ben-Yishai was described by CBS as a "military analyst." CBS reporters also turned to Ofra Benjio (CBS–August 2) for analysis. Benjio was described as a spokesman from Tel Aviv University but is not listed in *The World of Learning 1990* (1990, 735-736) as a professor at that university.

Shlomo Gazit (NBC–August 2) was another "Middle East analyst" to whom network reporters in Israel turned for analysis. Gazit is more accurately described as a former Israeli intelligence officer. He served as the director of intelligence for the Israeli defense forces from 1964 to 1967, head of the Occupied Territories from 1964 to 1967, and director of Israeli military intelligence from 1974 to 1979.

On two occasions (August 2 and 23), CBS reporters in Israel used Ze'ev Schiff as a news shaper. Schiff is the military correspondent for *Haaretz*, Israel's most prestigious daily newspaper, and a former fellow at the Carnegie Endowment. Schiff has also written several books on the Arab-Israeli conflict and is considered one of Israel's best-informed analysts, but one that has close ties to the Israeli High Command (Sid-Ahmed 1976, 16).

Network reporters based in Jordan and Egypt also went to think tanks to find news shapers, just as their counterparts in the United States and Israel did. Not counting economists, 11 of the 22 Egyptians and Jordanians who served as news shapers in August came from think tanks. Six of the 21 were journalists; the other five were academicians. However, the distinction between journalists, academicians, and think tank fellows is much less clear in the Middle East than it is in the United States, even though the distinction in the United States is sometimes blurred.

In Cairo, one of the two leading think tanks is sponsored by the *Al-Ahram* newspaper. The think tank is the Al-Ahram Center for Political and Strategic Studies, which produced Ali Dessouki, Mohammed Sid-Ahmed, and Saad Eddin Ibrahim, who appeared as network news shapers in August. Dessouki appeared once (NBC–August 9), Sid-Ahmed appeared three times—once on ABC (August 9), CBS (August 2), and NBC (August 25), and Ibrahim also appeared three times—twice on NBC (August 10 and 13) and once on CBS (August 10). Dessouki is a professor at Cairo University, Sid-Ahmed is a former politician and journalist, and Ibrahim is a sociology professor at the American University in Cairo. Of the three, Ibrahim is the best known in the United States. Six of his books are available in English and have been widely distributed in the United States. Like other news shapers who appeared in August, Ibrahim had appeared previously on the news to provide analysis. He appeared in the 1987-1988 sample (CBS–January 19, 1988, and NBC–January 20, 1988).

The most frequently appearing Mideast news shaper was Kamel Abu Jaber, a professor at the University of Jordan and fellow at the Jordan Center for Middle East Studies. He appeared four times in August, making it onto every network. His simplistic evaluations for the rising anti–U.S. sentiments in the Arab world, such as describing Arabs as "frustrated people" (NBC–August 19) and concluding that Arabs think that Americans hate them (ABC–August 21), made him the most popular news shaper in the Mideast.

Appearing twice in NBC reports originating from Amman was George Hawatmeh, a *Jordan Times* editor. He was only one of several journalists who appeared. The others were Cairo magazine editors Imaad Adib (CBS–August 4) and Safinas Khasen (NBC–August 12), *Al-Ahram* editor Hamdi Fouad (ABC–August 17), and Tahseen Bahseer (ABC–August 24), who is not only a journalist, but a former Egyptian official.

Network reporters based in London also turned frequently to think tank denizens for analysis. They turned to Heino Kopietz (ABC–August 13) and Michael Dewar (NBC–August 2, and CBS–August 13 and 15) of the IISS and David Barr (CBS–August 9) of the Gulf Center for Strategic Studies. Kopietz and other spokesmen for the IISS were used as news shapers before by network reporters. Kopietz appeared four times in 1986, three times in 1987, and once in 1988. Three other spokesmen for the IISS appeared in the 1987-1988 sample, but Dewar was not one of them. The gulf crisis appearances were a first for Dewar, who is a British colonel, teacher at the Army Staff College in Camberley, Surrey, and author of *The British Army in Northern Ireland* (1987).

The other London-based analysts to whom reporters turned were such frequently seen analysts as the *Economist*'s George Joffee, writer Anthony Sampson (CBS–August 15), "Middle East expert" Peter Mansfield (ABC–August 6 and 15), London School of Economics professor Fred Halliday (CBS–August 2 and 4 and NBC–August 2), and the *Middle East Economic Digest*'s David Butter (CBS–August 9). Sampson (CBS–September 23, 1987), Butter (CBS–August 3, 1987), Mansfield (ABC–August 5, 1987), and Joffe (ABC–August 3 and 10, 1987) popped up in the 1987-1988 sample, just as Saad Eddin Ibrahim had. Halliday did not appear in the sample, but appeared often as a news shaper between 1986 and 1988. He appeared five times in 1986, three times in 1987, and twice in 1988. Over the years, Halliday shaped news on a wide range of topics, including NATO and the Warsaw Pact (NBC–September 21, 1986), the Afghan guerrilla alliance (CBS–April 14, 1988), and Iran (ABC–November 10, 1986). In a gulf crisis analysis, he psychoanalyzed Saddam Hussein (CBS–August 2, 1990), comparing the Iraqi leader to Benito Mussolini and Adolf Hitler.

Also appearing in August were two other reporters for the *Middle East Economic Digest*, Jonathon Crusoe (ABC–August 9) and Pamela Smith (CBS–August 9 and 28), and a writer for the *Armed Forces Journal*, Francis Tusa (CBS–August 4). With Colonel Dewar, they were the only new faces to appear. Although their faces were new, Dewar, Crusoe, and Smith nevertheless came from the same institutions that produced the old faces—the IISS and the *Middle East Economic Digest*.

When the appearances by British stockbrokers, foreign think tank analysts and journalists, and Jordanian economists are added together, foreign analysts accounted for 61 (31.4 percent) of the 194 August appearances. This percentage was much larger than in the 1979-1980 and 1987-1988 samples. The large number of foreign news shapers was due to the vast number of network news reports that originated in the region and the large number of countries involved in the conflict. Besides the United States, there were sizable detachments of Kuwaiti, Saudi, Syrian, French, and British troops and smaller detachments from other countries deployed in the region. Jordan, Israel, Yemen, Iran, and the Soviet Union were also involved in the conflict, although not as combatants.

GENERALS, ACADEMICIANS, AND GENERALS TURNED ACADEMICIANS

Following President Bush's decision to send U.S. troops into Saudi Arabia, the networks scrambled to find "consultants" who could explain to viewers how U.S. troops in the Middle East would fight a war. The three networks went for the top brass, hiring either retired admirals or generals. CNN hired a retired colonel, Harry Summers. Summers appeared once on NBC (August 8) before landing his CNN contract.

The retired brass supplemented the views of the academicians and think tank analysts, whom the networks were using to shape their news. For "scholarly" analysis, CBS turned to its longtime Mideast consultant, Johns Hopkins University professor Fouad Ajami. Ajami appeared as a news shaper three times in August.

ABC hired Anthony Cordesman as its consultant. He appeared five times during August. During the appearances, ABC News viewers were told that Cordesman was "a professor at Georgetown University's National Security Studies program." His authorship of the book *The Lessons of Modern War: The Iran/Iraq War* was also played up by the network, but his Republican government credentials were played down. Cordesman was a director of intelligence analysis in the Department of Defense during the Nixon administration. In 1973, he became the assistant to the deputy secretary of defense. Cordesman moved to the Department of Energy in 1976, before Jimmy Carter became president, thereby escaping the Democrats' purge of the Defense Department. Like many other former federal officials, Cordesman went into the consulting business when he left government in 1980. In 1983, he was hired at Georgetown.

Ajami and Cordesman were the only academicians hired as network news consultants, but they were not the only professorial news shapers. Also appearing were Columbia University's Edward Said (CBS–August 15), the University of Southern California's Loren Lipson (NBC–August 19), the University of Wisconsin's

Gary Milholin (NBC–August 30), and Georgetown University's Barry Carter (NBC–August 11), Michael C. Hudson (CBS–August 14), and Robert Lieber (NBC–August 6). Of the 14 appearances by Ajami, Cordesman, and the other professors, eight were by Georgetown University professors and 13 of the 14 were by professors at private universities. Even if one counts the four appearances by retired admiral William Crowe, who now teaches at the University of Oklahoma, as being made by a public university professor, appearances by public university faculty constituted only 5 of 18 appearances by university professors. Crowe, of course, was hired as a news consultant by ABC because he was a former member of the Joint Chiefs of Staff and presidential adviser, not because of his academic credentials.

The other civilian consultant hired by ABC was Judith Kipper, an employee of the Council on Foreign Relations and the Brookings Institution. She appeared five times in August. Three of the appearances were on same day as Cordesman appeared, assuring that viewers got a big dose of opinion, rather than fact, on those days.

In addition to these civilian analysts, the network anchors depended heavily on these hired military consultants for opinion:

- Retired Admiral William Crowe, ABC's chief military analyst, chairman of the Joint Chiefs of Staff from 1985 to 1989, and a principal military adviser to presidents Reagan and Bush. Crowe has been a professor at the University of Oklahoma since retiring from the military in 1989.

- Retired Lt. Gen. Bernard Trainor, hired by ABC after it became clear that war was inevitable. He was a latecomer to ABC, and didn't appear at all in August. His contract with ABC allowed him to appear on other media, which he did. He appeared on NPR and "MacNeil/Lehrer." Trainor retired from the Marine Corps in 1985 and became the *New York Times'* military correspondent. In 1990, he became the director of the national security program at Harvard University. In addition to working at Harvard, Trainor serves as a director of the Institute for Foreign Policy Analysis, a right-wing think tank in Massachusetts.

- Retired Lt. Gen. William Odom, NBC's chief military analyst, served at the U.S. embassy in Moscow from 1972 to 1974. He was on the NSC staff between 1977 and 1981, and then became the army's assistant chief of staff for intelligence. In 1985, Odom was appointed director of the National Security Agency, the nation's most secretive intelligence agency. After retiring from the U.S. Army in 1988, Odom went to the Hudson Institute, a right-wing think tank that has contracts with the departments of Defense and State.

- Retired Gen. George Crist, CBS's chief military consultant, is a career military man who advanced through the grades with service in Korea, Haiti, Vietnam, and Europe. He was a planner and political adviser during the 1983 U.S. invasion of Grenada. From 1982 to 1984, he was vice director of the joint staff of the Joint Chiefs of Staff and later became Commander-in-Chief, U.S. Central Command. He became a private consultant after retiring from the military.

• Retired Gen. Michael Dugan is another CBS military consultant. He was the air force chief of staff who was fired by defense secretary Dick Cheney for using "poor judgement at a sensitive time" (*Time*, October 1, 1990, 55). Dugan told reporters about U.S. plans to use air power to defeat Iraq and kill Saddam Hussein. The aspects of Dugan's comments that most distressed Cheney were advocacy of bombing Iraqi cities—including downtown Baghdad—and his lack of concern regarding political constraints.

The paid consultants were not the only former military officers who shaped news. The CSIS's William J. Taylor is a retired colonel, as are Harry Summers and "national defense specialist" John M. Collins (NBC–August 9). Collins currently works for the Congressional Research Service, Library of Congress (*Congressional Staff Directory* 1988, 688). Former CIA chief Stansfield Turner (NBC–August 10) is a retired admiral. Overall, retired military officers comprised 25 of the 133 appearances by U.S. news shapers.

The majority of the retired military officers who appeared as news shapers—William Crowe, William J. Taylor, William Odom, Stansfield Turner, Harry Summers, and Bernard Trainor—are members of the Council on Foreign Relations, as are a majority of the consultants and academics who appeared. Judith Kipper, Fouad Ajami, Barry Carter, Robert Lieber, and Edward Said are Council members. Michael C. Hudson, who is not a member, participates in Council functions (see Council on Foreign Relations 1988, 76). Even London School of Economics professor Fred Halliday, who is a British citizen and therefore ineligible for Council membership, has ties to the elite U.S. foreign policy organization. Halliday spoke at the Council on June 12, 1990 (Council on Foreign Relations 1990, 80). And all but two of the former U.S. officials who appeared in August were also Council members.

THE FORMER OFFICIALS

Of the 133 appearances by U.S. news shapers, 34 were by ex-officials. The ex-officials were rarely described as such in their appearances. For example, Richard Murphy was described as a Council on Foreign Relations spokesperson during his 5 appearances. He was never described as a former official. Barry Carter was described as a Georgetown University professor, not as a former NSC member during the Nixon administration. Lawrence Korb (NBC–August 19 and CBS–August 26) and Robert Litan (NBC–August 9) were simply described as Brookings Institution fellows.

Of the 34 appearances by ex–officials and legislators, 4 were by individuals who are clearly Democrats. The Democrats were George McGovern (CBS–August 30), Robert Litan (NBC–August 9), Stansfield Turner (NBC–August 10), and Zbigniew Brzezinski (CBS–August 19). McGovern was called a "prominent Vietnam dove" during his appearance, rather than a former senator or presidential candidate. Brookings' Litan served on President Carter's Council of Economic Advisers from 1977 to 1979, but this wasn't reported by the networks.

The majority of the appearances by ex-officials were by individuals who served in Republican administrations or both Republican and Democratic administrations. The Republicans include Lawrence Korb (NBC–August 19 and CBS–August 26), Lawrence Kudlow (ABC–August 4), and Goeffrey Kemp (ABC–August 6). The three K's—Korb, Kudlow, and Kemp—served in the Reagan administration. James Aikens (CBS–August 15) was a career foreign service officer until being appointed director of the Office of Fuels and Energy in 1968. He was promoted to White House energy adviser in 1972 and ambassador to Saudi Arabia in 1973. Joseph Sisco (CBS–August 10 and 28) also began in the Foreign Service. He was appointed deputy director of the Office of U.N. Political and Security Affairs by President Eisenhower in 1958. Sisco also held several lower-echelon posts in the Kennedy and Johnson administrations. In 1969, President Nixon made him an assistant secretary of state. Sisco left government in 1976.

Most ex-officials are like James Schlesinger, Anthony Cordesman, and Richard Murphy, who began their government careers during the Nixon years but continued in government after Jimmy Carter assumed the presidency. President Nixon appointed Murphy to the post of director of Arabian peninsula affairs in 1970. He later became ambassador to Mauritania and Syria. During Carter's presidency, Murphy was made ambassador to the Philippines. When Ronald Reagan was elected, Murphy became the ambassador to Saudi Arabia and then assistant secretary of state for Near Eastern affairs.

William Quandt (ABC–August 17) also began his career in the Nixon administration. He left the Rand Corporation to become a staffer in President Nixon's NSC. He also served as a senior staff member of the NSC in the Carter administration. Robert Kupperman (NBC–August 18) held several posts in the Nixon and Ford administrations before joining the CSIS. The IIE's Jeffrey Schott worked in the U.S. Treasury Department from 1974 to 1977 and was a delegate to multinational trade talks between 1977 and 1980 and deputy director of the Office of International Energy Policy during President Reagan's first term.

Fred Bergsten followed the opposite path of his IIE colleague Jeffrey Schott. He began his career in a Democratic administration and then worked in a Republican administration. Bergsten began his government career as a State Department economist in 1963. After President Nixon was elected, Bergsten was appointed to the NSC. He served in the NSC until 1971, when he went to the Brookings Institution. Bergsten returned to government in 1977 as the assistant secretary of treasury for international affairs.

Nicholas Veliotes (ABC–August 16 and 24) was described as a former ambassador and former assistant secretary of state during his appearances. Veliotes was a career foreign service officer who was made ambassador to Jordan by President Carter. He was appointed assistant secretary of Near East affairs by President Reagan in 1981 and ambassador to Egypt in 1983.

John Sawhill (NBC–August 23) and Barry Carter (NBC–August 11) also started their political careers in Republican administrations. However, they describe themselves as Democrats. Sawhill was appointed head of the Federal Energy

Administration by President Ford following the Arab oil embargo of 1973-1974. His differences with the Ford administration led to his resignation in 1975. Sawhill returned to government in 1979 as deputy secretary of energy in the Carter administration.

Barry Carter (NBC–August 11) joined the government in 1969 as a program analyst in the Defense Department. In 1970, he was appointed to the NSC. He later served as a counsel to the U.S. Senate Select Committee on Intelligence and as a foreign policy adviser to the Mondale-Ferraro presidential campaign.

OTHER SOURCES OF INFORMATION

Viewers who preferred Dan Rather or Tom Brokaw to Peter Jennings still had many opportunities to hear the wisdom of ABC's Middle East sages—Anthony Cordesman, Judith Kipper, and William Crowe. These news shapers appeared on a variety of news programs in addition to "World News Tonight." If viewers watched the special ABC telecast of President Bush's addresses on August 8 and August 22, they would have seen and heard Admiral Crowe. If viewers tuned to the ABC News specials of August 2, August 16, August 23, or August 28, they would have seen and heard Judith Kipper. If they missed Kipper on these occasions, they could have caught her by watching "Nightline" on August 1, August 3, August 6, or August 8. If they missed Admiral Crowe during the regular newscasts or the news special, viewers could have heard him on "Nightline" on August 2, August 6, or August 17. Viewers who missed one or more of Anthony Cordesman's five appearances on ABC's "World News Tonight" had the opportunity to make up for it by watching "Nightline" on August 1 or August 24.

Viewers who watched Kipper, Crowe, or Cordesman on "Nightline" also encountered the other oft-appearing pundits. Viewers who heard Judith Kipper on August 6 also heard retired Col. Harry Summers and Andrew Duncan, another representative of the IISS. Crowe appeared with Edward Luttwak on "Nightline" on August 17. Ex–secretaries of state Henry Kissinger and Alexander Haig, two of Ted Koppel's favorite guests (Hoynes and Croteau 1989), appeared with Cordesman on August 24.

"Nightline" featured a Georgetown university professor review on August 3. Koppel interviewed professors Robert Lieber and Michael Hudson. On August 7, "Nightline" showcased retired CIA chiefs Stansfield Turner and Richard Helms. On August 9, it was Arab think tank night. Kamel Abu Jaber and Mohammed Sid-Ahmed appeared. When the "Nightline" and evening news appearances of these "representatives" of the Arab world are combined, they accounted for nine network television appearances in the month of August. Lawrence Korb was the only think tank analyst who appeared on August 29, but "Nightline" did feature other think tank spokesmen two nights later. PIRINC president John Lichtblau, the IIE's Philp Verleger, and the Worldwatch Institute's Christopher Flavin appeared on August 31.

CBS usually turned to Fouad Ajami and George Crist for analyses during their news specials and late night news reports. NBC used far fewer news shapers during its news specials than the other two networks, but when it did use news shapers, they were always the usual suspects—Charles DiBona, William J. Taylor, Edward Said, and Richard Murphy. During the evening newscasts, just as in news specials, NBC used fewer news shapers than did the other two networks. Of the 194 news shapers who appeared in August, 77 appeared on CBS, 66 appeared on ABC, and 51 appeared on NBC.

Many analysts who appeared on the three television networks also appeared on CNN. Retired admirals Stansfield Turner (August 24) and Eugene Carroll (August 18 and 22) appeared on CNN, as did retired colonel turned CSIS scholar William J. Taylor (August 31). Anyone who missed one or more of Richard Murphy's five network news appearances had an opportunity to catch him on CNN on August 30.

Viewers who missed Washington Institute for Near East Policy analyst Hirsch Goodman on ''World News Tonight'' had the opportunity to catch his colleague Seth Carus on CNN on August 29 and August 30. Brookings' Elisa Harris was on CNN the first day that Carus appeared, and the Carnegie Endowment's Peter Zimmerman was on the second day. Despite these appearances, CNN tended to use a much wider array of news shapers than did the three television networks. People who never appeared on network television managed to find their way onto CNN. Even though different faces appeared on CNN, analysts from liberal publications such as *Mother Jones* and the *Nation*, professors from public universities, and analysts from liberal think tanks like the World Policy Institute and Institute for Policy Studies were virtually absent from the cable network, just as they were absent from the three broadcast networks.

Network television and CNN completely neglected analysts associated with the Institute for Policy Studies and World Policy Institute, but newspaper reporters weren't exactly beating down their doors, either. A Data Times computer analysis of the *San Francisco Chronicle, Chicago Tribune, Washington Post, Cleveland Plain Dealer, Dallas Morning News,* and Minneapolis *Star Tribune* indicates that print reporters went to the same sources as network television reporters for expert opinion. A search of articles that appeared in these newspapers between August 2, 1990 and February 25, 1991 shows that Brookings Institution analysts expressed their opinions 440 times, CSIS analysts sounded off 126 times, and Rand Corporation spokespersons provided analyses 112 times. By contrast, World Policy Institute analysts were cited 3 times and Institute for Policy Studies analysts were quoted 26 times. Except for the lengths of the quotes, newspapers provided readers with nothing different than what they received from television. Newspaper readers and televison viewers were exposed to the same news shapers.

10

WASHINGTON REPORTERS: THE POWER ELITE

Veteran reporter James Doyle (1990) characterized Washington reporters as a "moneyed elite," but these journalists are more accurately described as a group within the "power elite." Research suggests that a power elite, which is comprised of a relatively small number of Americans, collectively debates and establishes U.S. government policy. This power elite, according to C. Wright Mills (1956) and G. William Domhoff (1970), includes many of the United States' wealthiest individuals but is not restricted to a traditional upper class or aristocracy.

Members of the power elite have much higher incomes than the typical citizen, making them appear as a moneyed elite, but they are socially and psychologically different from other wealthy citizens who are not members of the power elite. For example, many physicians and small businessmen have incomes equal to or higher than those of Washington reporters, but the physicians and businessmen are not likely to be members of the power elite. According to Mills, members of the power elite are "self-conscious members of a social class. People are either accepted into this class or they are not, and there is a qualitative split, rather than merely a numerical scale, separating them from those that are not elite" (1956, 11).

While referred to as a class, the power elite is not a class in the traditional sense. It consists of networks "whose members know one another, see one another socially and at business, and so, in making decisions, take one another into account" (Mills 1956, 11). Members of the power elite are members of the same organizations and cliques, attend the same parties and social gatherings, and are alumni of the same private universities—"the MIT–Harvard–Yale–Columbia–Princeton–Johns Hopkins–University of Chicago complex," as Domhoff (1970, 254) called it. The leaders of the journalism pack, the prestige reporters, belong to many of the same clubs and have degrees from the same universities as others in the power elite. Prestige reporters like William Beecher and Sanford Ungar are members of Washington's Harvard Club; Leslie Stahl is a trustee of her alma mater, Williams College; and Leslie Gelb is a trustee of his alma mater, Tufts University; and Beecher, Ungar, and Gelb, like many prestige journalists, are members of the Council on Foreign Relations, the most important of the elite organizations (Domhoff 1970, 1990).

Washington reporters, as Sen. Daniel Patrick Moynihan noted, are "Ivy Leaguers. . . . Journalism has become, if not an elite profession, a profession attracted to elites. This is noticeably so in Washington, where the upper reaches of journalism constitute one of the most important and enduring *social* elites in the city" (1973, 319). Hess corrected Moynihan's analysis, observing instead that

nearly 35 percent of the Washington press corps attended colleges or universities rated as highly selective, a category that includes, in addition to the Ivy League, such other institutions as Amherst, Brandeis, Bryn Mawr, Carleton, the University of Chicago, Haverford, Johns Hopkins, Massachusetts Institute of Technology, Mount Holyoke, Oberlin, Reed, Rice, Smith, Stanford, Swathmore, Wellesley, Wesleyan, and Williams. (1981, 117)

The 35 percent who attended these colleges invariably work for the prestige press.

Although most power elite members come from families who previously had members in the power elite, the power elite is not a caste that excludes individuals because of their birth. Individuals who have worked their way to the top in the military, business, politics, or the press can become members of the elite group. The children of upper-middle-class families who attend the "right schools" and make the "right contacts" also have an opportunity to become members of the power elite. As Domhoff observed, self-made millionaires and successful businessmen can become members of exclusive social clubs and organizations if they have "the right manners and attitudes" (1970, 31). The right manners and attitudes, organizational memberships, and group contacts are prerequisites for joining—and remaining—a member of the power elite.

However, it is much more difficult to become a member of the power elite if one is not born a member. If an individual is not born into the elite, attendance at the "right schools" and knowing the right people will not by themselves bring an individual into the power elite. An invitation from an established member of the elite is necessary. Henry Kissinger was brought into the power elite by McGeorge Bundy, who was his mentor at Harvard (Domhoff 1970, 119). Kissinger, in turn, brought William Hyland into the power elite.

Individuals who did not attend the "right schools" or who do not have the "right backgrounds" can ascend into the power elite, but they are usually promoted to it only after putting in long and distinguished apprenticeships in the bureaucracies that serve the elite. Retired Lt. Gen. Bernard Trainor worked his way through the ranks to become a member of the power elite; he was not born a member. Trainor attended the College of the Holy Cross and the University of Colorado, not Princeton, Yale, or Harvard. He joined the U.S. Marines in 1951 and was eventually promoted to Lieutenant General. His teaching at military colleges and his authorship of *History of the United States Marines Corps* (1968) eventually attracted the attention of the elite. He was hired at the *New York Times* as a military correspondent after retiring from the U.S. Marines in 1985. He became a director of the Institute for Foreign Policy Analysis and the head of the national security program at Harvard University's John F. Kennedy School of Government in 1990.

William Hyland also worked his way up through the bureaucracy, but in the CIA rather than the military. Hyland received his undergraduate degree at Washington University in St. Louis, served in the U.S. Army from 1950 to 1952, and then did graduate work at the University of Kansas City. He joined the CIA in 1954 and put in 15 years there before being appointed to the staff of the NSC in 1969. Hyland quickly moved up in the federal bureaucracy with the assistance of Henry Kissinger.

The long apprenticeships of Trainor and Hyland can be contrasted with the quick ascendancies of individuals with the "right upbringing." Cambridge-born Robert Hunter worked as a management intern with the Department of the Navy even before he received his B.A. degree from Wesleyan University in 1962. After graduating from Wesleyan, Hunter received a Fulbright Scholarship and then served as a White House assistant during 1964-1965. From there, Hunter went to the IISS as a research associate and then to the London School of Economics for a doctorate. After returning from London in 1970, he was named a senior fellow at the Overseas Development Council and a lecturer at Johns Hopkins University and in 1973 became Sen. Edward Kennedy's foreign policy adviser. Hunter became a senior staff member of the NSC in 1977.

Like Hunter, Richard Holbrooke began his rise from within the power elite. He received his B.A. from Brown University in 1962, served as a foreign service officer from 1963 to 1969 in Vietnam and Paris, and then went to Princeton for a Ph.D. After completing his doctorate in 1970, Holbrooke was appointed head of the Peace Corps in Morocco. He then became a Carnegie fellow and managing editor of *Foreign Policy* magazine.

Robert Litan's ascendancy was even quicker. He received a B.S. in economics from the University of Pennsylvania's Wharton School in 1972 and immediately became a research assistant at the Brookings Institution. Litan then served as an energy consultant to the National Academy of Sciences, received master's and law degrees from Yale in 1977, and was next appointed to President Carter's Council of Economic Advisers. Litan, Holbrooke, and Hunter are frequently quoted news shapers.

The same patterns of ascendancy are found among members of the elite press. Individuals with the right pedigree move up very quickly, while those from more humble origins put in long apprenticeships. Daniel Schorr graduated from City College in New York and then worked as an assistant editor with the Jewish Telegraphic Agency from 1934 to 1941. He was employed by Aneta News Agency until 1943, when he joined the U.S. Army. After the war, Schorr worked as a freelance reporter for the *Christian Science Monitor, London Daily Mail,* and *New York Times.* In 1955, he secured a job as CBS's Moscow correspondent.

Like Schorr, Michael Getler graduated from City College. He began his journalism career as a reporter for American Aviation Publications, where he worked from 1961 to 1968. Getler then worked for Ziff-Davis Publications, winning an award from the Aviation/Space Writers Association in 1969. The following year he was hired by the *Washington Post* as a defense correspondent.

Jack Germond also worked his way up. He graduated from the University of Missouri in 1951 and then worked for the *Evening News* in Monroe, Michigan. In 1953 he went to work for Gannett Newspapers as a reporter. In 1969 he became head of Gannett's Washington bureau and in 1974 the political editor of the *Washington Star.* When the *Star* went under in 1981, Germond went to the *Baltimore Sun.*

By contrast, William Beecher graduated from Harvard University in 1955 with a B.A., pursued graduate studies at Columbia University during 1956, and then went to work at the *St. Louis Globe-Democrat.* In 1959 he moved to Washington, D.C., as a reporter for Fairchild publications, and in 1960 he became the *Wall Street Journal's* Washington correspondent. Hedrick Smith graduated from Williams College in 1955 and went to Balliol College, Oxford, for graduate studies in 1955-1956. When he returned to the United States, Smith joined the Air Force, and upon being discharged in 1959, he went to work for United Press International. In 1962, he went to work for the *New York Times.*

Bob Woodward's ascent in journalism was even quicker. Woodward graduated from Yale in 1965, served in the navy from 1966 to 1970, worked as a reporter for the *Montgomery County Sentinel* for a year, and then joined the *Washington Post.* Sanford Ungar worked as a stringer for the *Boston Globe* while studying at Harvard. He then pursued a graduate degree at the London School of Economics and worked as a stringer for *Time.* After completing his graduate degree, Ungar went to work for United Press International in Paris and then became a *Newsweek* correspondent. In 1969, he joined the *Washington Post.*

Although it was possible for individuals like Schorr and Germond to move into positions at prestige media after long apprenticeships with nonprestige media, there are indications that upward mobility is becoming increasingly difficult for reporters without the "right credentials." The salaries of Washington reporters have soared during the last two decades, making reporting a more desirable occupation for individuals born into the upper classes. As John Herbers noted, "the prevailing orientation of Washington journalists began to change from populist-working middle class to moneyed elite in the early seventies. It took well into the eighties to be fully evident" (Doyle 1990).

Long apprenticeships are now a detriment to becoming a Washington reporter, not a stepping stone. Most reporters begin their Washington careers during their twenties or thirties. Hess (1981) found that 57.7 percent of Washington journalists began their Washington reporting careers while in their twenties, and 33.5 percent began their careers while in their thirties. Less than 10 percent of Washington reporters started in the capital when 40 years of age or older. A follow-up study of Washington-based regional reporters also found Washington reporting to be "a calling without senior citizens" (Hess 1991, 62).

REPORTERS AND NEWS SHAPERS

Previous research on the power elite (Mills 1956; Domhoff 1970) is enormously useful for explaining why prestige reporters, who set the standards followed by nonprestige reporters, ceaselessly turn to the same group of news shapers when policy issues are being reported: The news shapers, like the reporters who use them, are members of the power elite. The prestige reporters can identify the elite news shapers because "they move in packs with the affluent and powerful in Washington (just doing their job, of course), then swarm with them in summer to every agreeable spot on the Eastern seaboard between Canada and New Jersey," as Hodding Carter III (1984b, 25) observed. That is, prestige reporters are part of the power elite's political, economic, and social networks. The research also explains why these reporters seek out the views of political leaders, corporate chieftains, and the top brass of the military, but not the views of labor union spokespersons, members of grassroots political organizations, or minorities (Whitney, et al. 1989; Hoynes and Croteau 1989). Political leaders, corporate heads, and military chiefs are members of the power elite; labor organizers, political activists, and minority spokespersons are not.

Besides being part of the network of the power elite, prestige reporters are also part of Washington's revolving door, which moves elite members from one part of the elite network to the other. Reporters become think tank analysts, government officials, or professors, government officials become think tank analysts, professors, and reporters, and think tank analysts become reporters, professors, and government officials.

Typical of those in the revolving door are Leslie Gelb, Robin Wright, Jeane Kirkpatrick, David Gergen, and Robert Hormats. Gelb taught at Wesleyan University and was a Defense Department official, senior fellow at the Brookings Institution, senior associate at the Carnegie Endowment, and reporter for the *New York Times* before becoming an editorial page editor at the *Times*. Wright was a reporter for the *Washington Post* and *Christian Science Monitor*, a visiting scholar at Duke University, a Poynter fellow at Yale University, and a Carnegie Endowment fellow before joining the *Los Angeles Times*. Kirkpatrick has served as a Georgetown University professor, Reagan administration official, AEI senior fellow, and syndicated columnist. Gergen has been in and out of Republican administrations, a lecturer at Harvard University, an AEI fellow, and an editor at the *U.S. News and World Report*. Hormats was a Nixon administration official, guest scholar at the Brookings Institution, visiting lecturer at Princeton University, and vice president at Goldman Sachs.

Most people in Washington don't walk through as many doors as Gelb, Kirkpatrick, or Gergen, but there is a high degree of movement nonetheless. William Beecher went from the *New York Times* into the Defense Department and then to the *Boston Globe*. While serving as the military correspondent for the *Times*, Beecher was also a captain in the army reserve. Sanford Ungar left NPR to become a Carnegie Endowment fellow and then became a professor and dean at American University. Ben Wattenberg worked under President Johnson and Sens. Hubert Humphrey and Henry Jackson and became an AEI senior fellow and writer for the *U.S. News and World Report*. Hedrick Smith was a resident at the AEI between stints as a reporter.

Gordon Adams (1981), Domhoff (1990), and other researchers have suggested that the revolving door is an integral part of maintaining stability within the power elite. The revolving door reduces uncertainty among different groups in the power elite by allowing one group in the elite to see and understand the problems confronted by others. This reduces uncertainties and tensions that can arise between different elite groups. The movement between groups creates common bonds, common understandings, and additional contacts that strengthen the power elite. The result is the integration of the press, government, and other elite institutions "into a stable power structure that is not easily displaced" (Domhoff 1990, 21).

By viewing Washington insiders and pack-leading Washington journalists as members of the power elite, one also understands why the nation's capital functions as a closed circle: Members of the elite are "self-conscious members of a social class" who insulate themselves "from those that are not elite" and "take one another into account" when making decisions (Mills 1956, 11). The closed circle produces a conventional wisdom with narrow parameters. Hodding Carter III noted that, because of

the closed circle in the nation's capital, intelligence for pundit and politician alike is defined by the ability to echo conventional wisdom in well-turned phrases that neither disturb nor illuminate. People who are widely known as political geniuses around the city earned their reputations by resolutely refusing to embrace any new idea or cause before its time. To be considered unconventional, eccentric or "extreme" is more to be feared in these circles than to be proved wrong. (1984a, 31)

Carter's description is consistent with the theory of the power elite and clearly observable in practice. The description is consistent with the theory because members of the power elite are the primary beneficiaries of the status quo. Members of the status quo are not receptive to ideas that are radical or extreme, either from the left or right, because such ideas advocate changes in the status quo. This explains why the conventional wisdom is always center-right and why organizations either further to the right, such as the Heritage Foundation, or further to the left, such as the Institute for Policy Studies, provide far fewer news shapers than "Republican centrist" groups like the AEI or Brookings Institution. Simply stated, the status quo is near the middle, and so are most prestige journalists, as Hess (1981) noted. These journalists "have made it in modern America—ostentatiously, gloriously and rewardingly—and they are not about to play Samson in the temple" (Carter 1984a, 31).

This does not suggest that prestige reporters will always seek out center-right news shapers because they are political conservatives who favor the status quo. On the contrary, many reporters are undoubtedly self-described "liberals," as Lichter, Rothman, and Lichter (1986) contend. However, even these "liberals" subscribe to Washington's conventional wisdom, which capital-based news shapers dish out. The reporters accept the conventional wisdom because they are in a different world—socially and geographically—than the rest of America. As members of the power elite, they are socially separate from the nonelite. As Washingtonians, they live in a "city [that] has no white working class, no industries, no factories. . . . The normal stresses of American life are barely visible here, and apply mostly to the black population on the other side of town" (Doyle 1990).

Conservative, or more accurately "Republican centrist," news shapers dominate opinion because they dominate discourse in Washington. This is the outgrowth of having had Republican administrations for 18 of the past 24 years. As a consequence, if "liberal" reporters want to take the opinions of their elite peers into account when writing a story, as Mills (1956) contends members of the power elite do, their news reports will inevitably contain many conservative, but few liberal, opinions.

Not only do Washington reporters take elite news shapers into account when seeking analyses, but so do administration officials, congressional leaders, and virtually everyone else in Washington. When administration officials seek policy advice, they turn to the same think tanks and private universities that reporters turn to for news shapers. As the AEI's 1987 *Annual Report* noted, "AEI's scholars are extensively involved in Washington's policy debates. They are sought by congressional committees, cabinet secretaries and the president for their advice and counsel" (p. 2). These institutions also provide the government with appointees, and the government and prestige press provide think tanks and elite universities with "visiting scholars."

The same news shapers also dominate Washington forums, discussion groups, and congressional testimony. For example, the majority of those who testified before the Senate Foreign Relations Committee during December 1990 concerning U.S. policy in the Persian Gulf were the same individuals who shaped news coverage of the crisis: the AEI's Richard Perle, the CSIS's Robert Hunter and Zbigniew Brzezinski, Carnegie's Geoffrey Kemp, Georgetown University's Michael Hudson, Brookings' William Quandt and Judith Kipper, Harvard University's Laurie Mylroie, the Center for Security Policy's Frank Gaffney, and ex-ambassador Nicholas Veliotes (U.S. Senate 1990). However, the Senate committee heard testimony from individuals that the networks and prestige media did not use to shape gulf news: George McGovern, Arthur Schlesinger, Jr., and John Kenneth Galbraith.

The degree to which the power elite take their members into account and exclude the opinions of non-elite members is clear from an analysis of their books, speeches, and writings. Their writings and speeches are replete with citations and quotations from members of the power elite, but devoid of citations from anyone else. A book edited by Johns Hopkins University professor Simon Serfaty, titled *The Media and Foreign Policy* (1990), exemplifies the closed circle among the power elite. The book, which claims to address important questions concerning press-government relations in the making of foreign policy, consists entirely of chapters written by members of the elite press, think tank denizens, private university professors, and former government officials. Its contributors include former Reagan officials and advisers Kenneth Adelman, Richard Burt, David Gergen, Michael Ledeen, Robert MacFarlane, Robert Oakley, and William Odom. At the time of the book's publication, Adelman was national editor of the *Washingtonian* magazine, Burt was national security correspondent for the *New York Times*, Gergen was editor of the *U.S. News and World Report,* Ledeen was at the AEI, MacFarlane was at the CSIS, Oakley was with the Carnegie Endowment, and Odom was an adjunct professor of political science at Yale University and a fellow at the Hudson Institute. All of the other contributors were former lecturers or fellows at Johns Hopkins, Harvard, Duke, or Georgetown, fellows at the Brookings Institution or Carnegie Endowment, or former and current reporters for the *Washington Post,* the *New York Times,* the *U.S. News and World Report,* or NPR. Although it purports to be a study of the news media and government, the book does not discuss the revolving door between the press, think tanks, private universities, and government.

CONVENTIONAL WISDOM

Carter's (1984a) contention that the "political geniuses" around Washington "have earned their reputations by resolutely refusing to embrace any new cause or idea before its time" is supported by this study. The news shapers used by Washington reporters come from pro–status quo institutions; experts from anti-status quo institutions are never interviewed. When the topic is the Soviet Union, Eastern Europe, and the future of European socialism, analysts like Robert Legvold of Columbia University's Harriman Institute are used by elite reporters as news shapers. Experts like Bogdan Denitch are not. Denitch, a City University of New York professor, is author of *The Legitimation of a Revolution: The Yugoslav Case* (1976), *The Socialist Debate* (1990), *The End of the Cold War* (1990), and *Limits and Possibilities: The Crisis of Yugoslavian Socialism and State Socialist Systems* (1990) and editor of *Opinion-making Elites in Yugoslavia* (1973) and *Legitimation of Regimes* (1977).

The reason why elite reporters go to Legvold but not Denitch for analysis cannot be attributed to geographic convenience. Legvold and Denitch both teach in New York City. If anything, the City University of New York's Graduate Center on Forty-second Street is closer to the network television studios and the *New York Times* building than is Columbia University. It cannot be attributed to their academic accomplishments, because Denitch has written more books than Legvold. The answer is that Legvold is a member of elite institutions such as the Council on Foreign Relations and Columbia University, which are the repositories of conventional wisdom. Denitch is the opposite. He is a member of anti-elite institutions, those challenging conventional wisdom. Denitch is a member of Democratic Socialists of America and an editor of *Dissent* magazine.

The elite media's reliance on news shapers who espouse conventional wisdom does not guarantee that the wisdom is either accurate or even consistent, because conventional wisdom in Washington can change quickly. For example, Iraq's invasion of Kuwait rapidly changed the conventional wisdom. Until the invasion, Washington experts contended that Saddam Hussein was a trustworthy and practical, albeit ruthless, politician. This conventional wisdom was promoted by Harvard University professors Daniel Pipes and Laurie Mylroie and CSIS senior fellow Frederick Axelgard. Pipes and Mylroie wrote articles calling for closer U.S.-Iraq ties, and Axelgard wrote a book titled *A New Iraq?* (1988), which argued that "there is a new Iraq, more stable in its leadership, stronger and more united, wiser and better balanced in foreign policy" than before the Iran-Iraq war (*CSIS Publications* 1989). These monumental errors of analysis didn't stop reporters from going to the CSIS, Pipes, or Mylroie for "expert analysis" after Iraq's invasion of Kuwait. In fact, Mylroie, who is also a fellow at the Washington Institute for Near East Policy, was more frequently quoted after the invasion than before. She was cited only three times in the *Washington Post, Los Angeles Times*, and *San Francisco Chronicle* between January 1, 1988 and August 31, 1990, but 22 times between September 1, 1990, and April 1, 1991.

Reporters for these and other prestige newspapers repeatedly turned to her for expert analysis because she had the "right credentials"—a Harvard professorship and a think tank title—and was coauthor of a book, *Saddam Hussein and the Crisis in the Gulf* (1990), which she wrote with *New York Times* editor Judith Miller. The book was written in three weeks and was designed to cash in on the Gulf crisis. It lacked an index and citations but was nevertheless reviewed in the *New York Times Book Review* and the *New York Review of Books*. Not surprisingly, the *New York Times* review (November 11, 1990) concluded that the book was "a frequently riveting account of how Saddam Hussein, ruthless visionary that he is, has driven his country and manipulated much of the world to satisfy his grandiose ambitions" (p. 7). The conclusion is not surprising given that the book was coauthored by a *New York Times* editor. By contrast, a review in *Business Week* (November 26, 1990) concluded that the book was "largely a synthesis of others' work" (p. 12).

In the book, Miller and Mylroie describe Saddam Hussein as a vicious, "xenophobic" dictator. They excoriate the policy toward Iraq that was pursued by the United States for several years before the August invasion and decry President Bush for not "talk[ing] straight to the American people" about why the United States was in the Gulf. While criticizing Hussein and the U.S. preinvasion policy, the book never mentions that Mylroie was one of Hussein's U.S. apologists and an advocate of close U.S.–Iraq ties. With Daniel Pipes, Mylroie wrote "It's Time for a U.S. 'Tilt.' Back Iraq" for the *New Republic* (1987). The article suggested that the United States supply "remotely scatterable and anti-personnel mines, and counterartillery radar" to Iraq, along with increased credits, reduced tariffs, and upgraded intelligence. Such actions could lead to "a more fruitful relationship in the longer term," these "experts" argued. This view can be contrasted with those expressed in the book:

Giving Iraq the benefit of the doubt has been the result of a curious blend of cynicism and naivete on Washington's part . . . Washington overlooked human rights and other abuses and persuaded itself that what for Saddam was a temporary and tactical political repositioning was, in effect, a basic shift in his orientation and objectives.

In an article in *Orbis,* the publication of the rightist Foreign Policy Research Institute, Mylroie (1988) didn't argue that Saddam Hussein's human rights abuses should prevent closer U.S.—Iraq ties; she argued the opposite. Mylroie listed numerous reasons why the United States needed to cultivate better relations with Iraq: Saddam Hussein's widespread domestic support, his support for the status quo, Iraq's oil pricing policy, its large oil reserves and support for the U.S. military presence in the Persian Gulf.

William Paterson College professor Stephen Shalom documented Mylroie's about-face in a February 25, 1991, article in the *Nation.* He concluded that Mylroie "didn't just misjudge Iraq. She served as an apologist for and supporter of Saddam Hussein, a man whom after the invasion of Kuwait she presented as eternally evil" (p. 243). Shalom's documentation left little doubt about Mylroie's expertise, but it apparently had no effect on elite reporters. She continued to be a source of wisdom for reporters even after Shalom's article appeared in print (see *New York Times,* March 21, 1991, 2, and Minneapolis *Star Tribune*, March 31, 1991, 10A). Her "right credentials" overshadowed her mistakes.

While repeatedly seeking out the analyses of Laurie Mylroie, Judith Kipper, Fred Halliday, and others with debatable expertise, reporters somehow neglected the analyses of leading Iraq scholars such as Marion Farouk-Sluglett and Peter Sluglett. Marion Farouk-Sluglett and Peter Sluglett wrote *Iraq since 1958: From Revolution to Dictatorship* (1987), and Peter Sluglett wrote *Britain in Iraq* (1980). The two books are considered important works of scholarship about Iraq. A review in *Choice* magazine (March 1988) described *Iraq since 1958* as a "well-written history from two fine scholars" (p. 1158). Farouk-Sluglett and her husband are with the School of Oriental Studies at Durham University, not the London School of Economics, where Fred Halliday teaches. In contrast to the London School, Durham isn't perceived to be an "elite" institution. Few, if any, members of the U.S. power elite receive their educations there. This might explain the absence of analyses from the Slugletts in the prestige press.

THE PROBLEM

Washington journalists have demonstrated that they are as trustworthy in selecting news shapers as disc jockeys were in selecting records to air during the 1950s. One of the broadcasting scandals of the 1950s concerned the power that disc jockeys exercised over the exposure and consequent popularity of popular recordings. Records repeatedly aired were likely to become hits, while records that were neglected never made it onto the charts. The power that disc jockeys had in making and breaking records led record companies to pay disc jockeys for playing their recordings. This practice became known as "payola."

During congressional hearings concerning payola, disc jockeys admitted to accepting payments for airing records but saw nothing wrong with the practice. WILD-AM disc jockey Stan Richards compared payola to politicians' accepting campaign contributions. The contributors give "in the hope that something good will happen," but it doesn't mean that the recipient of the gift has been influenced (Barnouw 1970, 125).

In 1960, Congress banned payola and radio broadcasters revised their system of selecting records to play on their stations. The power of record selection was taken away from disc jockeys and placed in the hands of program directors, whose activities could be monitored easily. Disc jockeys were thereafter required to select and play records from their station's playlist, which was compiled by a program director.

Journalists, like the disc jockeys of the 1950s, see nothing wrong with the current method of selecting experts. This myopia exists despite evidence that the most frequently used "experts" are often wrong, say little of consequence, represent a very narrow range of views, and have political axes to grind. The political axes of the news shapers are rarely revealed to news consumers, unless the news shaper is politically liberal.

Journalists, like the disc jockeys of the 1950s, raise some individuals to prominence, while neglecting others. Individuals who are raised to prominence can and do negotiate lucrative book deals, promote their books, receive consulting contracts, sell magazine and newspaper articles, and receive pay for speeches. The opportunities that are available to leading news shapers has led some to exaggerate their credentials and others to manufacture their credentials.

In Southern California, the leading "military and defense expert" was Andy Lightbody, who reportedly made 2,100 radio and television appearances, where he discussed the arms race, new weapons technology, and the conflict with Iraq. He was also widely quoted by print journalists, including reporters for the *Los Angeles Times*. During the Gulf conflict, he appeared almost hourly on KNX-AM, a CBS-owned radio station, and "on other CBS radio network stations around the country" (Pinsky 1991). He was hired by Fox's KTTV Channel 11 to provide nightly analysis about the Gulf war. The prominence that Lightbody received as a result of his shaping gulf war news allowed him to charge $2,000 for speaking engagements.

According to Lightbody's résumé, he was a graduate of Loyola University, a former air force officer, and author of articles and books on military hardware. In reality, Lightbody's degree was from the University of Beverly Hills, "a defunct, never-accredited institution," and he was never in the U.S. Air Force, although he had once been an ROTC cadet. The highest aviation certificate that he attained was a student pilot's license, and the books and articles that he produced were "picture books and magazines—some published by his father-in-law—full of Pentagon and defense contractors' handouts" (Pinsky 1991).

Lightbody made over 2,000 broadcast appearances and provided innumerable quotes to print reporters before *Los Angeles Times* reporter Mark Pinsky decided to investigate Lightbody's credentials. Pinsky's investigative article, titled " 'Military Expert' Has Gap in his Credentials" (1991), revealed that Lightbody had fabricated his credentials. After the exposé was published, KNX-AM terminated its contract with Lightbody, and reporters who previously believed Lightbody to be one of the country's leading military experts shunned him.

The case of Andy Lightbody is less of an aberration than it appears. The country's most frequently cited Middle East expert, Judith Kipper, also has a gap in her credentials. Kipper served as an ABC News consultant, and appeared on "Nightline," CNN's "Newsmaker Sunday," the "MacNeil/Lehrer NewsHour," and NPR. She was quoted 28 times in the *San Francisco Chronicle,* Minneapolis *Star Tribune, Washington Post,* Cleveland *Plain Dealer, Dallas Morning News,* and *Chicago Tribune* between August 2, 1990, and February 25, 1991. Kipper became a leading expert even though she "doesn't speak Hebrew or Arabic" and "has never written anything on the region much longer than an op-ed," according to David Segal (1991). Her credentials came from "making a number of trips to the Middle East" and knowing the right people—CBS's Walter Cronkite, AEI's William Baroody, and ABC's Peter Jennings. These contacts allowed Kipper to become the country's preeminent Mideast "expert" without having any "political, academic, diplomatic, or military experience in the Middle East" (Segal 1991).

Unfortunately for the news consuming public, the "experts" with dubious credentials are about as accurate in their assessments as the "usual suspects" who dominate foreign affairs discussions. Not one "expert" who commented about the Gulf crisis predicted the rapid collapse of the Iraqi army or the popular uprisings against Saddam Hussein in the Shiite south and Kurdish north. These pundits left the American public unprepared for what eventually unfolded. Even the U.S. government, which relied on many of the same pundits for advice, was left unprepared. When President Bush called on the Iraqi citizenry to overthrow Saddam Hussein, he was apparently unaware that Iraqis would heed his call. They did, and thousands died as a result.

The foreign policy pundits who shaped news about the gulf crisis couldn't have been more wrong. Zbigniew Brzezinski advised CNN viewers that the United States would get "bogged down in a protracted mess in the Middle East." He predicted that the Iraqis would use chemical weapons when war broke out. Using a "sophisticated" computer model, Brookings' Joshua Epstein determined that U.S. casualties would be between 3,300 and 16,000. That was less than the 20,000 casualties that Brzezinski predicted. The CSIS's Edward Luttwak boldly asserted that Gen. Norman Schwarzkopf and other army generals were not competent to wage an air war. He predicted that under the best of circumstances, the United States would sustain several thousand casualties. James Schlesinger argued that a diplomatic solution to the Gulf crisis was necessary because an embargo wouldn't work. The embargo would fail, he insisted, because other nations would cheat. Schlesinger, like the other experts, predicted that Arab public opinion would turn against the United States. In an article in the *New Republic*, Jacob Weisberg (1991) described these pundits as "Gulfballs" and awarded them such prizes as "Best Fictional Screenplay" and "Best Stunt Work" for their predictions.

WHAT CAN BE DONE?

Because reporters repeatedly turn to the same individuals and institutions for expertise, have failed to get a diversity of opinions, and have even gone to bogus experts for analysis, the responsibility for selecting news shapers should be assigned to news organizations, not individual reporters. Just as the responsibility for selecting radio station playlists is now vested with program directors instead of disc jockeys, so too should the responsibility for locating experts be vested with competent, trained individuals. News organizations should assign the task of finding news shapers to their librarian, who can maintain a constantly changing and updated file of experts that journalists can draw upon. Librarians, unlike journalists, are trained to find and evaluate publications that news shapers have written and find and examine reviews of their books. Librarians are capable of using biographical and publication indexes, which are needed to evaluate news shapers' credentials. Most journalists lack the skills to do this type of backgrounding, but even if they have the skills, they lack the time to do the research.

Assigning the responsibility for backgrounding, selecting, and locating experts to librarians has advantages for the public and reporter. First, it would reduce pack journalism and increase the diversity of voices. Journalists, unlike librarians, rely primarily upon other journalists and mass media articles to locate "experts." This invariably produces pack journalism. Few journalists have used or even heard of data bases, such as RLIN or OCLC, that most librarians know and use. These data bases can be used for locating experts, and other reference materials can be used for backgrounding them.

Second, librarians would not be interviewing or otherwise rubbing shoulders with news shapers and are therefore less likely to become source-dependent, as some journalists have become. Many reporters have cultivated a small group of sources on whom they have become reliant. Because librarians have little or no contact with the sources, they are unlikely to say, "I just trust [Norman Ornstein's] judgement. If I were going to buy a used car I'd call him," as *Los Angeles Times* reporter Robert Shogun said (Waldman 1986, 37).

Third, having the librarian select and locate experts would eliminate a task that many reporters find burdensome and difficult. Some reporters claim that finding experts is a difficult task and, because reporters face deadlines, they cannot "beat the bushes and launch a search of the city or the country for them," as Sam Donaldson (1990) put it. Having the librarian do the search would save the reporter time. Moreover, the reporter would not need to explain to an editor why the news shaper was used, if he or she were not one of the same, familiar faces.

Finally, it assigns responsibility to a specific individual or group. At the present time, no reporter can be held responsible for pack journalism or the use of questionable experts, because most reporters go to the same small group of news shapers for wisdom. Pack journalism disperses responsibility rather than making individuals accountable for their work.

More important than finding and using a diverse group of bona fide experts is the need to cut back on their use. During the past decade, there has been a threefold increase in the use of news shapers on network newscasts, indicating that techniques of reportage have changed during the past decade. Television reporters go more frequently to "experts" today than they did a decade ago. In the 1979-1980 sample of network newscasts, only 88 news shapers appeared. This was 1 news shaper per three newscasts. In the 1987-1988 sample, there were 260 news shapers, or slightly more than 1 news shaper per nightly newscast. During August 1990, the first month of the Gulf crisis, the average newscast featured 2 news shapers.

In the 1979-1980 sample, television reporters turned to news shapers to discuss complicated issues that could not be visually presented, such as issues concerning the economy. Economists were used to shape news about the recession, inflation, and unemployment. News shapers were rarely used to discuss domestic political or policy issues. By 1987-1988, this had changed. News shapers were being used to shape news about relatively simple, but subjective, issues such as which presidential candidate won the debate. In the past, such issues were left to the public to decide. Network producers and reporters apparently now believe that the public needs an "expert" like William Schneider or Norman Ornstein to tell them who won.

The increased use of news shapers parallels the diminishing length of the average sound bite. As the number of news shapers per newscast has increased, the length of the average sound bite has decreased. By 1988, the average sound bite was just under ten seconds. These short sound bites have allowed politicians and political candidates to emphasize "photo ops" and one-liners over speeches and image over substance. Candidates no longer need to discuss complicated issues and policies, because complicated issues don't lend themselves to the ten-second sound bite. Instead, politicians and their consultants create one-liners that the spin doctors can embellish upon. No matter how nonsensical the statement (e.g., "a thousand points of light"), the spin doctors can be trusted to give it meaning and substance.

Print journalists followed the lead of television reporters in using news shapers. Like television news reports, print stories are now liberally (or, more accurately, conservatively) laced with the opinions of news shapers. Newspaper stories are no longer just "hard news."

In some instances, print reporters have gone even further in using news shapers than television reporters have: Some newspaper stories now consist entirely of the opinions of news shapers. Stories such as "Scuds Scarce, but Is That Good or Bad?" (*San Francisco Examiner*, February 6, 1991, A9), "Experts: Fed Policy Split Has Halted Credit Easing" (Minneapolis *Star Tribune*, April 20, 1991, 1D), and "Early Success Gives Rise to Cautious Optimism" (*USA Today*, January 17, 1991, 3A) are based entirely upon news shapers' statements. The *San Francisco Examiner* article was based solely on the speculations of Washington Institute for Near East Policy analyst Mike Eisenstadt and military intelligence "consultant" Jeff Richelson. The opinions of former secretary of state Alexander Haig, CDI founder Eugene Carroll, CSIS analyst James Blackwell, the Heritage Foundation's David Silverstein, and a few other former officials and academics were the sole content of the *USA Today* report. The *Star Tribune* story was based entirely on the analyses of David Jones and a few other corporate economists.

All of the blame for the widespread use of news shapers should not be directed at the networks or Washington reporters. Much of the blame needs to be directed at President Reagan and his advisers, who often refused to go on the record or answer questions from the press (Hertsgaard 1989). Because the administration was unwilling to speak directly to the press, Washington reporters looked to others who were willing to speak. These individuals were primarily former officials, who stayed around Washington as think tank analysts, Ivy League professors, political consultants, or journalists. Soon individuals from these institutions became the primary sources of this nation's political wisdom.

Although not solely responsible for the widespread use of news shapers, Washington journalists are responsible for tolerating the behavior of Reagan administration officials. If journalists had consistently reported on the administration's policy of orchestrating "photo ops" and "pseudoevents" rather than publicly discussing policies, the public would have been better served.

Washington journalists are also responsible for selecting news shapers who come almost exclusively from the ranks of the power elite. Although the Reagan administration might have been a contributor to the widespread use of news shapers, it can't be blamed for journalists' choosing a very narrow, elite group to shape news. These choices were made by reporters and editors. Elite journalists chose individuals from elite institutions to shape their news; they turned their backs on all individuals except these. Reporters from regional newspapers mimicked the elite reporters and brought pack journalism to new heights or, more accurately, new lows. Only news organizations and their reporters can change this situation.

APPENDIX:
METHOD AND SAMPLE

Two samples were selected from network evening newscasts. One sample was selected from newscasts airing between January 1, 1987, and December 30, 1988. The other sample was selected from newscasts airing between January 1, 1979, and December 30, 1980.

The selection procedure consisted of first randomly selecting three two-week clusters from 1987 and three two-week clusters from 1988, for a total of twelve weeks of programming. Unlike the study of Whitney et al. (1989), weekend as well as weekday newscasts were included in the sample. The selected intervals were: January 15-28, 1988; February 1-14, 1987; May 7-21, 1988; August 1-14, 1987; September 14-28, 1987; and November 8-21, 1988. The six intervals contained 86 days, or a maximum 258 newscasts by the three networks.

After the 1987-1988 sample was selected, the 1979-1980 sample was selected. The 1979-1980 sample was matched to that of the 1987-1988 sample to assure that the same days were studied in both samples. The clusters in the 1979-1980 sample were January 15-28, 1980; February 1-14, 1978; May 7-21, 1980; August 1-14, 1978; September 14-28, 1978; and November 8-21, 1980.

The actual newscasts were not analyzed, but the summary transcripts published by Vanderbilt University in the *Television News Index and Abstract* were. To assure that the titles of news shapers published in the *Television News Index and Abstract* were the same as those broadcast by the networks, tapes of 12 newscasts were viewed at the Vanderbilt Archive and compared with the summary trancripts. The comparison showed that the titles of individuals in the transcripts were identical to those appearing in the newscasts, except that the transcripts frequently attached the title "spokesman" or "spokesperson" to appearances by individuals associated with think tanks and universities, when no such title appeared in the broadcasts. For example, James Chace was described as a Carnegie Endowment spokesman in the transcript but was simply described as from the Carnegie Endowment in the broadcast (CBS–May 9, 1988). This difference has no effect on the coding categories used in this study.

The transcripts were coded as to whether they concerned domestic political issues, foreign affairs, or other content. Domestic issues were operationalized to include elections; internal economic matters such as actions of the Federal Reserve Bank; the budget deficit; hearings, investigations, and inquiries by congressional committees and special prosecutors, including the investigations concerning "Irangate"; and court decisions. Foreign affairs included issues related to the military, national security, or defense, including appropriations for weapons systems; international economics or aid, including reports concerning the U.S. trade imbalance; terrorism; and the internal affairs of foreign countries. The "other" category included news reports on the arts, science, sports, human interest, personalities, entertainment, or student affairs. Whitney et al. (1989) used the latter as separate categories in their analysis. All of the stories coded as "other" were deleted from the analysis, producing a study of the news shapers who discussed domestic and foreign affairs.

The categories of news shapers used in this study were derived from categories derived by Herman and Chomsky (1988):

Former Politicians and U.S. Government Officials: people who are no longer in government, including the advisers, aides, speech writers, and press secretaries of former politicians and officials

Economists: individuals described as "economists" and "economic analysts" or "industry analysts" during newscasts

Think tank spokespersons: individuals who are associates of foundations, centers, or institutes that conduct research and publish policy papers

Experts, Analysts, and Consultants: individuals who were described by the networks as such in newscasts, except when described as economic or industry analysts

Journalists: editors, reporters, columnists, and broadcast news reporters who work for U.S. media but do not work for the networks

Academics: individuals described as professors, political scientists, historians, or sociologists or whose title is not given but who are described as spokespersons or representatives of universities

Other: including lobbyists, pollsters, psychiatrists, and teachers who provide background information but are not involved in the news event.

The coding of individuals into these categories excluded appearances by individuals who appeared as news makers rather than news shapers. Former government officials, such as Robert McFarlane or Oliver North, who were involved in the actual news event, were not counted as news shapers. Journalists who discussed their experiences, contacts, and stories were also excluded. (For example, see Carl Rowan's comments of May 10, 1988 for the television network newscasts.)

Once the news shapers were identified, their institutional and political affiliations were determined using standard biographical reference sources such as *Who's Who in America, Who's Who in American Politics, Contemporary Authors*, and *Biography Index*, which were located using the *Biography and Genealogy Master Index*. For individuals not listed in these sources, other techniques were employed.

The political affiliations and posts of former government officials were determined using editions of the *U.S. Government Manual* and the *Congressional Staff Directory*. The university affiliations of individuals described as professors, historians, and sociologists were determined using the *National Faculty Directory*. Political consultants and experts were identified using the *Political Resource Directory*. In instances where the individual had authored a book or article, biographical information was retrieved from it.

This information was used to politically classify analysts, experts, consultants and former government officials. Officials in the Eisenhower, Nixon, Ford, and Reagan administrations were coded as "Republicans"; officials in the Truman, Kennedy, Johnson, and Carter administrations were coded as "Democrats." The biographies were also used to determine the accuracy of the descriptions provided by the networks.

REFERENCES

Adams, Gordon. (1981). *The Politics of Defense Contracting*. New Brunswick, NJ: Transaction.

Adatto, Kiku. (1990). "The Incredible Shrinking Sound Bite." *New Republic*. May 28, 20–23.

Alt, James E. (1987). "Review of *Britain's Economic Renaissance*." *Political Science Quarterly* 42, 118–120.

American Enterprise Institute. (1987 to date). *Annual Report*. Washington, DC: American Enterprise Institute.

American Enterprise Institute. (1989). *AEI Sourcebook*. Washington, DC: American Enterprise Institute.

American Institute for Political Communication. (1972). *"Liberal Bias" as a Factor in Network Television Reporting*. Washington, DC: American Institute for Political Communication.

Atwater, Tony, and Green, Norma. (1988). "New Sources in Network Coverage of International Terrorism." *Journal Quarterly* 65, 967–917.

Barnet, Richard, and Muller, Ronald. (1974). *Global Reach*. New York: Simon and Schuster.

Barnouw, Erick. (1970). *The Image Empire*. New York: Oxford University Press.

Bennett, David. (1988). *The Party of Fear*. Chapel Hill: University of North Carolina Press.

Ben-Yishai, Ron. (1981). "Israel's Move." *Foreign Policy*. 1981, 43.

Berger, Peter, and Thomas Luckmann. (1967). *The Social Construction of Reality*. Garden City, N.Y.: Doubleday-Anchor.

Berkman, Ronald, and Kitch, Laura. (1986). *Politics in the Media Age*. New York: McGraw-Hill Books.

Bluestein, Paul. (1988). "Conservative Think Tank Ready for Fight." *Washington Post*. January 18, F5-6.

Brookings Institution. (1989). *The Brookings Institution 1989 Report*. Washington, DC: Brookings Institution.

Brown, Jane, Bybee, Carl, Weardon, Stanley, and Straughton, Dulcie. (1987). "Invisible Power: Newspaper News Sources and the Limits of Diversity." *Journalism Quarterly* 64, 45-54.

Carnegie Endowment. (1989). *Staff and Projects, Fall 1989*. Washington, DC: Carnegie Endowment for International Peace.

Carter III, Hodding. (1984a). "Potomac Pundits Get Reintroduced to New Ideas." *Wall Street Journal*. March 8, 31.

Carter III, Hodding. (1984b). "Journalistic Pundits Move in 'Right' Circles." *Wall Street Journal*. August 16, 25.

Cato Institute. (1988). *Cato Institute 1988 Annual Report*. Washington, DC: Cato Institute.

Clancey, Maura, and Robinson, Michael. (1985). "General Election Coverage, Part I." *Public Opinion*. January, 52-54, 59.

Columbia Broadcasting System (1971). "Analysis of Method." Appendix C. In *How CBS Tried to Kill a Book*. See Efron and Chambers 1972.

Congressional Staff Directory. (1986 to date). Mount Vernon, VA: Staff Directories.

Contemporary Authors. (1974 to date). Detroit: Gale Research Company.

Cooper, Marc, and Soley, Lawrence. (1990). "All the Right Sources." *Mother Jones*. February/March, 20-27, 45-48.

Council on Foreign Relations. (1988 to date). *Council on Foreign Relations Annual Report*. New York: Council on Foreign Relations.

Crouse, Timothy. (1972). *The Boys on the Bus*. New York: Random House.

CSIS Publications. (1989). Washington, DC: Center for Strategic and International Studies.

Current Biography. (1970 to date). New York: H. W. Wilson Company.

Dickson, Paul. (1971). *Think Tanks*. New York: Atheneum.

Dionne, E. J. (1989). "The New Think Tank on the Block." *New York Times*. June 28, 24.

Domhoff, G. William. (1970). *The Higher Circles*. New York: Random House.

Domhoff, G. William. (1990). *The Power Elite and the State*. New York: Aldine de Gruyter.

Dominick, Joseph. (1977). "Geographic Bias in National TV News." *Journal of Communication* 27, 94-99.

Donaldson. Sam. (1990). "How to Get on TV" (interview). *Mother Jones*. February/March, 24-25, 45.

Doyle, James S. (1990). "Journalists, Inc." *Washington Monthly*. March, 20, 22-23.

Easterbrook, Gregg. (1986). "Ideas Move Nations." *Atlantic Monthly*. January, 66-80.

Efron, Edith. (1971). *The News Twisters*. Los Angeles: Nash Publishing.

Efron, Edith, and Chambers, Clytia. (1972). *How CBS Tried to Kill a Book*. Los Angeles: Nash Publishing.

Emery, Michael, and Emery, Edwin. (1988). *The Press and America*. Englewood Cliffs, NJ: Prentice-Hall.

Encyclopedia of Associations, 24th ed. (1989). Detroit: Gale Research Company.

Epstein, Edward. (1973). *News from Nowhere*. New York: Random House.

Fairness and Accuracy In Reporting. (1990). "All the Usual Suspects: 'MacNeil/Lehrer' and 'Nightline.' " *Extra!* Winter, 1-11.

Ferrell, Robert. (1986). "Review of *The Uncertain Crusade*." *Journal of American History* 73, 817-818.

Foundation Grants Index. (1989 to date). New York: The Foundation Center.

Fialka, John. (1989). "Mr. Kissinger Has Opinions on China—And Business Ties." *Wallstreet Journal* September 15, 1.

Frank, Reuven. (1969). "The Ugly Mirror." *Television Quarterly* 8, 82–96.

Gamarekian, Barbara. (1985). "Fostering a Middle East Dialogue." *New York Times Biographical Service.* August, 959–960.

Gamarekian, Barbara. (1989). "In Pursuit of the Clever Quotemaster." *New York Times.* May 12, 10.

Gans, Herbert. (1979). *Deciding What's News.* New York: Pantheon Books.

Gans, Herbert. (1985). "Are U.S. Journalists Dangerously Liberal?" *Columbia Journalism Review.* December, 29–33.

Gerard, J. (1989). "TV Notes: 'Nightline' Criticized by Monitoring Group." *New York Times.* February 6, 18.

Gergen, David. (1984). "Reel Two, Take One." *New Republic.* December 3, 16–18.

Goedkoop, Richard. (1990). Review and Criticism. *Journal of Broadcasting and Electronic Media* 34, 230–232.

Hansen, Kathleen, Ward, Jean, and McCleod, Douglas (1987). "Role of the Newspaper Library in the Production of News." *Journalism Quarterly* 64, 714–720.

Hecht, Ben. (1928). *The Front Page.* New York: Covici-Friede.

Heritage Foundation. (1988). *Architects of Public Policy: The Heritage Foundation Annual Report 1988.* Washington, DC: Heritage Foundation.

Herman, Edward, and Chomsky, Noam. (1988). *Manufacturing Consent.* New York: Pantheon.

Herman, Edward, and O'Sullivan, Gerry. (1989). *The "Terrorism" Industry.* New York: Pantheon Books.

Herschensohn, Bruce. (1976). *The Gods of Antenna.* New Rochelle, NY: Arlington.

Hertsgaard, Mark. (1989). *On Bended Knee.* New York: Shocken.

Hess, Stephen. (1981). *The Washington Reporters.* Washington, DC: Brookings Institution.

Hess, Stephen. (1989). "Confessions of a Sound Bite." *Washington Post.* October 22, C5.

Hess, Stephen. (1990). "Is Electronic News Dishonest?" *Communicator.* April, 22, 27.

Hess, Stephen. (1991). "Reporters Who Cover Congress." *Society.* January/February, 60–65.

Hoynes, William, and Croteau, David. (1989). "Are You on the *Nightline* Guest List?" *Extra!* January/February, 1–15.

Hume, Ellen. (1990). Why the Press Blew the S & L Scandals. *New York Times.* May 24, A25.

Hyland, William. (1987). *Mortal Rivals.* New York: Random House.

Jenkins, Brian. (1982). "Statements about Terrorism." *Annals of the American Academy of Political and Social Science* 463 (September), 11–23.

Johnson, Ronald. (1986). *Shootdown: Flight 007 and the American Connection.* New York: Viking Press.

Johnstone, John W., Slawski, Edward, and Bowman, William. (1972). "The Professional Values of American Newsmen." *Public Opinion Quarterly* 36, 522–540.

Kalb, Marvin. (1978). "What Will Henry Kissinger Do for an Encore?" *New York Times Magazine.* April 16, 29–31, 54–68.

Karpman, I. J., ed. (1978). *Who's Who in World Jewry.* Tel Aviv: Olive Books of Israel.

Kelly, Joseph. (1971). *The Left Leaning Antenna.* New Rochelle, NY: Arlington.

Kenworthy, E. W. (1969). "Agnew Says TV Networks Are Distorting News." *New York Times*. November 14, 1, 24.

Kern, Montague, Levering, Patricia, and Levering, Ralph. (1983). *The Kennedy Crises: The Press, the Presidency and Foreign Policy*. Chapel Hill: University of North Carolina Press.

Kuczin, Sam. (1972). "Book Review of *The News Twisters*." *Journalism Quarterly* 49, 192.

Kupperman, Robert, Van Opstal, Debra, and Williamson, David. (1982). "Terrorism, the Strategic Tool: Response and Control." *Annals of the American Academy of Political and Social Science* 463 (September), 11–23.

Kuttner, Robert. (1984). "Revenge of the Democratic Nerds." *New Republic*. October 22, 14–17.

Kuttner, Robert. (1985). "What's the Big Idea?" *New Republic*. November 18, 23–26.

Lazarsfeld, Paul, and Merton, Robert. (1948). "Mass Media, Popular Taste and Organized Social Action." In *The Communication of Ideas*, ed. Lyman Bryson. New York: Harper and Brothers.

Lewis, Anthony. (1978). "Hire and Salary." *New York Times*. January 26, A21.

Lewis, Anthony. (1980). "The Kissinger Secrets." *New York Times*. June 9, 23.

Lichter, S. Robert, Amundson, Daniel, and Noyes, Richard. (1988). *The Video Campaign*. Washington, DC: American Enterprise Institute.

Lichter, S. Robert, Rothman, Stanley, and Lichter, Linda. (1986). *The Media Elite*. Bethesda, MD: Adler & Adler.

Linden, Patricia. (1987). "Powerhouses of Policy." *Town and Country*. January, 99–106, 170–179.

Lowenstein, Douglas. (1980). "Covering the Primaries." *Washington Journalism Review*. September, 38–42.

Luttwak, Edward. (1979). "Cubans in Arabia? Or, the Meaning of Strategy." *Commentary*. December, 62–66.

McDowell, Edwin. (1979). "Henry Kissinger." *New York Times*. November 25, 106 VII.

Magner, Denise. (1991). "An Expert on the Arab World Helps TV Focus on the Gulf War." *Chronicle of Higher Education*. February 6, A3.

Mann, Jim. (1988). "Taiwan a Big Contributor to Think Tanks." *Los Angeles Times*. September 5, 10.

Marchetti, Victor, and Marks, John. (1975). *The CIA and the Cult of Intelligence*. New York: Dell Publishing.

Mills, C. Wright. (1956). *The Power Elite*. New York: Oxford University Press.

Moynihan, Daniel Patrick. (1973). *Coping*. New York: Random House.

Muscatine, Alison. (1986). "Georgetown University and Its Media Stars." *Washington Post National Weekly Edition*. May 26, 10–11.

Ogden, Rollo. (1907). *Life and Letters of Edwin Lawrence Godkin*. New York: Macmillan.

Page, Benjamin, Shapiro, Robert, and Dempsey, Glenn. (1987). "What Moves Public Opinion?" *American Political Science Review* 81, 23–42.

Patterson, Thomas. (1980). *The Mass Media Election*. Praeger: New York.

Perrin, Dennis. (1990). "*The New Republic*: The Center as Left." *Extra!* July/August, 7.

Petroleum Industry Research Foundation. (1988). *PIRINC: Petroleum Industry Research Foundation*. New York: PIRINC.

Pincus, Walter. (1989). "Kissinger Says He Had No Role in China Mission." *Washington Post*. December 14, A52.

Pinsky, Mark. (1991). " 'Military Expert' Has a Gap in His Credentials." *Los Angeles Times*. April 1, F1, F8.

Plane, Donald, and Oppermann, Edward. (1981). *Business and Economic Statistics*. Plano, TX: Business Publications.

Political Resource Directory. (1989). Rye, NY: Carol Hess Associates.

Prados, John. (1986). *President's Secret Wars*. New York: William Morrow and Company.

Research Centers Directory. (1989 to date). Detroit: Gale Research Company.

Robinson, Michael, Clancey, Maura, and Grand, Lisa (1983). "With Friends like These . . ." *Public Opinion*. June/July, 2–3, 52–54.

Rosenthal, James. (1985). "Heritage Hype." *New Republic*. September 2, 14–16.

Roshco, Bernard. (1975). *Newsmaking*. Chicago: University of Chicago Press.

Rosten, Leo. (1937). "The Social Composition of Washington Correspondents." *Journalism Quarterly* 14, 125–132.

Schudson, Michael. (1978). *Discovering the News*. New York: Basic Books.

Schulzinger, Robert. (1984). *The Wise Men of Foreign Affairs*. New York: Columbia University Press.

Segal, David. (1991). "Shrink Rap." *New Republic*. March 25, 18.

Serfaty, Simon, ed. (1990). *The Media and Foreign Policy*. New York: St. Martin's Press.

Sesser, Stanford. (1969). "Journalist: Objectivity and Activism." *Quill*. December, 6–7.

Shalom, Stephen. (1991). "Saddam Who?" *Nation*. February 25, 241–243.

Shoup, Lawrence, and Minter, William. (1977). *Imperial Brain Trust*. New York: Monthly Review Press.

Sid-Ahmed, Muhammad. (1976). *After the Guns Fall Silent*. New York: St. Martin's Press.

Sigal, Leon. (1973). *Reporters and Officials*. Lexington, MA: D. C. Heath and Company.

Smith, James. (1991). *The Idea Brokers*. New York: Free Press.

Smith, III, Ted J. (1988). *The Vanishing Economy*. New York: Media Institute.

Stein, Jeff. (1980). "Old Spies and Cold Peas." *Inquiry*. December 29, 21.

Stempel, III, Guido. (1965). "The Prestige Press in Two Presidential Elections." *Journalism Quarterly* 42, 15–21.

Stevenson, Robert, Eisenger, Richard, Feinberg, Barry, and Kotok, Alan. (1973). "Untwisting *The News Twisters*: A Replication of Efron's Study." *Journalism Quarterly* 50, 211–219.

Stone, Peter H. (1985). "Businesses Widen Role in Conservative 'War of Ideas.' " *Washington Post*. May 12, F3–F5.

Strentz, Herbert. (1989). *News Reporters and News Sources*, 2d ed. Ames: Iowa State University Press.

Tebbel, John. (1974). *The Media in America*. New York: Mentor Books.

Tuchman, Gaye. (1972). "Objectivity as a Strategic Ritual." *American Journal of Sociology* 77, 660–679.

Tuchman, Gaye. (1978). *Making News*. New York: Free Press.

U.S. Senate. (1990). "U.S. Policy in the Persian Gulf." *Hearings before the Committee on Foreign Relations* (2d Session), December 6, 12, and 13 (S. Hrg. 101–1128), pts. 1 and 2.

Waldman, Steven. (1986). "The King of Quotes." *Washington Monthly*. December, 33–40.

Weisberg, Jacob. (1991). "Gulfballs." *New Republic*. March 25, 17–19.

Whitney, D. Charles. (1987). "Essay Review—Counterpoint." *Journalism Quarterly* 64, 871–873.

Whitney, D. Charles, Fritzler, Marilyn, Jones, Steven, Mazzarella, Sharon, and Rakow, Lana. (1989). "Geographic and Source Biases in Network Television News 1982–1984." *Journal of Broadcasting and Electronic Media* 33, 159–174.

Who's Who in America. (1980 to date). Chicago: Marquis Who's Who.

Wilentz, Amy. (1986). "On the Intellectual Ramparts." *Time.* September 1, 22–23.

Willrich, Michael. (1990). "Renting the Fourth Estate." *Washington Monthly.* March, 13–23.

World of Learning 1990. London: Europe Publications.

Writer's Market 1988. (1987). Cincinnati: Writer's Digest Books.

Zaroulis, Nancy, and Sullivan, Gerald. (1985). *Who Spoke Up?* New York: Holt, Rinehart and Winston.

INDEX

ABOUT THE AUTHOR

LAWRENCE C. SOLEY is a professor at the University of Minnesota's School of Journalism and a contributing writer for *City Pages*, the Twin Cities' weekly. In addition to *City Pages*, Soley's articles have appeared in a variety of newspapers and magazines, including the *Boston Phoenix, Dissent, Mother Jones*, and *Stamps*. With coauthor Marc Cooper, he received the Sigma Delta Chi award for ''All the Right Sources,'' which was published in *Mother Jones* magazine

Soley's articles have also appeared in a variety of scholarly publications, including the *Journal of Communication, Journalism Quarterly*, and the *Journal of Advertising*. He is the author of *Radio Warfare* (Praeger, 1989) and coauthor of *Clandestine Radio Broadcasting* (Praeger, 1987).